DOUBLE TRAP

Other Books by John Melady

Acts of Courage
Cross of Valour
Explosion
Escape from Canada!
Heartbreak and Heroism
Korea: Canada's Forgotten War
The Little Princes
Overtime Overdue: The Bill Barilko Story
Pilots
Search and Rescue
Star of Courage

DOUBLE
TRAP

The Last Public Hanging in Canada

by John Melady

THE DUNDURN GROUP
TORONTO

Copy-Editor: Andrea Pruss
Design: Andrew Roberts
Printer: Transcontinental

Library and Archives Canada Cataloguing in Publication

Melady, John
Double trap : the last public hanging in Canada / John Melady.

ISBN-10: 1-55002-571-6
ISBN-13: 978-1-55002-571-2

1. Melady, Nicholas. 2. Hanging--Canada--History--19th century.
I. Title.

HV8699.C2M44 2005 364.66'092 C2005-903478-5

1 2 3 4 5   09   08   07   06   05

Conseil des Arts Canada Council Canada ONTARIO ARTS COUNCIL
du Canada for the Arts CONSEIL DES ARTS DE L'ONTARIO

We acknowledge the support of the Canada Council for the Arts and the Ontario Arts Council for our publishing program. We also acknowledge the financial support of the Government of Canada through the Book Publishing Industry Development Program and The Association for the Export of Canadian Books, and the Government of Ontario through the Ontario Book Publishers Tax Credit program, and the Ontario Media Development Corporation.

Printed and bound in Canada.
Printed on recycled paper.

www.dundurn.com

Dundurn Press
8 Market Street, Suite 200
Toronto, Ontario, Canada
M5E 1M6

Gazelle Book Services Limited
White Cross Mills
Hightown, Lancaster, England
LA1 4X5

Dundurn Press
2250 Military Road
Tonawanda NY
U.S.A. 14150

DOUBLE TRAP

*In memory of Thomas R. Melady, D.V.M.
whose encouragement, advice, and good
humour helped so much.*

TABLE OF CONTENTS

NICHOLAS MELADY.

ACKNOWLEDGMENTS

I WOULD NOT have been able to research and write this book without help and encouragement from several people. And while I do not wish to forget anyone who assisted me, I do want to express my gratitude to as many of you as possible. If your name is not here, and you helped me, I am still indebted to you, and I thank you. I am just sorry if I failed to acknowledge your contribution.

First and foremost, my thanks to Kirk Howard, my publisher, for seeing the project through, to Tony Hawke, Barry Jowett, and Andrea Pruss for your editorial skills, and to Jennifer Scott and Andrew Roberts for your work on the design. It was through your efforts that the book took shape.

Jean-François Lozier, Genealogical Consultant at the National Archives in Ottawa, was of help, as was Paul McIlroy at the Archives of Ontario. Several individuals, whose names I often did not know, assisted me in the Osgoode Hall library in Toronto, at the D.B. Weldon Library at the University of Western Ontario in London, at the Stratford-Perth Archives in Stratford, and at the Central Reference Library in Toronto.

I owe special thanks to several people at the Museum & Historic Gaol in Goderich. Among them are Jeremy Allin, Dan McPherson, Lara Vanstone, and Kevin Whitworth. All were cheerful and generous with their time. Museum Curator Patricia Hamilton went out of her way to assist me in so many aspects of my research. She gave me advice, suggestions as to where I might find information, and help with photocopying, yet she always remained enthusiastic and professional. I owe much to her.

In addition, Jeannette Finnigan and Rebecca Dechert Sage assisted me in the library in Seaforth, while Reg Thompson was equally helpful at the library in Goderich. *Huron Expositor* publisher Tom Williscraft gave me permission to use the newspaper's sketch of Nicholas.

Father Joe Hardy, Graydon Carter, Susan Hundertmark, and Tom Nigro read all or part of the manuscript and provided helpful feedback, and I thank them. In my inquiries concerning the Van Egmond House, three people were most generous with their time and advice. They are Vivienne and Bob Newnham and Kyle Rea.

One of my neighbours, Kevin Coyne, discussed the subject of the book with me and in so doing asked several probing questions, all of which helped me clarify the story line that I wanted to develop. Kevin helped me more than he probably realized.

And finally, but most important of all, my wife, Mary, who lived with the seemingly endless ups and downs of the research and writing. She gave me advice when it was asked for, encouragement when it was needed, and insight always. I thank her so much.

John Melady
Seaforth, Ontario
June 2005

INTRODUCTION

THE EVENTS DESCRIBED in this book happened more than a century ago, so all the people depicted have faded into the distant past. At one time, however, all were alive; each played a role in a society that was as vibrant, exciting, and unique as our own. These people laughed, loved, dreamed, and did the best they could with the talents they had. Some certainly did a better job than others.

In telling their tale, I have endeavoured to give them life, but whether I have succeeded or not will to some degree be in the perception of the reader. I was obviously not able to interview any of the people in the story, so I had to improvise at times in order to put flesh on their bones. For example, I have James Kehoe fixing a farm wagon just before he runs and hides from Constable Tom Stephens, who is coming to make an arrest. The wagon repair is conjecture on my part, but at least he *could* have been doing such a job. It would have been commonplace on a farm. On the other hand, I located documentary proof that he ran to the barn and hid in the hay.

All the dialogue in the book is factual, as is the courtroom testimony. My sources were legal documents, newspaper accounts, public record archives, and biographical references as they pertained to such people as judges, lawyers, civic personalities, and those who held official positions of various kinds.

The times depicted in the book are as accurate as I could make them, as are the personalities and events portrayed. In this regard, there were so many instances where the main characters were in court that it was occasionally difficult to be clear about who was doing what to whom. For this reason, I apologize in advance for sequences that some readers may find rather opaque. On the other hand, all of the events described in the book *did* happen; perhaps that is why they may seem so incredible to us today.

And lastly, to those of my relatives who did not want me to write this book: I understand your reserve, and I accept your criticism. Yet while none of us are at all proud of what happened within our family, we have to admit that these events are all part of history now, and we might as well acknowledge and deal with them.

CHAPTER 1 | TO DIE IN THE MORNING

THE NIGHT BEFORE the hanging, a mysterious stranger came to the death cell door. He did not enter or speak; he merely stood in the shadows, stared at the condemned man for a couple of minutes, then disappeared. Seconds later, the echoes of his footsteps grew faint and were gone.

Even though the prisoner had never laid eyes on his visitor before, he would soon see the man again. In fact, the silent stranger was the last person the prisoner would ever see. That was because the figure at the door was the hangman, and he had gone to the cell to look at the man he would kill in the morning. He had to be sure of his victim's weight, body type, and height in order to make his death quick, proper, and, in a grotesque sort of way, even humane.

The executioner was an experienced man. He was of average height, meticulous, dour in appearance, and extremely secretive. He did his job and he did it well, but almost never mentioned what it entailed. To his neighbours, he was a businessman who travelled at times. His family said he was a civil servant. None knew what else he did. And of course, he did not want them to ask.

Often, the name Arthur Ellis was used as a pseudonym for the hangman. This man's real name was Jesse Marshall. He lived in Toronto, but plied his trade wherever it was required. When his services were called for elsewhere, he would tell his family about an important meeting he had to attend. Then he would pack a bag, put on his good suit, and leave town. Overnight accommodation at the end of the journey would be provided free of charge at either the home of the local sheriff or a hotel.

On the night of Monday, December 6, 1869, he was given a room in Goderich, Ontario, then a town of some three thousand people on the shores of Lake Huron, in the county of the same name. He had been summoned there to hang a young murderer, and would be paid $37.70 for doing the job. To say he was welcomed would probably be simplistic; however, at a time when executioners were often less than reliable, Marshall's arrival would have been a relief for those who had asked him to come. Hangmen sometimes did not show up, and often, when they did appear, they were drunk, incompetent, or woefully unprepared for the terrible task at hand. There were documented instances when the hangman could barely stand and botched the job, strangling the victim or, even worse, decapitating the poor wretch. No wonder the executioner was generally shunned by society and took pains to remain anonymous.

Fortunately, the execution Marshall would do on this occasion would proceed without a hitch.

The hanging would be in public, from a scaffold built on the east side of the local jail. The plank floor of the structure and the trap through which the killer would plunge were both level with the top of the prison wall and had actually been built against the wall itself. The trap was on the outside of the wall. A railing had been erected on three sides of the platform, while on the fourth was a wooden staircase the condemned man would climb from the jail yard below. He would never walk outside again, only touching the ground when he was cut down and his still-warm corpse was placed in the cheap wooden coffin that would be there to receive it. The coffin had been made to order at Warerooms, an area household furnishing emporium.

The scaffold and the stairs that had been erected for the hanging would be dismantled and removed after the execution by the carpenter who built them. That man was Charles Horton, and his bill was $39.50 for his efforts. He was brought from London for the work because no carpenter in Goderich would touch the job. When they learned this, some city newspapers joked about the sensitivities of the local tradesmen.

No one knows who got to keep the wood, because it was never used for the same purpose again. Only one other hanging was ever done at the jail, and it was hidden behind the eighteen-foot walls some four decades later.

The man that Marshall came to hang was my cousin, Nicholas Melady, Jr.

Nicholas was twenty-four years old, tall, handsome, and well-liked by almost everyone except the two people he helped kill. One of them was his father, the other his stepmother. Both were murdered at their farmhouse a couple miles southeast of the village of Seaforth, about twenty-two miles from Goderich. The deed was a particularly bloody one, performed after dark on June 6, 1868. Nicholas was not alone that night, but he was the only one convicted of the crime. Exactly eighteen months later, he sat in his cell and prepared to pay with his life for his part in what had been done.

His surroundings were spartan at best. Goderich Gaol, as it was called, still exists. It is a well-preserved national historic site, built high above the Maitland River on the outskirts of the town between 1839 and 1842. The building is certainly substantial, but it is not beautiful. Massive, two-foot-thick stone walls encase the structure, while the octagon-shaped centre section holds the turnkey's office, a medical room, and what once passed for a library. Four cellblocks radiate out from the inner core: two on the ground floor, two above it. Between the blocks are exercise yards.

Individual cells are decidedly primitive. The one in which Nicholas spent his final night was six feet wide, seven feet long, and eight feet high. A two-inch-thick wooden platform served as the bed. The cell walls were hand-hewn timbers, all twelve to fourteen inches thick. The door was double oak, bolted from the outside. A ten-inch-wide window in the innermost wall of the cell, opposite the door, provided him with a view of a stone wall a few steps away. Immediately outside his window was an exercise yard.

Even today, little effort is required to imagine the atmosphere, particularly during the dark fall and winter days when rain or snow enveloped the place and rendered each cell as cold, clammy, and ugly as any place on earth.

Conversely, in the July and August humidity of southern Ontario, the heat in the lock-up must have been unbearable. When Nicholas was there, the place was lit by lanterns after dark (electricity and air conditioning were far in the future), and the stench from the latrine pails used at night was overpowering. A ramshackle privy in the corner of the yard outside was used during the day.

There was always the noise of cell doors being slammed, prisoners cursing, the incessant buzzing of flies, and the occasional, animal-like screeching of the "lunatics" who were incarcerated there along with everyone else. While some inmates were well past middle age, most were young, and some children were locked up with their parents because they were vagrants arrested for begging in the streets. There were lots of drunks, brawlers, an occasional hooker, and plenty of thieves. But because he was there for murder, Nicholas was in a unique category.

Once he got past the feeling that he might be exonerated, or could even escape, he became resigned to his lot and co-operated wholeheartedly with his jailers. When his final appeal failed, he wept bitterly at first, but then found solace in his faith and began to count the hours.

Outside his cell, he could hear the hammering as his scaffold was built.

In the twenty-four hours before his death, Nicholas had several visitors in addition to the hangman. These included family members, employees of the judicial system, clergy, and newspaper reporters. The latter gave us a final glimpse of how this condemned man coped with his fate, bade farewell to loved ones, and prepared to meet his God. These members of the press had generous access to the prisoner and were able to ask him virtually anything. And they did.

The investigation of the murders had been haphazard, controversial, and time-consuming. After an initial flurry of activity immediately after the killings, the police and legal officers of the day seemed to sit on their hands and do little to conclude the matter. They lost evidence, lied in court, delayed needlessly, and jailed the obviously innocent. At one point, several people were accused of the crimes, placed behind bars, and then, in time, quietly released and sent home.

But one element always stood out. Virtually anyone who knew anything at all about the murders was convinced that Nicholas had not acted alone. However, when reporters asked him about this, the condemned man refused to incriminate others. Instead, he declared, "No, I have to die for this, but that is no reason why I should bring anyone else into the same position." When a *Toronto Globe* correspondent asked Nicholas if his brothers and sisters had had anything to do with the killings, Nicholas turned to the writer and said, "My brother, nor any of my sisters, had no more to do with it than you have." Then he sat down, wrote a statement for the press, and asked that it be published after his death.

The assembled reporters described the condemned man's last hours and, ultimately, his final minutes. The stories they filed were reasonably detailed, but not always exactly the same. For example, the *London Free Press* told readers that Nicholas "slept soundly until about five" the night before he was hanged. The *Stratford Herald*, on the other hand, reported that the prisoner wakened at 4:00 a.m., "after a broken sleep." The latter would seem to have been more accurate.

In any event, shortly after Nicholas was up and dressed on the last morning of his life, two nuns from the local Sisters of Mercy convent came to see him. They talked together, then recited the rosary, and they stayed on when Father Bartholomew Boubat arrived to say Mass in the small day room that was just a few steps from the cell. The forty-seven-year-old, French-born Boubat had been a priest for twelve years at the time and had recently been appointed pastor of St. Peter's church in Goderich. He was looked upon as a cultured, kind man who quickly established a rapport with the condemned man and remained at his side for the brief time remaining to him. Boubat never forgot this murderer, and he often spoke of him in the remaining five years of his pastoral tenure in Goderich.

As for the man who was about to die, the *Toronto Globe* reported that while "the culprit seemed to enter into the observance [of the Mass] with intelligence and solemnity," the "most terrifying thing of all was still to come for the poor wretch."

Nicholas had four sisters and one brother. Of the sisters, Alice was just one year older than he. The two were very close, and indeed, she had spearheaded a last futile appeal to the provincial government for clemency. The black-haired, blue-eyed young woman was inconsolable as the hours wound down. Though only five feet, three inches in height, she appears to have figuratively towered over those who witnessed her parting with her brother.

"About seven o'clock," wrote the correspondent for the *Globe*, "his sister Alice, who was passionately attached to him, entered his cell. She could not speak, but just clutched his hand and bathed it with tears and kisses." A writer for the *Huron Expositor* witnessed the parting as well, and his report was equally maudlin: "To say that this was sad would be but a partial description, for it was heart-rending in the extreme. The last long clasp of brother and sister was here exemplified in a superlative and touching manner. The cheeks of strong men who were spectators were watered with tears from eyes, which perhaps had been for years dry of all such sympathetic affections." Finally, jailer Edward Campaigne stepped into the cell, took the young woman by the arm, and, as gently as he could, led her away.

Then Thomas Melady, the prisoner's older brother, went to say his final farewell. He handled the parting in much the same way as his sister. Tom "broke down and cried like a child," observed the *Stratford Herald* reporter. "The prisoner however, did not cry, as he said himself, his heart was too dry to cry," the article added. "Thomas is a fine stalwart farmer," the *Globe* observed, "but all he could say when he went into the cell was 'poor little Nicholas, poor little Nicholas,' and he cried and sobbed like a babe, and wrung his brother's hand, no doubt in his own mind going back to other times when he and Nicholas were boys together." During these farewells, the paper continued, "Nicholas restrained himself wonderfully; he seemed to feel more for the anguish of his friends than his own." When other relatives were there a day or so earlier, his decorum had been much the same.

As soon as the last two family members had gone, Father Boubat talked to the prisoner until about 8:20 a.m., when John Macdonald, the Huron County sheriff, entered the cell and spoke to the priest. Jesse Marshall, the executioner, then stepped forward.

When he realized who the hangman was, "Melady turned deathly pale," observed one reporter, while another thought the prisoner "was close to fainting."

And no wonder. The executioner had blackened his face and hands just before coming to do his work. This was because the hanging would be public, and he had no wish to be identified by anyone in the crowd that waited outside. The black-faced official's role was grim, so his appearance that morning must have been particularly chilling for the man who would die.

Marshall never actually said anything to the prisoner, either then or later. He had such a deep-seated fear of recognition that he remained silent to prevent the reporters present from identifying him by voice. The *Expositor* representative wrote that the hangman was "fiendish looking," but refrained from describing him further.

The executioner motioned for Nicholas to hold out his hands with the palms inward. His wrists were tied together in front of his body so tightly that there would be no chance of him slipping them loose. The prisoner watched the hangman perform this task, standing, in the words of one reporter, "as erect as his trembling knees and emaciated muscles would permit."

In public executions at the time, a hood was placed over the condemned person's head. In Nicholas's case, the hood was white, and cost the county thirty-five cents. Marshall carefully adjusted the head cover on his victim but made sure it did not obscure the face. After all, the prisoner had to see where he was going as he walked to the gallows. Only if he had been unable or unwilling to walk would he have been carried to his death. Such a circumstance occasionally took place, but not on this day.

Just before 8:30 on that raw December morning, the executioner nodded to the sheriff, and the death procession began. Father Boubat opened the prayer book he carried and, in a soft, French-accented voice, began to read the twenty-third Psalm as he and Nicholas walked together the few steps to the door that led to the prison yard. A gust of bitter wind blew across the snow-covered ground as the pair stepped outside and turned to the stairs at the wall. Sheriff Macdonald was close behind, and the hangman followed. "Melady ascended the scaffold with tottering steps, still with an air of firmness," observed the *Expositor*. Once he and Father Boubat reached the gallows floor, both knelt down, recited the Lord's Prayer together, then stood and waited for Marshall to do his deed. Those who watched did so in silence.

The white hood was pulled down, the new, inch-thick rope was placed around the condemned man's neck, and the knot that would break that neck was adjusted just below and behind his left ear. Finally, Father Boubat pressed a crucifix to the doomed man's lips. Nicholas kissed it and, in the words of a newspaper reporter, "uttered his last earthly prayer: 'Lord have mercy on my soul.'"

Then the hangman turned his victim partly away from the crowd below and sprung the trap. The drop was seven feet.

Apart from a few muscular contractions of the limbs, death came quickly to Nicholas Melady. His corpse hung in place for the required time of thirty minutes; as soon as the attending physician gave the word, it was cut down and lowered into a plain pine coffin. By the time family friends had removed it, many in the crowd were ashen-faced at what they had just seen.

The three hundred or so who watched the hanging were quiet throughout and, as the *Stratford Herald* reporter observed, conducted themselves "without any demonstration whatsoever." Most who were there were relieved that they had arrived in time to see the spectacle. The execution was originally scheduled for later in the morning, and by ten o'clock, thousands of others streamed into Goderich to witness the event.

They were too late. They had missed Canada's last public hanging.

Three weeks after Nicholas Melady was hanged, a new federal government Order-in-Council took effect. It stipulated that from January 1, 1870, executions would no longer be public, thereby ensuring that this death would become an infamous footnote in the history of the nation. It followed, by ten months, the execution of one Patrick Whelan for the murder in Ottawa of politician and father of Confederation Thomas D'Arcy McGee.

The death of Nicholas Melady was the final event in his long and bitter journey. He alone paid with his life for what was done on that warm spring evening eighteen months before. But the events of that night would continue to be as controversial as they were revolting.

CHAPTER 2 | THE LAW AND THE LAND

THE SHADOW OF the gallows has hung over my family for over a century. But we rarely mention the matter, not just because it is somewhat embarrassing, but because we have never really known the whole story. On those rare occasions when the subject comes up, we still switch to something safer: who is hospitalized; last night's game; the need for rain. After all, the killings took place a long time ago, so perhaps it is best to forget them. Doing otherwise might be too painful.

And yet, some of us have always wondered about those deaths — all three of them. Why did they happen? How did they happen? What mysteries lay at their root? Were they properly investigated? Were the trials fair? Did the third person deserve to die? Did others? Today, no one knows the answers to most of these questions. In fact, no one may ever know all the facts.

Of course, many years have passed. When the tragedy occurred, this nation was new. Great swaths of forest blanketed much of the land, many roads were corduroy at best, and the western plains were still unploughed. Those coming to Canada at the time were among the first white people to arrive. And while aboriginal peoples were the original inhabitants, incoming settlers from overseas were generally referred to as pioneers in this vast land. They came to eastern North America first, then followed the lakes and rivers to the Prairies, the mountains, and ultimately, the shores of the western sea. Partway there, they discovered what we now call Ontario.

Settlement in this province also began in the east, along the mighty St. Lawrence River, in towns like Prescott, Brockville, and Kingston. From there, by water, bush road, and eventually rail, the newcomers moved west. York, the settlement that in time would spawn the towers of Toronto and the millions who live and work in them, soon became the most important town in what came to be called Upper Canada.

A brilliant drunk was prime minister, and the union he had toiled to establish was fragile at best. Because settlers were coming in so quickly, and the nation was growing so fast, governing it and them would take every skill that John A. Macdonald possessed. But the young country would remain intact, flourish, and, in time, take its place as a land of plenty and peace.

But not for all. Perhaps plenty for those who toiled with diligence — but peace? Not for Nicholas Melady, Sr. He was probably never at peace. Nor was he ever truly happy. He came from poverty, lived with constant adversity, and, in the end, died horribly.

He was born in Longford County, Ireland, like his father before him, and his father's father. All had been tenant farmers: men of the soil who in large measure failed, not because of their work ethic or the quality of the land they leased, but because of ever-increasing demands of absentee landlords they rarely saw. In Ireland he had had little, and in the first few years after he immigrated to Canada he may have had less. But at least here, he had opportunity.

In Ireland, he had been a product of his father's first marriage. There were siblings, but little is known of them today. Following the death of his wife, Nicholas's father remarried and had a second family; a son from this union was my great-grandfather. His name was Thomas Melady.

As far as we know, Thomas had a typical, if impoverished, upbringing in the land of his birth. Because of the dictates of the English Penal Laws, under which Roman Catholic boys in Ireland were not to be educated, we can assume he had little, if any, formal schooling. He would have worked on the land, along with his father, but when he got the chance to leave Ireland and the hardship that was there, he grasped the opportunity.

Family lore tells us that shortly before he left home, he was helping to cut turf and transport it by wheelbarrow to a shed for drying. It was 1839, and he was sixteen years old. The peat bog where he worked was essentially a long, hand-cut trench in the marshy ground, about six feet below the level of the surrounding fields. The day was damp, the work hard, and the satisfaction involved in the task almost non-existent. But that morning, he was told that a letter had arrived from Canada for him. Someone — it is unclear who — read it to him, and the young peat cutter got the news that he had awaited for weeks. He was being asked to come to Canada, where a new life awaited him. Whether he knew, or even cared, what this new life would offer is debatable. The message meant opportunity, and he intended to grasp it. He knew little of the land to which he would go. The youngster threw down his wheelbarrow and announced to those with him: "That's the last turf I'll ever wheel in Ireland." And he kept his word. We do not know for sure who wrote to him, although it was likely Nicholas, his half-brother.

As soon as he could arrange passage, Tom said emotional goodbyes to those he loved and then left Ireland on a sailing ship, one of the 221 filthy barques that transported so many destitute Irish to the New World. After three months on the storm-tossed North Atlantic, land was sighted, and the ship moved into the Gulf of St. Lawrence. Then there was a stop at Grosse Ile, the infamous quarantine station, thirty miles or so east of Quebec City. There, on that rocky, windswept, forested island where thousands of starving, desperately ill Irish would find but a grave, Tom went ashore, but because he was healthy, he was allowed to go on.

The young man walked off the sailing ship at the port of Montreal, and a week or so later, as soon as he could arrange passage, he boarded a smaller Durham boat: a forty-foot-long, flat-bottomed vessel capable of manoeuvring through the St. Lawrence rapids above Montreal. In due course, he arrived at Prescott, Ontario, and disembarked for good in the bustling harbour immediately below Fort Wellington, the imposing structure built during the War of 1812. He then walked for most of a day through the bush to the tiny village of Merrickville, some twenty-five miles north of the St. Lawrence. He lived and worked for a time on a farm there, but not long afterwards made his way across the province to Adjala Township, near present-day Barrie. Later, young Tom journeyed south and west to the Seaforth area, acquired land, and remained there for the rest of his life.

He went to Adjala because Nicholas was homesteading nearby. Thomas may have hoped his older half-brother would be a mentor or protector of sorts, but this did not happen. Nicholas was a hard-driving, ruthless man who was almost impossible to work with or please. Within a month, the two parted company and Tom moved on. In Barrie, he befriended a one-armed man named Downey, who convinced him to leave Adjala and go to the Huron Tract, where a settlement outfit called the Canada Company was leasing and selling land. Whether Downey was of lasting help is not known, nor is his particular connection to their destination, although he had relatives in the Tract and likely wanted to join them. The fact that he was handicapped seems to have been the one characteristic that people remembered.

The Huron Tract, as it was called, was a vast swath of virgin forest, encompassing close to two and a half million acres, most of which lay in southwestern Ontario between Guelph and Goderich. Tom was particularly attracted to acreage in Hibbert Township, on the western edge of Perth County. Once in Hibbert, he leased one hundred acres, built a cabin, and set about felling trees.

Nicholas remained where he was. He was nineteen years older than Thomas and had arrived in Canada as a young man. Once here, he had worked hard, saved his money, and scraped together £100 by the winter of 1834. On February 22 that year, he used the cash to buy land that became available in Tecumseth, the township that bordered Adjala. The plot acquired was only fifty acres, rock-strewn and hilly, but at least it was his, and Nicholas was on his way. In time, he would add to his holdings and become a wealthy man.

During his time in Tecumseth, he married and became a father. His wife, the former Margaret Farrell, bore him a daughter, Mary, before he bought his land. A second daughter, named after her mother, was born in the summer of 1835. Four other children, two boys and two girls, would round out the family. The youngest of the six, Nicholas Jr., came along in 1845. This boy was destined to become even more infamous than his father would prove to be. Because no hospitals existed in the bush, all the children were born at home.

Meanwhile, Nicholas Sr., or Old Melady as he came to be called, continued to improve his lot, but those early years were hardscrabble. The trees and brush that thrived on his land had to be cut, cleared, and burned. The stones that seemed to be everywhere had to be removed by hand and either piled in selected spots or placed along what would become fence lines. As soon as possible, wheat, corn, and other crops had to be planted to provide fodder for the first few chickens, cattle, and pigs that were bought, bred, and butchered for family sustenance. There was always a garden. The potato was the most important item, but there were also carrots, cucumbers, peas, cabbage, turnips, and other vegetables for the table. In addition, wild fruits such as strawberries, raspberries, and blueberries were picked and preserved for the long winter months. The main meats were always beef and salt pork. Women baked everything from bread to pie. Often venison was part of the diet.

The first accommodation in the bush would have been a log cabin, likely a mere shack, erected quickly with whatever tools were at hand. It would have been small and uncomfortable. In most cases the interior was dark, smoky, and drafty, and often the roof leaked. Initially, the floor was the earth, and the heat came from a fireplace. The farther from the fire you were, the colder it was. On winter nights, water inside the building would freeze. In summer, the interior was hot, stuffy, and damp.

There was not a lot of furniture, other than a makeshift bed, table, chairs, and a cupboard. These items were handmade. As children came along, a rudimentary sleeping loft might have been built, but in many cases, the cabin was a single room. There was no plumbing, no electricity, and no respite from work. Everyone pitched in and toiled from dawn to dusk. And this meant all family members. Children laboured alongside their parents at every job, from picking stones to chopping wood to baking bread.

Education out of the home was rudimentary, and not many children went beyond three or four years of what we would call elementary school. Youngsters who went further were few, largely because, once they were in their teens, they were sorely needed on the farm. In general, schools that did exist had one room, and pupils from seven to seventeen were all there together. The schoolroom itself was small, low-ceilinged, poorly lit, and either too hot or too cold, depending on the time of year. The walls and floors were rough boards at best, and the desks often accommodated two and even three youngsters. Children wrote on individual slates with chalk, or in workbooks or "scribblers" when they were available. Paper was often in short supply. Apart from an old Bible and perhaps a dog-eared atlas and a history of England, there were few books. The boys and girls in the schoolroom were taught together, but they generally played apart during the recess and noon breaks. They often used separate doors to enter and exit the building, and when they came inside, they hung coats and caps on hooks near the door or, as the schools got larger, in what were called cloakrooms. When outside, the children played with a ball and bat and perhaps a skipping rope, or on a swing attached to a tree limb in the yard. There was lots of tag, hide-and-seek, and soccer, though the game was generally called football at the time. Apart from a teeter-totter (a board over a big chunk of tree trunk), virtually no schoolyard play equipment existed.

There was an outdoor privy, of course: a tiny, smelly, fly-filled building, half-concealed by bushes at the back of the property. The "convenience" was used in winter and summer. When the snow was deep, a path had to be shovelled to the door. Drinking water came from a pump in the yard, or else was brought in a pail from the nearest house. As in the homes, however, water left in the classroom overnight would be frozen solid on winter mornings. Generally, either the teacher or one of the older boys at the school arrived early and lit the fire. There was rarely what we might call a janitor or custodian who would do this. Children often had to wear their coats and caps for the first hour or so, until the classroom became warm enough to be comfortable. But by then it was often too hot, and the pupils would complain of the heat. Students walked to school, and indeed, the location of the building was generally based on how far a youngster could walk to get there. Tales of long treks in winter storms to a cold schoolhouse were based on fact.

Teachers often had little education themselves and were expected to rule with an iron fist. If they failed to do so, they did not last. They were hired as much for their ability to keep order as their ability to teach. Oftentimes, those hiring the teacher were barely literate themselves, but then, as now, they wanted more for their children. The teacher was often a young, single woman who paid a nominal rent to stay at a local home. More often than not, it would be at the home of children she taught. In many cases, these women came to a community to teach and then met and married someone from the same region. Sometimes, the new teacher was the first young woman that the single men in the settlement had seen. And whether beautiful or plain, she generally had her choice of suitors.

Entertainment for both adults and children was limited in these communities. There was visiting at other homes, lots of storytelling, card-playing for some, and, in the summer, picnics. In many instances, settlers with musical talent played the fiddle at community gatherings in the local schoolhouse — often the only building around that was large enough to accommodate a crowd. Life was hard, but there was always time for laughter. Homemade hooch was often a factor in the merriment.

That, then, was the environment in which Old Melady raised his family.

Over time, he prospered; he cleared more land, increased his livestock holdings, grew larger crops, and sold both for profit. With the returns, he obtained more land: at least two additional fifty-acre farms in Tecumseth alone. Then, like his half-brother, he gravitated to the Seaforth area. He had heard that the land there was better than where he was.

While Old Melady was wheeling and dealing in Tecumseth, his half-brother Thomas was leasing and clearing a Canada Company hundred-acre property at Lot 30, Concession IV of Hibbert. Here, vast stands of maple and other trees took forever to remove, but the young man did his best in the face of insurmountable odds and limited funds. Unfortunately, on this land, all his work would be in vain. He fell behind in his rent, and despite travelling at least twice to Toronto to renegotiate the terms of his lease, he ultimately lost the farm and the owners retained title.

But then Old Melady arrived on the scene with plenty of cash. He gave the Canada Company businessmen £175 and bought the acreage for himself. The deal closed on February 14, 1853. Because a good deal of the terrain had already been cleared and had become workable, acquiring it was certainly a bargain. Thomas, the half-brother who had done all the work, lost out. There is no record of his ever being paid for his labour.

Thomas learned from the matter, however, and when he was granted a lease on property that became available nearby, he managed to hang onto it. Even though he eventually bought the land, added to it, and continued to farm there for years, he always harboured a measure of bitterness about the way his older sibling had treated him. The two remained on speaking terms, however, and occasionally worked together in the company of others at barn raisings and the like. In time, they became more reconciled, and much later, in 1866, they were jointly appointed Overseers for the Highways by the Hibbert Township Council. This indicates that by then, Thomas, as well as Nicholas, had a substantial farming operation. They were two of eleven appointed to ensure that the roads in the areas of their properties were maintained according to the standards then in place. Prior to municipal tax assessments that included road maintenance, the job was done by property owners themselves, or by others they hired to do the work for them.

Back when he first came to Tom's land, Old Melady learned that the soil was even better than he expected, so he decided he wanted more of it. To that end, he bought three other hundred-acre farms on that same 1853 Valentine's Day. All were close to the property Thomas had lost, but were in adjacent Tuckersmith Township, in Huron County. On one of these, Lot 2, Concession III, Old Melady would eventually build a large house.

It would be the last he would ever own. Thirteen years later, his bloody corpse would be carried from it. But that is getting ahead of the story.

Despite becoming, overnight, a major landowner in Huron and Perth, Old Melady had no intention of leaving Tecumseth just yet. His home, his family, and his other holdings were still there.

During his last years in Tecumseth, he continued to add to his assets and improve his farms, and he became increasingly well-to-do. He travelled regularly between Tecumseth and Seaforth, and occasionally took one or more of his children with him. They probably stayed with his oldest daughter, Mary, who had already met and married a prosperous farmer from Hibbert named Tom McGoey. The McGoeys lived on Lot 26, Concession IV of Hibbert, fairly close to the properties Old Melady had recently purchased. Also around this time he became a grandfather.

But things began to go wrong in Tecumseth, and he found himself involved in several disputes with farmers in the area. There were arguments about property lines, missing cattle, and the like, and while most of the squabbles were relatively minor at first, they eventually increased in seriousness until the police took notice. Any time he was involved in a disagreement, Old Melady never conceded that he might be in the wrong.

Virtually all of his troubles grew out of the fact that he was a hot-tempered bully who simply could not get along with people. The fact that he drank too much often made bad situations worse. In one month in 1859, for example, he was in court twice. On August 4, he was convicted in Barrie on two charges: trespassing on a neighbour's property and threatening the same neighbour when the man objected. Nicholas Jr., then fourteen, was not only present with his father on both occasions, he was also found guilty of the same offences. Years later, as will be shown, the pair would become adversaries before the law, but on this occasion, they acted together. Both were fined and told to keep the peace.

Neither did so. The two were back in the courtroom again on August 16. George McManus, the presiding Justice of the Peace, seemed to have become tired of the nonsense. He convicted the pair of assault and threatening. He also doubled the fines and told the pair they would face ten days in jail if they did not pay.

They paid, or at least the father paid for both. At this point, it should be noted, father and son were quite close. They worked together on the Tecumseth farms, and Nicholas could do no wrong in his father's eyes. Because he was the youngest in the family, the boy had always been his father's favourite child. In due course, however, that would change.

Old Melady was just coming into his own as far as contact with the law was concerned. He continued to get into trouble, and finally, following another incident, he was arrested, tried, and convicted on a much more serious charge. Unfortunately, the nature of the crime is missing in the records, and National Archives inmate case files date from 1886 only. However, fragmentary newspaper references imply that it may have been arson. He could well have torched someone's barn during one of his drunken rages. At any rate, the outcome is known. He was sent to the penitentiary for three years.

Much later, in another courtroom in another place and time, a trial witness who knew him in Tecumseth testified that Old Melady left there out of fear for his life. Had he not, the witness declared, he would have been killed by a fellow named Lester. Unfortunately, further information about the matter was not recorded, and the woman who made the state-ment was not asked to elaborate. Today, we know neither Lester's full name nor the cause of the conflict.

Whatever the problem, it definitely precipitated his move from Tecumseth. In the summer of 1863, not long after his release from prison, the family packed their belongings and travelled to their new home in Huron County. Sadly, Margaret, Old Melady's long-suffering wife, passed away the same year. He found himself a widower with plenty of money but few friends.

CHAPTER 3 | IMPOSSIBLE TO PLEASE

WHEN HE CAME to Huron County in 1863, Old Melady moved into the new, storey-and-a-half frame house local builders had constructed for him on Lot 2, Concession III of Tuckersmith Township. The large building was on the south side of what would have been little more than a wagon road at the time. There were several rooms, along with a basement that provided ample storage space for winter food. A cast-iron stove and a fireplace provided warmth, with plenty of hardwood readily available to burn.

The structure faced north towards the road and sat well back from the front of the property. On the east side of the building was the rather pretentiously named Bayfield River. The only time this watercourse was much of a river was during the spring runoff. Then it often became a raging torrent, and ice jams routinely tore out one and sometimes both of the wooden bridges that were half a mile or so from Old Melady's home. The rest of the year the stream meandered southward through the middle of the property and then veered west into the trees until it could no longer be seen from the house. Other than in the springtime, or after a prolonged period of rain, the river was always fairly shallow, and in the late summer it often dropped to a mere trickle in places. However, because it never ran dry, it was a valuable natural resource for watering livestock. A well had been dug by hand twenty feet southeast of the house, and water from it was meant for human consumption. Several mature trees encircled the dooryard.

At the time he had the house built, Old Melady would have had a shed of some sort constructed for his horses and whatever other animals he may have brought with him. Horse-drawn buggies, large farm wagons, and what were called buckboards, or light wagons, were the mode of non-public transportation, and virtually all farmers kept horses. In winter, travel was by sleigh or cutter, so those who did not have at least one horse walked or hitched rides with neighbours. Many settlers travelled on horseback as well. In the spring of 1868, five years after his arrival, Old Melady contracted to have a larger barn erected on the property. He had become increasingly prosperous, and the barn he had been using was inadequate. He had cows that were milked by hand morning and night, along with calves that were together in pens, so the first barn was jammed to the rafters. The upper mows of the structure were always filled in the summer with the long hay crop his cattle consumed in winter.

At the time he made the move to Huron, only two of his six children were still at home. They were Alice, then nineteen, and Catherine, who was twenty-one. Both older daughters were already married: Mary was Tom McGoey's wife, and Margaret had married a young man named James Kehoe. In due course, the Kehoes would move near Old Melady, to a farm just across the river to the east. He bought this hundred acres in 1858 and then leased it to Margaret and James. And even though he had sold one farm in Tecumseth back on June 10, 1857, he still had plenty of land. His Huron holdings alone now amounted to three hundred acres. The hundred acres in Hibbert was in addition to this. For the most part, the soil on all these farms was a rich black loam.

The two sons had moved out some time earlier. The older of the two, another Thomas Melady, went to the United States, found employment, and, apart from brief visits home, remained away from Canada — and away from his father. During this period and later, many young men from Ontario drifted across the border to work on American farms and for lumber and construction companies there. With his farm background, Thomas had no trouble finding a job. Because he had helped clear land in Tecumseth, he was equally at home wielding an axe in the bush, sowing wheat in a clearing, or building the stone wall foundation for a barn.

Nicholas Jr. lasted longer at home, but then left — more than once.

As part of his farming interests, Old Melady was busy selling cattle at the stockyards in Toronto. Over time, he marketed hundreds of animals there, and they all had to be driven to the city, so father and son attempted to work together on the enterprise. Even though hired hands were there to help, the journey was a long and difficult one. There were no trucks, of course, or even trains near his land at the time; while the route followed on the cattle drives was presumably the most direct, even then, it would have been at least thirty miles.

The livestock taken to Toronto were likely Shorthorn, the English/Scottish breed that had been introduced into Canada thirty years earlier. These animals could be used for either dairy purposes or for their meat. A few cows were milked, but most ran with their calves and were kept to build up the herd. Once young heifers were old enough they were bred, while the fattened steers were marketed in the city. Old Melady made a lot of money from this venture, and because Toronto was expanding so rapidly, the town was a steady source of cash. Satisfying the insatiable urban need for food was a never-ending proposition.

Each year, his herds got larger; the need for beef was more pressing, so profits increased proportionately. The cattle drives were done on horseback, on trails through the bush, in all kinds of weather. And even though we sometimes think of such jobs as both adventurous and even romantic, they were not necessarily so. The work often had to be done on days that were too hot or too cold, and even though it was usually boring, it was sometimes dangerous. Men were out in lightning storms, on horses that sometimes spooked or bucked when being saddled. Men were injured by their mounts, sometimes severely, although deaths from the kick of a horse were relatively rare. There were occasional instances of lightning killing cattle drivers who made the mistake of sheltering under trees in storms.

It was after the delivery of one herd that Nicholas and his father had a serious disagreement over something. It is probable that Old Melady expected his son to work for free, but whatever the cause, the matter seems to have simmered for a time. When the steers were sold and Old Melady was flush with cash, the two erupted into a heated argument. Father and son were alike in temperament, and neither would back down from confrontation. Old Melady apparently refused to pay, or paid too little, so Nicholas told him he could keep the job and then left home for the first time. As far as we know today, Old Melady never admitted that his own intransigence might have been the reason. He had money, and he felt he could always go and hire whomever he wished and pay them less than Nicholas wanted. That idea did not prove to be particularly successful, however. Because of his belligerence and temper, Old Melady was rarely able to keep help for long — even when he paid appropriately.

For the next while, the son lived with an aunt in Monroe, Michigan, a small town southwest of Detroit. However, after a cooling-off period, he was persuaded by the aunt to return to Tecumseth. She came with him, presumably hoping to ameliorate the relationship between her hot-headed brother and his boy. Because Old Melady found he needed more help than he could hire, he too had suggested his son return, and he offered Nicholas a cash advance if he would stay. The mere fact that the father asked for help was almost out of character for him. It implied that he had been the one in the wrong, even though he could not and would not ever admit it — least of all to Nicholas.

Nicholas was a hard worker and was interested in farming, but he could not co-exist for long with his father on the same land. Old Melady was beginning to realize this, so he promised that in time, Nicholas could have the hundred acres in Hibbert as his own. He could farm there, buy more land if he wished, and be a success. He could also be some distance away from constant correction. Nicholas liked the proposal, and, perhaps against his own better judgment, he took his father at his word and agreed to stay at home and help out. He set to work, did not complain, and gradually assumed more and more responsibility. His father even let him make some of the decisions relative to cropping and land clearance. Two of the cattle drives to Toronto were carried out successfully and without rancor.

For a time, the arrangement worked well. Nicholas was young, strong, muscular, almost six feet in height, and well-suited to farm labour. Much later, newspaper reports would refer to this period as a time when father and son seemed to get along and to work together with a minimum of friction.

In all likelihood, Nicholas used whatever free time he had, and possibly his evenings, to further his education. He also may have attended school when he was in Michigan. These efforts paid off. A newspaper story about him published in the *Stratford Herald* on December 15, 1869, mentioned that he had received "a good English education." He was, the paper affirmed, "a good writer, indeed far better than any of his rank in life." He also "conversed freely and sensibly." Obviously, young Nicholas was a man with a future. For his time he had all the education he needed to succeed in farming and marketing, and the inherited skills to do both. He also had an excellent mind.

But the good times did not last. In all, Nicholas remained at home for seventeen months. He and his father worked together reasonably well at first and tried to avoid irritating each other. One day, however, the pair had another dispute, and Old Melady reneged on his earlier promise. Because he was being threatened in Tecumseth and knew he had to get out quickly, he was in no mood to negotiate anything. Also, because more of his holdings were now in Huron, and as he would be living close enough to keep an eye on the Hibbert farm himself, he told Nicholas he could not have it after all. There was a prolonged, heated argument, but Old Melady would not relent.

Bitterly disappointed, the son went back to Michigan. There are no records around that indicate how long he was there this time, or even where he actually lived. The aunt had returned to Monroe, however, so he likely stayed with her. Presumably, he found employment there, and he may have even considered settling down and becoming an American. However, this did not come to pass. After his release from prison, Old Melady had to get rid of cattle that he owned in Tecumseth. While he was in prison, no one else had dared make many decisions concerning which cattle to sell and which to keep. For this reason, when he got back from prison, the cattle had to be culled; there were just too many of them. He therefore held one last cattle drive from Tecumseth, probably no more than a month before leaving for Huron. Records that survive mention that Nicholas actually came home from Michigan, helped with this drive, and then went right back to the U.S. as soon as the cattle were sold. But Nicholas would not remain in the United States

Back in Ontario, Old Melady was becoming established in Huron, but the long hours of work and worry that farming entailed were taking their toll. In 1864, he was sixty years old, and while he was still tall and powerfully built, he had neither the desire nor the ability to toil as he once had. Even though he had always been known to drink heavily, he now started to do a lot more of it.

He often drank alone, mainly because he was an ugly drunk. For that reason, he alienated many who might have befriended him. And while he was hot-tempered even when cold sober, drinking companions soon realized that he became explosive after too much alcohol. He became totally obnoxious and would do his best to start a fight, so those who knew they could never beat him physically simply avoided him. On days when drinking at home lost its appeal, he would hitch up a horse, climb into his buggy, and make the three-mile drive to Seaforth, already a flourishing community of about a thousand souls. From the time its first resident had built a log cabin there some twenty years earlier, the settlement had grown rapidly. When the railway arrived in 1858, the impetus for growth was enhanced. Houses went up, as did stores, churches, a school, and several hotels. One of these was called the Carmichael.

This hotel, on the southwest side of the main corner of the town, was probably the most prestigious. Old Melady would go there, drink to excess, flash a wad of money, and almost always get into a drunken argument with whoever happened to be nearby. Like all disputes between inebriates, the subject matter was invariably puerile and pointless. Then the old drunk would blubber in his beer about how much he missed Nicholas.

So it was that during the winter of 1863, after he had been in his new home for a few months, Old Melady contacted his younger son and more or less pleaded with him to come home. The entreaty was thought through before it was made, so it may well have been quite sincere. Old Melady was desperately lonely. He missed his wife, and he undoubtedly needed another pair of hands on the farm. His daughters Catherine and Alice helped when they could, cooked his meals, and tried to keep him out of trouble. But they had no real love of farm labour, and they too would often leave home and spend time with their sisters, Mary McGoey and Margaret Kehoe. It was as if the two youngest daughters could only tolerate their father's antics on a somewhat less than regular basis.

In his message to Nicholas, Old Melady renewed his offer of land. For a second time, Nicholas took the bait. He too was lonely, so he came home in early April, in time to help with the spring seeding. His father welcomed him with unaccustomed warmth, and once more promised the Hibbert farm. Again, Nicholas set to work to earn it.

By then, a good portion of the land the father owned was cleared, so there would have been much spring planting to do. This involved long, dusty hours in the fields, at a job that was very labour intensive. There are no records extant as to hired hands Old Melady employed for the task, but given the size of his operation, there might have been three or four. And because he still had land in Tecumseth that had to be seeded as well, some likely worked in both places.

While he was out in the fields during the spring, Nicholas was at least some distance away from his father. However, at mealtimes and at night, they were together in the house. Such close proximity again led to bickering, and because both were quite stubborn, neither wanted to lose an argument. Nicholas was now nineteen years old, and he would no longer let his father dictate all of the terms all the time. As always, his father refused to tolerate a difference of opinion.

It was therefore not surprising that there was another eruption. Although neither the specific reason nor the exact location is certain, we do know that it was at a Seaforth hotel. There, father and son were drinking together when they started to bicker; their voices were raised, and in no time they were flailing at each other. Neither was injured, but the ruckus got completely out of hand. A crowd gathered, and try as he might, the beleaguered hotel keeper found it impossible to restore order. The police were called, and both combatants ended up in court — each charged with assaulting the other.

In convictions registered on May 5, 1864, Justice of the Peace John Fitzgerald fined both men, but the aggressor was definitely Old Melady. He was fined two dollars and costs; Nicholas was fined one dollar. Each was ordered to keep the peace and to pay the Huron County Treasurer forthwith. The money was paid. Then the two went back to the farm — chastened but not repentant.

For a few weeks, there seems to have been a fragile peace. The seeding was completed, and given the excellence of the soil in the Seaforth area, the crops flourished. Summer was at hand, and by the third week in June, haying season started. By any measure, harvesting hay was even more strenuous than planting the crops had been. Fields of clover, timothy, and alfalfa had to be cut by hand, coiled to dry, and then transported by horse and wagon into the barn in order to feed the livestock during the winter. Taking off hay was hot, backbreaking, and mind-numbing, but apparently Nicholas did his share, kept a low profile, and stayed out of trouble.

Then there was yet another upheaval. Again the location of the incident is not known for sure, but in all probability it was the Carmichael, still Old Melady's preferred haunt on Main Street in Seaforth. Nicholas and his father were there along with Jim Kehoe, Margaret's husband. The three sat around a beverage room table, drank to excess, and got loud. It was not a sedate social gathering.

During the fight that seems to have been inevitable, Jim played peacemaker. Judicial records note his presence but give no indication of any charges against him. Old Melady and Nicholas both were charged, and again it was the father who was the instigator. In the trial before Justice Robert Hays on June 24, 1864, at the Huron County Court in Goderich, Old Melady was convicted of assault on his son, fined eight dollars, and ordered to remit forthwith. Nicholas was convicted on the same charge, but his fine was only a dollar. And while he was given three weeks to pay, he did not do so. The Return of Convictions statement for the period mentions that he "left the place." Nicholas had gone back to Michigan.

At this time, those who appeared before the courts were publicly identified, their charges listed, and the judgments indicated. As well, the magistrate who was involved was named, and sometimes even the police officer who investigated the case. These documents were published periodically in the larger papers of the day and were avidly pored over by readers. The reports were the gossip columns of the day.

So now Old Melady was alone again, or at least he didn't have Nicholas to get on his nerves. For his part, Nicholas seems to have decided to stay away for good. He probably assumed he would never get the Hibbert farm and was undoubtedly fed up with going home, working hard, and getting nothing for doing so. He is on record later as complaining about this in conversations about the circumstances of his employment while he was at home. He often said he could barely afford to live when he worked at home. His father fed him and made sure he worked hard, but never wanted to pay for the labour. Old Melady, it seemed, was more interested in spending his money on alcohol than on his farmhands or his son.

As far as can be determined, Nicholas stayed out of trouble while he was away. But Old Melady did not.

About five months after his younger son left the country, Old Melady seems to have resumed his rambunctious ways — perhaps because he no longer had his wife to provide some restraint, or because he simply had too much money at his disposal and did not know what to do with it, or just because he was bored. This time, however, he ran into a problem of different nature.

A woman was involved. Unlike his late wife, this individual had no intention of backing down in the face of his belligerence. Unfortunately, today we know little about her, apart from her name. Old Melady and one Bridget Flood had some kind of a confrontation in Carronbrook, the village that would later be called Dublin, about five miles northeast of the Huron farm. Carronbrook was a small place, one of the many settlements that sprang up along what was called the Huron Road, the main east-west artery that linked the Canada Company lands between Guelph and Goderich.

Melady was in Carronbrook on Monday, November 14, when he encountered Bridget. As usual, he had been drinking that day, and when the two exchanged words, she became quite upset. No one knows what was actually said, but in response to it, Bridget started to beat on him. Old Melady did not take kindly to this, so he had her charged.

Three weeks later, on December 9, the pair found themselves before two Justices of the Peace, again in Carronbrook. The judicial report of the matter may be mildly amusing today, but to Old Melady, the resolution of the case must have been as surprising as it was unwelcome.

The charge against Flood, in the parlance of the times, was as follows: "That Bridget Flood, of the Township of Hibbert, did assault and beat with a stick one Nicholas Melady over the head and shoulders, contrary to the form of the statute in such case made and provided."

Old Melady explained his version of events, presumably painting himself as the hapless victim in the case. The justices listened to his submission because they were obliged to do.

Then Flood had her turn. She must have provided a detailed rationale for her actions, because whatever she said was convincing. Unfortunately, there is no mention in the surviving documents as to what Old Melady actually did to her, or said to her, that led to the beating. At any rate, when Justices of the Peace R.H. Sarvis and James Pierce had heard and considered all the facts, they rejected Old Melady's testimony entirely and decided that he was solely responsible for what had happened to him. The ruling they handed down was blunt, and it undoubtedly got Old Melady's attention.

"We do therefore dismiss the same, and do adjudge that the said Nicholas Melady, Complainant, do pay to the said Bridget Flood, Defendant, the sum of five dollars for her costs incurred by her in her defence in this behalf," the Justices wrote. Then they added, "If the said sum for costs be not paid within ten days, we order that the same Nicholas Melady be imprisoned in the Common Gaol for the space of fifteen days." Melady paid, and the case was closed.

But his troubles were far from over.

CHAPTER 4 | A Decision to Get Even

IN THE FIRST few months following his humiliating loss to Bridget Flood in the Carronbrook court, Nicholas Melady, Sr., worked his land, played with his grandchildren, and started another fight. His older two daughters had young families, and by all accounts, he enjoyed the children. Because none of them lived far from him, he saw them often, carted them around, and delighted in their development. This was particularly true of Margaret and James Kehoe's little girl and boy. They came to his house, sometimes daily, and he was glad to have them there. On those occasions, and to the surprise of all, he was actually a loving patriarch.

But because he was who he was, a problem soon arose with the children's parents — or more correctly, with their father.

Shortly after their marriage, the Kehoes lived for a time in Guelph, Ontario, but Margaret missed being closer to her three sisters. She had few friends in Guelph, and given the difficulties of travelling by road between there and Seaforth, she found it impossible to visit her family very often. She took the train now and then, but the cost of a ticket was onerous, especially because neither she nor Jim had money for anything that could be termed frivolous. She prevailed upon her husband to move to Huron. He was initially reluctant to do so, mainly because he had never been terribly fond of Old Melady and wondered about living anywhere near him. However, because of his wife's insistence, Jim finally agreed to go.

Because they could not possibly afford land of their own at the time, the Kehoes ended up living next door to Margaret's father on the farm he bought in 1858. Old Melady was quite happy to lease the property to family members, but they were expected to clear the land, crop it, and then pay him a rather high rent. This had to be paid in full, on time, twice a year. And while the exact amount does not show up in any records of the time, news stories refer to the sum as being substantial. Old Melady gave nothing away, even to his daughters, so coming up with the necessary cash proved to be more of a struggle than the renters had anticipated. Cutting the trees, working the land, and cropping it were the easy parts.

At first, the Kehoes got along surprisingly well with Old Melady. They visited back and forth, and he was solicitous of their well-being. However, it was not long before his drunken antics became annoying, and gradually, even Margaret's relationship with him, although respectful, became strained. She did not object to the fact that her children went to see their grandfather whenever they wished, though, because she wanted them to have a positive relationship with him. After all, they did not have a grandmother on her side of the family now, and they were too young to notice the coolness among the adults.

Jim Kehoe's affection for his father-in-law was never warm, but in spite of that, they saw each other fairly often, worked together when they had to, and drank together on occasion. Still, Jim found that being beholden to Old Melady was demeaning always, and irritating often. Even though money was tight, he and Margaret did the best they could. When he was out of his wife's earshot, Jim sometimes told others how he felt. One of those he confided in was a neighbour, a man named Joseph Nigh.

Nigh lived across the road from Old Melady, not far from the Kehoes. He saw both parties regularly, and he and Jim liked each other and got along well. At a later time, Nigh would describe Old Melady as "contrary," while he thought Jim was a man who was "honest and upright." Because he was aware of Jim's frustration with his father-in-law, he sympathized with the young man.

The problem worsened, as Nigh would later explain, when Old Melady suddenly decided that he no longer wanted his daughter and son-in-law living where they were; he preferred, in Nigh's words, to have them "off the place" entirely. And even though Nigh did not explain his neighbour's rationale for this, he assumed it was more than likely about unpaid rent. But whatever the precise cause, Old Melady's attitude certainly annoyed Jim Kehoe. It actually bothered Nigh as well, but he kept his feelings to himself. In discussing the matter, Nigh did not mention, or perhaps did not know, how Margaret reacted. He just knew that Old Melady was forever badgering Jim, apparently hoping his son-in-law would just get fed up and go. Nigh was rather embarrassed by the tirades, and when they occurred, generally wished he was somewhere else. He always felt sorry for Jim when these arguments erupted.

But suddenly, the young couple had something of a reprieve. Old Melady still pressured them to get off his land, but he became less combative about it. In fact, he suddenly became much more accommodating and less dictatorial in his demands. The change was as unexpected as it was remarkable — until the reason came out. Old Melady had fallen in love.

Today, we have no idea how they first became acquainted, but Nicholas Melady, Sr., and a young widow began to see each other on a fairly regular basis. Her name was Ellen Kelly, and her late husband, John, had farmed in Hibbert. When he passed away, she continued to live in the family home there. She was in her late thirties when she became romantically linked with Old Melady, had one son for certain, and may have had other children as well. The son would probably have been eighteen or nineteen at this time.

As might be expected, there were those in the community who questioned Ellen's motives. A few said she truly loved Old Melady, but others were sure she "latched onto" him because he had money. The latter might well have been true, but it might also have been an observation born of jealousy. Old Melady had always been interested in other women, or so claimed the community gossips. So while they thought his actions now were completely in character, they also were of the opinion that a man of his age who was dating was just being a ridiculous old fool.

During the months when Old Melady was "courting," to use an expression of the time, his daughter Catherine was doing the same thing. She was still living at home, but she had met a man to whom she was quite attracted. His name was David Donovan, and he was a hard-working, muscular twenty-three-year-old with black hair, blue eyes, and a five-foot-eleven-inch frame. He and his brother Tom farmed together about four miles south of the Melady home. David was a bit younger than his twenty-five-year-old girlfriend, but the age difference was obviously unimportant. The two fell madly in love and soon began making plans to spend the rest of their lives together. In accordance with Roman Catholic practice, they contacted a priest and made arrangements for their wedding.

On Tuesday morning, May 28, 1867, Catherine and David were married in the St. Columban church in Irishtown. This was a small village three miles northeast of the Melady home. The church was located on the Huron Road, and at the time of the wedding, it was the only Catholic one in the entire area. The Irishtown settlement would later be renamed St. Columban, and it remains so today. Catherine's sister Alice was the maid of honour at the wedding, and one of the guests was their brother Nicholas, who came home for the occasion. He was reluctant to return at first, but the young couple wanted him to be present, and they sent several messages pleading with him to come.

Later on, the bride and groom probably wished they had never contacted him in Michigan, because his homecoming set in motion a series of events so terrible, no one involved could ever have anticipated the enormity. Once again, the long-standing feud between Nicholas and his father was at the centre of the storm.

Fortunately, the wedding itself went off without a hitch. The newly-weds and their guests had a wonderful day, and everyone had good memories of the time. There was a reception at the home of the bride; the liquor flowed, and the partying continued for hours. Even though Old Melady might have been cantankerous, his neighbours had no scruples about drinking his booze. They knew he could afford it.

The morning after his sister's wedding, Nicholas was approached by his father, who made yet another promise regarding the Hibbert farm. He needed his son's help, but he was too stubborn to come right out and admit it. This time, what he said seemed to carry more weight than previously, perhaps because Ellen Kelly was present and vouched for the sincerity of the words. However, she may not have known much about the previous offers and the rancor that had accompanied each one of them. Several people in the community did know, but there is no indication that she was one of them. She took Nicholas aside and told him she thought the offer was fair and was something he rightfully deserved. Her words were reassuring, and what she said was what he wanted to believe. Nicholas was still very skeptical, and with plenty of reason, but Old Melady insisted that this time, he really meant what he said, and he would keep his word. Nicholas could have the farm that fall.

The young man was delighted with the offer and envisioned going to the land, working it, building on it as soon as he could, and remaining there — likely for the rest of his life. However, he was still not ready to take his father's word at face value, so he suggested that together, they get a non-involved third party to verify the promise.

Old Melady agreed — reluctantly — and after some discussion the two decided the witness could be the St. Columban parish priest, Father James Murphy. Both Nicholas and his father knew Father Murphy and respected the big, plain-spoken clergyman who had arrived in Irishtown three years earlier.

Father Murphy acted as requested. Whether he knew of the father-son feud is not known, but in all likelihood, he did. He may even have felt that finally, these two strong-willed men were going to put their differences aside.

Five months later, Father Murphy joined Ellen Kelly and Nicholas Melady, Sr., in marriage. Their wedding was at St. Columban, and the date was Monday, October 21, 1867. Nicholas Melady was sixty-three, his bride forty. They took up residence at the Melady homestead in Huron. The local gossips now had to admit that, no matter what her motives, Ellen had caught her man.

Old Melady must have been filled with a surprising measure of goodwill that week, because three days after he was married, he formally relinquished the Hibbert farm to Nicholas by signing a ninety-nine-year lease on it. The son, who, rather surprisingly, had come home again for this wedding, finally had the land he had been promised for so long.

While Nicholas was undoubtedly happy about the agreement, a problem immediately asserted itself. Because he had been living in Michigan off and on for so long, he had certain business matters to take care of there before he would be in a position to remain in Hibbert. For this reason, he decided to lease the land until such time as he was in a position to come back and operate it. He made some discreet inquiries within the local farming community and had little trouble in locating an interested party. The rental agreement arrived at was for a single season only. Nicholas intended to return as soon as he could, so he felt that renting was the best option in the meantime. He also needed whatever money the land lease would produce.

Because he knew his father so well, he thought it would be unwise to tell him about his plans, so it was not until the following spring that word leaked out. Nicholas did not want to be the recipient of Old Melady's ire, but when the son did not turn up in time to plant the crops, Old Melady wondered what was going on. He hitched up his horse and buggy and drove to the Hibbert farm, and when he saw another farmer working the land, he began to realize what must have transpired. He spoke to the renter, who was cultivating a patch of wheat ground at the time. The poor man was reluctant to say much, but in the face of Old Melady's persistence and increasing anger, finally blurted out the details of the land lease.

Old Melady exploded in fury. He got back into his buggy, slapped his horse with the reins, and raced away in a cloud of dust, cursing loudly as he went. Later that same day, he set in motion a stratagem he knew well. He drove to Stratford, laid an official complaint before a magistrate in that city, and took his son to court.

The resulting case was heard before a judge at the courthouse in Stratford, because the disputed land was in Perth County and the administrative headquarters for the jurisdiction was there. Old Melady hired two high-priced lawyers, C. Robinson and S.G. McGaughay, and instructed them to break the lease he had given to Nicholas and to get the land back right away. He told them he had turned the land over to his son for his use alone, and that the contract was broken once the property was sublet to any other party.

Nicholas had to use most of his rent money to get legal representation, but he was able to retain a young barrister named J. Idington to take the case. The lawyer went over every detail of the dispute with his client, and once he got into court, he did a fine job. He countered all the arguments the father's legal team made, raised plenty of objections to what was said, and, in the eyes of the judge, presented the better case. Mr. Justice John Hawkins Hagarty took little time to ponder the matter and quickly found for the defendant. Nicholas was relieved at the outcome, congratulated Idington, and probably felt the dispute had ended at last.

He could not have been more wrong.

Old Melady was incredulous, and could not believe that he had lost. He listened to the judge's decision, and then, as several spectators, among them a newspaperman, watched, flew into a towering rage and stormed out of the courthouse. He stood on the steps of the building and made an utter fool of himself. The reporter remained to one side, listened, and scribbled furiously. The others who were there could barely believe what they were hearing.

The target of Old Melady's venom was Nicholas in particular, but it was not restricted to him. As the *Stratford Herald* reported in a story on December 15, 1869, the verdict "was a signal for Old Melady to show what kind of disposition he possessed, and in what terms he held his family. In front of the court house, he abused Nicholas, calling him a bastard, and applying to his late wife terms that are unfit for publication and such that are only applied to the vilest of the sex." In the same article, the reporter pointed out that Old Melady was in court because he wanted to go back on his word. Attempting to do so, the writer claimed, proved that Old Melady was "devoid of principle" and "utterly lacking in truth because of his refusal to fulfill the promise made before the priest." From the overall tone of the story, it was obvious that the newsman was profoundly shocked at what he had witnessed.

The promise notwithstanding, Old Melady had lost in law. Yet, true to his nature, he had no intention of simply dropping the matter. Had he done so, his future, and the future of his youngest son, might have been different indeed.

In the period immediately before his father's marriage to Ellen, Nicholas had expressed certain reservations about it. In fact, a neighbour had heard him say that he would never allow his father to bring another wife home. In all likelihood, his love for his own mother coloured his views about any woman who would replace her. Until he learned that his father was going to remarry, he sometimes stayed with him on visits home. But as soon as he found out that Ellen would be living there, he never slept at his father's again. Nor, for that matter, did other family members. Alice, the last to leave, moved in with Catherine and Dave Donovan shortly before her father's wedding.

In April 1868, less than a week after the hearing in Stratford, Nicholas noticed that his father had become close to Ellen's son. And while the Kelly boy did not live at the Melady home, he was often there working on the farm. He helped look after the cattle, did some of the milking, and was particularly good with horses.

One morning, as he was walking past Old Melady's home, Nicholas observed his father and the new stepson putting a plough and a set of harrows onto a wagon. They had already hitched the horses, so it looked as if they were preparing to take the farm implements elsewhere. The two secured the load, climbed onto the wagon, and started up the lane towards the road. As they did so, Nicholas, who was now some distance farther along, wondered where the two were going, but at the same time he hardly dared to let himself believe what he guessed.

His hunch was accurate. Old Melady drove the horses east along the dusty concession road from his house and turned a corner that led south to the Hibbert farm. But Nicholas got there first and watched to see what was going to happen.

Old Melady drove up, climbed down from the wagon, and, despite the fact that he saw Nicholas standing nearby, told his stepson to get ready to unload the implements. At this point, Nicholas strode over, reminded his father of the judge's ruling, and asked what was going on.

At first, Old Melady ignored the question, instead helping lift the plough to the ground. He finally said that he intended to take possession of the farm by working it, court order or not. It was *his* land, and no judge was going to tell him what he could or could not do with it. Nicholas objected, but to no avail, so he ordered his father off the property. Old Melady told his son to go to hell and refused to budge. The two came closer to each other, both shouting, neither looking as if he had any intention of resolving the dispute amicably.

As the stepson watched in amazement, they came to blows.

The fight was over almost as soon as it began. Nicholas was younger, quicker, stronger, and fed up. He got the better of his father and again told him to leave the farm. Surprisingly, Old Melady went — straight to Seaforth. There, he located a police officer and laid a complaint against his son. The lawman promised to investigate, and he kept his word.

A few days later, the combatants appeared before local Justice of the Peace Robert Hays. This time, Nicholas lost. He was convicted of assault, fined, and ordered to keep the peace. Old Melady gloated as he returned to his home. Nicholas went to scrounge for the money he had been told to pay.

Yet little had been resolved. Somewhat incredibly, Old Melady seems to have looked upon this victory in court as some kind of vindication of all his actions. The day after the hearing, he and the stepson again took a team of horses to the Hibbert farm, hitched them to the plough that was already there, and began to use it. By the time Nicholas was informed of their actions and was able to reach the farm, the pair had ploughed half an acre in a field that fronted the road.

Once again, a heated confrontation ensued, but Nicholas, mindful of Justice Hays's order, kept his clenched fists in his pockets. But not Old Melady or his stepson. Together, they knocked Nicholas to the ground, told him they had ploughing to do, and demanded that he get off the land and stay off it. If he did not, Old Melady told Nicholas, he would be shot.

This time it was Nicholas who resorted to the courts. Again, the long-suffering Robert Hays had to deal with the matter. Court records of the time seem to indicate that Hays was not exactly unbiased — largely because of his feelings for the two before him. Nevertheless, he was now completely exasperated with the actions of the men before him and rendered the best judgment he could.

On May 12, 1868, he found both Old Melady and his stepson guilty of assault, and fined each of them twelve dollars and costs. He was aware of Old Melady's comment about killing Nicholas, but took no action on it because he felt the threat was a bluff. Old Melady threatened lots of people. Later on, Hays admitted that he really had been less than enamoured of Old Melady. "I thought very little of [him]," he declared, but Nicholas "bore good characteristics." Perhaps if Nicholas had not kept the peace, as ordered earlier, Hays would have felt differently.

But still, the matter of the property was not resolved.

As far as can be determined today, Old Melady paid his fine, then probably got drunk; while he was full of alcoholic bravado, he set about to plot his revenge. Young Kelly helped. The two left Seaforth, went to the Hibbert farm, and together began to tear down a rail fence that had been put up to keep cattle from wandering onto the road.

By the time Nicholas learned of this, he had come to the end of his patience. He felt he had done what he could to appease his father, but nothing had worked. For that reason, he made a decision to get even.

Unfortunately, the actions he would take in righting the wrong went far beyond what any civilized society allows.

CHAPTER 5 | THE OLD MAN'S LAST DAY

THE MEETING WAS held on a bridge over the Bayfield River, not far from Old Melady's house. There, after dark one warm evening at the end of May 1868, at least four, and perhaps five or six, young men met, did some drinking, and talked about what to do about the problem they were having with Old Melady and his new wife. The voices of those in the group were conspiratorial and whispered to begin with, but as the alcohol took effect, they became louder, argumentative, and insistent.

Nicholas was there. So were Jim Kehoe and the Donovan brothers, Tom and Dave. Tom McGoey might well have been present. There likely were others on the fringes of the group, but their identities are impossible to determine today. Nor do we know who initiated the get-together, but certainly Nicholas and Jim were upset at Old Melady at the time, so either of them might well have come up with the idea for the gathering. Both were angry because of the disputes over land: for Nicholas, the problem was the Hibbert farm; for Jim, the fact that Old Melady wanted Margaret and him off the property where they lived. Other family members were upset as well because they felt they might lose their inheritances, and they certainly did not want all the family possessions, money, and land to go to a gold-digger they neither liked nor trusted.

Everyone present knew there was always plenty of money hidden in Old Melady's house, and after they had consumed several drinks, they not only thought of all that cash, they wondered if it would be possible to help themselves to some of it. They laughed a lot at the outrageousness of this suggestion, but also congratulated themselves on stumbling onto such a splendid idea. If someone could get into his house and locate the money, it could be divided among them. Old Melady would be furious when he discovered his loss, of course, but he would not know for certain whom to blame for it. Then, sometime in the future, if he actually did bequeath what he had to the new woman and her family, at least he would not have it all to leave. The idea of a robbery quickly became tremendously appealing to the bridge group, and the blackness of the night provided the perfect atmosphere for the discussion of such an audacious venture. Just the idea of going into the house and robbing him was so exciting it sent shivers up and down the spines of everyone present.

As might be expected, there is no written record of either the get-together or the plans that were made. The knowledge that it occurred is based entirely on oral accounts that were subsequently passed along from generation to generation. It likely went on for at least two hours, and perhaps much longer.

I recall hearing of it from my father, who likened it to a party that, because of the amount of liquor consumed, got completely out of hand. "Donovan and Kehoe were big shots when they were full of booze," he once told me, repeating the opinion of his father from years earlier. Dad could become quite incensed when talking about the bridge meeting, but he was also convinced that regardless of what might have been planned that night, if Nicholas had avoided getting involved with anything having to do with Tom Donovan and Jim Kehoe, "all the rest would not have happened." That opinion, however, is purely conjecture. Nicholas was certainly capable of getting into plenty of trouble on his own. The other two were merely the sparks needed to bring about full-blown conflagration.

Another of my memories as a young boy is of being present and listening in the gathering darkness of a summer night as my father, his older brother, and their ninety-three-year-old uncle sat on the back porch of a house in Seaforth and talked in hushed tones of terrible events that involved our family and a man named Nicholas. I don't think the three realized I was listening, and if so, they might not have cared, yet what they said kept me from sleep that night and gave me nightmares for years afterwards. I no longer recall many of the details of their talk, but the effect on me is as vivid now as it was the night I heard it. I have since been torn between wishing I could remember more of what was said and thinking that it might have been better had I not heard anything at all. I am, however, annoyed at myself for not asking questions of the speakers, particularly at the time. Unfortunately, as youngsters, most of us pay too little attention to the stories of our elders. It is only later that we wish we had listened with more than feigned interest, learning that what they might have told us could have been both exciting and worthwhile.

Another now-deceased relative remembered hearing his late mother-in-law mention the bridge meeting. She would sometimes talk of it when prompted, and because she was born in 1885, she would have heard the account in her youth. No real effort had been made to ensure that the meeting was secret, so in all likelihood, the notoriety surrounding it grew as the years passed. In some instances, the numbers involved were revised upwards, and some even said two of Nicholas's sisters were present. And while that is unlikely to have been the case, they probably would not have objected if they had heard the plans made that night. Later on, though, the sisters maintained that they had no knowledge of any meeting anywhere.

Those at the bridge would have been well aware of the dispute Nicholas was having with his father, and probably everyone in the community would also have heard that Old Melady was trying to force the Kehoes from their home. Both matters would have been neighbourhood gossip, but the former dispute was reported in newspaper accounts as well. At the time, local papers did not just run stories of serious law-breaking; they also published lists of misdemeanours that by today's journalism standards would be considered trivial. For example, fines could be levied for driving a buggy too quickly, using profane language on a main roadway, turning a horse loose without removing its harness, or getting a dog to chase a cow. Those convicted of these offences, or of all kinds of others for that matter, were named in the press, along with mention of the penalty imposed by the courts. If the guilty person had to pay a fine, its size and the time by which it had to be paid were noted, along with if, in fact, it was actually paid.

Because the ongoing disputes between Nicholas and his father were included in the court records of the time, they also provide us with a lasting glimpse of the turmoil that swirled around Old Melady, those he encountered, and those he disagreed with on a daily basis. He used the courts so often to get back at people that his own neighbours took pains never to cross him. He pressed charges so often, for real and imagined slights, that he appeared to regard the law as his own personal bludgeon.

But that spring night at the bridge, there was undoubtedly much more discussed than just the problems of Nicholas and the Kehoes. The stakes had become considerably higher, and they involved every family member present, along with others who could not be there or perhaps were afraid to be there. And even though Old Melady was generally the focal point in most family conversations, on this occasion, his new wife was mentioned just as often. She was not only disliked by her new relatives, they had also convinced themselves that she was a shameless hussy who saw the main chance and went for it. Now, they resented her even more, for a reason not anticipated even a few months earlier: she was pregnant.

Seven months earlier, when she and Old Melady had married, even they may not have believed they would, or could, have children. They were apparently in love, both were single, and each was tired of living alone, but still, the marriage might have been one of convenience and practicality, little more. Others were sure that Ellen just wanted his money. But now that she was pregnant, several perspectives changed.

At first, the mother-to-be just scoffed when asked if she was expecting. She either pretended she was not or shrugged off the question. And even when she could no longer hide the obvious, she laughed at the possibility. During civic celebrations in Seaforth, on May 24, Queen Victoria's birthday, Ellen denied the pregnancy when Dave Donovan's sister inquired about it. "If it was so, she did not know it," was the way the sister was quoted in the *Huron Expositor* on September 24, 1869.

Old Melady, on the other hand, bragged about the fact that his prowess in the bedroom was there for all to see. To those who knew him, he might be Old Melady, yet in his own mind, he was still young, vigorous, and virile. But he was still as cantankerous as ever, and now he had found a new way to alienate his family. His weapon was the child in his wife's womb.

Quite often after he moved to Huron, he told various family members that they would not inherit any of his large estate when he died. Generally he would make such pronouncements when he was drunk or when he was fighting with the person he was addressing. On such occasions, he would tell that son or daughter that everything he had would go to the others. Later on, when he sobered up, he would change his mind or have no recollection of ever making the remark. Then he would say that he didn't mean whatever it was he might have said. Most of the time, however, he was in a dispute with at least one of his adult children, so that one would be out of his will for sure. If he loaned them money, he would demand payment, with interest, much sooner than expected; if he bought their cattle, he would claim to have been shortchanged on the weight; if they returned borrowed farm equipment, he would say that it had been damaged, and the borrower would be told to pay for repairs. Because of this, his children avoided unnecessary dealings with him. They came to visit, but those visits were always of short duration.

Each of them knew the pattern, and apparently most had been told at some time or other that they need not think they would ever inherit a dime because of their supposed transgressions, or because they were just like their mother, whom he often ridiculed. But when they were in his presence, he nevertheless expected compliance despite his incessant and increasingly erratic demands. And even though all of his sons and daughters did their best to get along with him, their efforts were rarely good enough.

But now that his wife was with child, his threats were taken much more seriously.

With the possible exception of Tom McGoey and his wife, who were, in the main, able to ignore his insults, his regard for the rest of his brood deteriorated noticeably almost from the day he remarried. And the closer he got to Ellen's family, the more his actions infuriated his children. With each passing day, he repeated his taunts about disinheriting them all. Initially, most of the threats had been made when he was drinking. Now they were also made on the rare occasions when he was sober.

Needless to say, these new threats were not appreciated. He told them his unborn child, his wife, and even her relatives would get all his land, his livestock, his money, and the home in which he lived. And in view of the way he had treated Nicholas, and continued to treat the Kehoes, the rest of the family was convinced that this time he intended to make good on what he was saying.

But what to do about it? Various suggestions were put forward, but we will probably never know the details of the plans the conspirators made at the bridge that night. They argued for a long time and in all likelihood found themselves swayed by both the effects of the alcohol they had consumed and by the most strident individual among them — although whether that was Nicholas or someone else is not known. However, Nicholas was undoubtedly the protagonist in a bloody drama that would be enacted at Old Melady's a few nights later. And while he did not act alone, nor did he pick the exact date and time for action, his name would soon be the main one linked to the terrible things that were about to transpire.

Old Melady spent most of Saturday afternoon, June 6, at the Carmichael in Seaforth. He arrived there alone, tied his horse in the open stable behind the hotel, and stomped through a back door to the beverage room. Because it had rained heavily all morning and he could not work on his land, he had decided to drive to town and drink with others, rather than by himself at home. There is no record of Ellen drinking with him.

We have no idea whom he talked to that day, but for some reason or other, he actually drank a bit less than usual. Some who saw him that afternoon knew that such sobriety was not the norm, and they mentioned it on later occasions. Perhaps he restrained his intake in order to reflect on his proud status as an expectant father, but we have no way of knowing. However, moderation or not, he still became loud, argumentative, and obnoxious. There were scores of patrons at the hotel, and they all heard him ranting. Much of what he said concerned the supposed ungratefulness of his own children.

Robert Hays, who was at the Carmichael at the same time, later mentioned that he was at a table almost next to Old Melady, and from that vantage point the Justice of the Peace was able to observe what was happening around him.

As usual, Old Melady became the unwanted focal point of the room. He sat with his back to a wall, dominated the conversation, bragged, and then began showing off. Hays noted that he was trying to impress everyone there by reaching into his pocket, pulling out a thick roll of bills, and flashing them above his head. Then he stood up, yelled at the drinkers who had been studiously ignoring him, and challenged them to tell him how much money he had in his hand. When no one spoke, Old Melady got even louder. One disgruntled patron bellowed, "Sit down and shut the hell up!," but nothing stopped him. He just kept showing the money and asking how much cash he had in his hand.

"He finally said there was five hundred dollars in the roll," Hays recalled, "and it looked like it." Old Melady then reached into another pocket and hauled out a second stash, which Hays estimated to have been about the size of the first. The Justice of the Peace did not mention further reaction, if any, from the patrons. Most had seen similar amounts of money produced on previous occasions. But five hundred dollars was a substantial amount when the average working man earned less than two dollars a day at the time, so a thousand dollars was a fortune. Likely none of the drinkers ever made that kind of money, and they resented the braggadocio and the ugly display of obvious wealth.

Sometime during the early part of that Saturday afternoon, three of the men who had been at the meeting at the bridge trooped into the Carmichael as well. The first to show up was Dave Donovan, but whether he spoke to or drank with Old Melady cannot be determined. In any event, the two would not have been together for long. The room was almost full when Donovan arrived, so he ordered a whiskey and stood at the bar.

After about twenty minutes, he was joined by his brother Tom, who arrived with Jim Kehoe. An hour or so earlier, these two had linked up in a blacksmith shop in nearby Egmondville. Because they had time on their hands, they decided they needed a drink and would walk into Seaforth to get it. But when they got to the Carmichael and noticed that Old Melady was there, they made the deliberate decision to go somewhere else. Dave Donovan went with them. None of the three wanted anything to do with Old Melady that day. In view of later events, no one knows if there might have been a specific or even sinister reason for this.

The place they adjourned to was Walsh's tavern, a rather seedy, single-storey, wood-frame establishment a stone's throw away on the east side of the main street. The three remained there for much of the afternoon, drank prodigious quantities of alcohol, and became three of the last best customers of the place. The tavern burned to the ground a week later, and few in Seaforth bemoaned its demise. The place was generally an embarrassment to the town fathers because it was often in the news — for all the wrong reasons. The management was regularly fined for what the *Huron Signal* newspaper termed "selling intoxicating liquor to

Indians." There were also other common infractions, in particular drunken brawls that almost always got out of hand. Scarcely a day passed when one or more of the local constables did not have to be called.

As the Donovan brothers and Jim Kehoe were extending their visit at Walsh's, Old Melady decided he had socialized enough for the day. He rose from his table and weaved his way to the Carmichael's stables for his horse and buggy. He untied his driver, backed his buggy out into the small clearing behind the hotel, and drove away. Half an hour later, he made it home. To a large extent, this would merely have necessitated setting the horse on the right road; she would have made the trip without being driven. Most horses would return home on their own, and Melady's grey driver had taken him there many times when he was too inebriated to guide her.

Finally, when Old Melady approached his own driveway, he noticed Joseph Nigh a short distance away, mending a rail fence that ran along the front of his property. He waved a greeting, and Nigh returned the gesture. Later on, Nigh estimated that this had happened "around five o'clock."

This time was later confirmed by a man named James Williams, a framer and carpenter hired by Old Melady to oversee construction of the new barn, about 120 yards southwest of the farmhouse. Earlier that afternoon, while Williams was working, Ellen Melady came out of her kitchen to talk with him. He later recalled that she looked well, as did Old Melady when Williams spoke to him while he unhitched the horse. Like Nigh, Williams estimated the time as being around 5:00 in the afternoon. Neither man commented on Old Melady's sobriety. Williams saw him hang up the harness, let the horse into a nearby pasture, and then walk towards his house.

Meanwhile, back in Seaforth, the happy trio at Walsh's decided to try another venue. They came out of the hotel, walked a block or so along the board sidewalk, then careened down the centre of the muddy street towards Egmondville and a place that had even less class than the one they'd just left. This watering hole operated under several names over the years. At one time it was known as Mrs. Robinson's, at another time Brydon's Hotel, but to most patrons it was generally called Bummer's Roost. The moniker evoked what the place had become. It was almost always crowded, and the echo of drunken laughter and yelling could be heard coming from the beverage room at almost any hour of the day and on into the night. The hotel was on the stagecoach line that linked Egmondville with the village of Bayfield, on Lake Huron, so the Roost was well known to thirsty travellers and locals alike. There is no trace of it today, although neighbours recall the cache of whiskey bottles unearthed when the property was graded some years ago. The site is now a lawn.

By the time they reached the Roost, the three drinkers had developed a marked degree of fellowship. They laughed, talked, jostled one another, and argued about what to do that evening. They may even have left to eat somewhere, but before dark, they were all back at the tavern looking for adventure, never giving any thought to cutting down on their alcohol intake or their inebriated chatter.

In all probability, the problem discussed at the bridge was reviewed. And in direct proportion to the amount of beer and liquor consumed, several solutions likely came to the fore. Because Nicholas had to have a role in whatever was done, it was felt that they should go and talk to him. However, in view of the hour, Dave Donovan thought he had better get home. He told his companions that his wife had no idea where he was, but that she would be "pretty ugly" when he returned so late. Even though the days were long in early June, it was already quite dark outside.

Ultimately, Tom Donovan and Jim Kehoe took it upon themselves to locate Nicholas. They bought a couple of bottles for the road and got ready to leave the Roost. They lurched to their feet and made their way to the street that ran along one side of the imposing yellow brick Van Egmond home, the local focal point built by a son of the village founder. Then they headed east. Today, for no discernable reason, the dusty wagon trail they walked is called the Front Road. As they walked, the Bayfield River would have been on their right, along with a flourishing tannery at the edge of the village.

Nicholas had been staying at the Kehoes', and they expected to find him there. However, about a mile out of Egmondville, they met him walking towards Seaforth. They greeted him like a long-lost friend, even though Jim had seen him that morning at home. The two immediately offered him some of their booze, drank with him, and then prevailed upon him to have lots more. After a while, Nicholas was almost as inebriated as his companions. They would later say that it was at that time that they decided to go to Old Melady's, not to rob him or go anywhere near his house but ostensibly to check on how his barn framing was going. How much of the construction they expected to see in the dark was never explained. Nevertheless, one mile and more drinks later, they neared Old Melady's house. They could see the outline of the building among the trees to their right.

Shortly before they came to the farm gate, they left the road, trudged across a neighbour's field of peas, and, after a couple of attempts, managed to climb over a rail fence and onto the Melady property. A short distance away was a woodpile, so they went over to it, sat down, and tried to figure out how to approach the task at hand. The barn framing was quickly forgotten. By this time, they were quite drunk, but they probably kept their voices down. They did have another drink to celebrate their arrival, however, so there was some muffled laughter.

A few yards away, the house loomed large in the blackness, and as no lamplight shone from any window, it seemed obvious that the couple inside had retired for the night. In fact, a while before, Ellen Melady had put on a long nightgown over her one-piece chemise, Old Melady had gotten into his nightshirt, and both had climbed under the covers. The coal oil lamp beside the bed was snuffed out, and the house fell silent.

It is impossible to determine how long the three young men remained by the woodpile. It might have been a few minutes; it might have been well over an hour. They sat and whispered, their voices gradually becoming conspiratorial and strained, betraying the nervousness they were starting to feel. Because of the darkness, they were not able to see each other's faces, so feelings of fear were not obvious.

We know from later accounts that they talked about Old Melady, his wife, and his money — money they were sure was hidden in the house, although none of them, not even Nicholas, knew exactly where. Nicholas had not been near the place since his father's wedding; in the interim, Ellen Melady might well have rearranged the furniture in the house, and she could have put her husband's money anywhere.

Finally, all three decided that if they were ever going to do what they came to do, the time was at hand. It should be mentioned that Tom Donovan was involved that night because he and Old Melady had hated each other for years. However, the initial cause of their enmity has been lost with the passage of time. Nicholas and Jim decided together that they would break into the house through a cellar window and then help themselves to a strongbox Nicholas said was there. They were sure it had to be worth locating, but the difficult part of the plan would be to find it and then get out before they were discovered.

Just before starting, they each took a last swallow of whiskey. Tom picked up an axe as he stood like a drunken armed guard, while Nicholas and Jim headed for the cellar window.

From this point onwards, the actions of the three would shock the residents of Huron County as they had never been shocked before. What was intended as nothing more than a robbery quickly became a tragedy.

CHAPTER 6 | A HORROR BEYOND WORDS

TOM AND MARY McGoey arrived first. In the early afternoon of Sunday, June 7, they drove to Old Melady's by horse and buggy. It was a glorious late spring day, sunny, warm, not a cloud in the sky. A soft breeze blew through the maple leaves and then swept across the partly grown fields of wheat. Because of the recent rain, the countryside was lush and green. Nesting birds seemed to be everywhere, and squirrels raced up and down tree trunks and along the top rails of the fences. At the bridge on the concession road over the Bayfield River, two boys were fishing. Neither admitted to having much luck.

The McGoeys were responding to an invitation. One morning three days earlier, McGoey had happened to meet his father-in-law in a harness shop in Seaforth. After some casual conversation about the fine weather and the condition of the crops, Old Melady mentioned that he had not seen his daughter Mary in a couple of weeks, and he suggested that she and her husband come up for a visit on Sunday afternoon. McGoey mentioned the matter to his wife, so after returning from Mass at St. Columban, they had their noon meal and then set out on the three-mile drive to her father's farm. Along the way, they called greetings to neighbours, many of whom were outside, enjoying the perfect weather.

It was about 2:00 p.m. when the McGoeys reached Old Melady's. Tom McGoey pulled up in front of the road gate and climbed down to open it, and Mary drove through. There were a few calves in the barnyard, and McGoey wanted to make sure they didn't get out. He closed the gate, got back into the buggy, and then drove down the lane towards the house. There was no sign of activity there at all.

After Tom tied the horse, the couple walked to a back kitchen door, chatting as they went. As they passed the vegetable garden, Mary remarked on how wonderful it looked. There did not seem to be a weed in sight, so Ellen was certainly good with plants. The garden was her pride and joy, and she spent hours tending the rows of carrots, radishes, lettuce, and assorted other vegetables.

Oddly, there was still no sound from the house, nor any indication that their arrival had been noticed. Ordinarily, Old Melady would have been watching to see who had driven into the yard and would likely have come out to either greet or challenge his visitors. But not today. When the McGoeys reached the door, they found it ajar. They looked at each other, mildly surprised, but neither said anything.

McGoey tapped on the door frame.

There was no response.

"That's odd," Mary observed. "Maybe they're napping."

McGoey rapped again. Mystified, the couple stood where they were for a few seconds, then Mary opened the door and stepped inside, calling a greeting as she went. McGoey followed just behind her. Both noticed a strange smell in the room.

At first, they had trouble comprehending what was before them.

"Look here!" Mary cried, pointing to the floor, her hand trembling. Instinctively, she stepped back, brought her hand to her mouth in shock, and blinked with disbelief. Her husband was looking beyond her.

"There must have been a fight here last night," he muttered, as his eyes swept the room. The kitchen table had been moved from its usual place, and a potted plant was upturned on the floor. A chair lay on its side. A dark, wine-coloured substance covered a large area of the wooden floor and then extended towards a closed hall door, twenty feet across the big farm kitchen. The substance was obviously blood, thick in places, and there were a lot of footprints in it. Here and there, it looked as if some-one had tried to wipe up the mess. There were slathered streaks of what could have been water intermingled with the pools of red.

Mary gasped inadvertently, clutched her husband's arm, and pleaded in a soft, anxious voice, "Let's go away!" She started to back towards the open door behind her. Her face was ashen, her heart pounded, and she found it hard to catch her breath.

McGoey hesitated, struggled with his own urge to flee, and instead moved gingerly around the mess on the floor across the room towards the hall. The blood was thicker there, a bit lighter in colour, and it seemed to ooze from under the door. He glanced back at Mary, then tapped softly on the door. Mary watched, listened, and again begged him to leave. But she also found it impossible to move and stared at the door, dreading what might be behind it.

When there was no response to his knock, McGoey rapped again, paused momentarily, then pushed the door open. He would never forget what he saw.

The crumpled, half-naked body of his father-in-law lay sprawled in a lake of blood, two paces away. A gaping hole was clearly visible in his head, and in the warmth of the afternoon, the sickly-sweet stench of blood was overwhelming. Mary could see her father lying there, and she shrieked at the horror.

McGoey recoiled abruptly, left the hall door open, and then half-dragged his wife from the building, desperate for fresh air and deliverance from the charnel house. Both gasped for breath as they fought sudden, overpowering waves of nausea. Then Mary, white-faced and hysterical, was clinging to him.

"Oh my God, my God!" she wailed. "Tom, what happened?" Her husband looked at her and tried to speak, but no words came.

Together, they ran for help.

Scarcely ten minutes later, McGoey returned to Old Melady's with Joe Nigh, while Mary remained with the neighbour's wife. The Nighs had emerged from their house together, alarmed because they heard Mary screaming as she and Tom ran down the lane. Mrs. Nigh immediately went to Mary, embraced her, tried to find out what was wrong, and attempted to calm the hysterical woman. As soon as he knew his wife would not be alone, McGoey quickly told Nigh what had happened and asked for his help. As they both raced across the road to Melady's, McGoey tried to prepare the neighbour for what he was about to see.

"The kitchen was terribly tracked with blood," Nigh explained later. "There were marks of at least two persons, one of them barefoot, another a stocking track. These were very plain in the blood on the floor, and the barefoot tracks were larger. There might have been a number of persons in the house at the time of the murder, as shown by the tracks."

The men went over to the hallway, taking particular care not to walk in any footprints. They found Old Melady lying face down in blood that was only partly congealed. The right side of his face was towards the floor, while the jagged wound McGoey had already seen was in the dead man's left temple. For some reason, his nightshirt was pulled up around his neck. The body lay across the threshold of the large master bedroom, which was off the hallway to the left. The right arm of the deceased was extended forward, as if he had been trying to defend himself or strike out at someone. Already, flies buzzed around the wound.

On this second visit to the death house, McGoey was able to force himself not to leave. Instead, he and Nigh stepped a foot or so closer to the corpse on the floor, far enough to see into the bedroom.

What they saw there was terrible beyond words. Ellen Melady lay on her back beside the bed, her feet towards the door. Her upper torso was drenched with blood, and her head, in Joe Nigh's words, was "frightfully mangled." Indeed, he said later that he barely recognized her.

"Her head was split up," Tom McGoey observed, "as if with an axe." Both men noticed a smashed chair near the head of the corpse and a broken pistol nearer her feet. There was so much blood pooled on the floor that at first, neither man noticed an axe partly obscured by the foot of the bed. Great splashes of blood had already dried on the curtains, the bedclothes, and the adjacent walls.

Realizing that help was needed right away, Joseph Nigh sent two messages with passersby on the road: one was to Seaforth for the coroner; the other was to Jim Kehoe, asking for immediate assistance. Jim did not respond for well over half an hour, even though his house was a five-minute walk away, at most. However, as Nigh would later say, "He did show up after a while." If Nigh wondered why he was so long in coming, he did not say. Nor did Jim explain why he took so long to get there. Presumably McGoey wanted his brother-in-law there for additional family support.

However, as soon as Jim arrived, he, Nigh, and McGoey set about checking the house for traces of the killers and signs of entry. All three knew that, because of his past, Old Melady would have made sure the house was locked before going to bed. McGoey knew the place was open when he and Mary had arrived that afternoon.

Doctor T.T. Coleman had been one of the first physicians in the village of Seaforth, and in 1868 he was also the coroner for the municipality and the surrounding area. Later, he became a successful businessman. Along the way, he entered politics; he was elected Seaforth's first reeve, and later its mayor when the town incorporated in 1875. He amassed substantial land holdings, and today Coleman Street in the town is named after him. He was always known as a fine doctor and a careful and thorough coroner. In the days immediately after the Melady murders, Coleman would also demonstrate his detective skills and legal expertise. But first, he went to the crime scene.

"I got there about 3:00 p.m.," he explained later, "and the bodies seemed unmoved." Coleman made a general assessment of what was before him, concentrating in particular on the wounds he saw and what he felt were the probable causes of death. He noted the gunshot wound in Old Melady's left temple and concluded that he had died from the shot, and that death had been instantaneous. He asked Tom McGoey about not only the time of his arrival but also exactly what he had seen when he got there. Once he was certain neither McGoey nor Nigh had touched the bodies or rearranged them in any way, the doctor turned his attention to Ellen Melady. Her death did not seem to have been as quick as Old Melady's. It was likely far more tortured as well.

"She was twisted in blankets," Coleman noted, "and her skull was almost torn off by the axe strike. She had also been hit over the head with a chair, and it had broken. Her brains were dashed out, and there were powder marks from a gunshot on her face."

The medical man had to step over the woman's body to fully check her injuries, but finally, satisfied that he had seen enough, he set about initiating a search for clues the killers might have left behind. He also placed the house under guard and told the first policeman who got there not to touch or move the bodies. Then he directed that autopsies should be done by his colleague, Doctor Henry Vercoe of Egmondville. A neighbour of Old Melady's immediately left to contact the physician in question.

Henry Vercoe was still a young man in his third year of practice locally. He had known Old Melady by sight, although the two men were never really acquainted. He had been visiting a patient who was seriously ill at home when Coleman's message arrived, so there was some delay in his acting on it. Vercoe did get to the murder scene around dusk that Sunday evening, but after looking at the remains and conferring with Coleman, he decided he could not perform proper autopsies by candle or coal oil lamp. He noted, however, that he was sure the deaths had occurred several hours earlier, even though some of the blood remained liquefied.

He later marvelled at the number of people who descended on the house. The crowds seemed to materialize quickly, and out of nowhere. Word of the tragedy spread throughout the community and far beyond it with an urgency that was remarkable, both because the deceased were well-known and because the killings were particularly violent. Total strangers and neighbours alike gawked, luxuriating in the gruesome details; after they had done so, they ensured that the news of the terrible event spread far and wide. Of course, with each telling and retelling, the enormity of the crime was expanded.

The first four police officers who arrived had to spend an inordinate amount of time on crowd control alone. One of these was Constable Michael McNamara, a former bricklayer from Egmondville. He arrived just before 4:00 p.m., while Constable Hugh Grant got there an hour or so later. They were soon joined by officers Thomas Stephens and Daniel Moran, and in the days that followed, by several others who would be assigned to the case and rotated in the times they attended. Most of the policemen viewed the bodies and were revolted by what they saw, but it was Doctor Vercoe who would become particularly familiar with the extent of the injuries and the effects of them. His work began early Monday morning, more than thirty hours after it was felt the murders had taken place. Prior to commencing his grim task, he directed that the doors and windows on the ground floor of the house be opened in order to let as much light and fresh air as possible inside. Then, as the police struggled to keep the curious outside, the doctor set out his instruments and got started.

Old Melady's remains were examined first.

Much of the blood on the hall floor was his, the doctor determined, and it came from the gunshot wound "in the left temple, and extending back." As well, the left side of the deceased's face was covered with powder marks, indicating, in Vercoe's words, that "the shot must have been very close." The doctor did not say, but simply assumed, that the broken gun on the floor was the weapon used. Before proceeding further, he had one of the policeman wrap up the revolver and then remove it from the room. He also gave the same instruction regarding the pieces of the chair that were on the floor, as well as the axe that McGoey and Nigh had noticed earlier. Then the doctor did a lengthy check on the bullet hole in Old Melady's forehead: "I found the wound exited to the back of the head. I found wadding an inch and a half inside the wound, and in the back, three buckshot balls. The shot went through the brain. There would have been no struggling after it. There were some powder marks on his hand, as if he held up his hand to protect himself."

Ellen Melady's injuries were much worse.

Vercoe began with a description of what the deceased was wearing: "A nightdress and chemise, and a handkerchief around her neck." He then made notes on the ravages to her person. Most of these had already been seen by McGoey, Nigh, and Coleman, but Vercoe elaborated on what was even more apparent on closer examination: "The upper part of her skull was smashed in, and there was a large, gaping wound across her temple. A chair had apparently been used, and part of the leg was in the wound. She had a broken skull and her brains were scattered about." The rest of the chair lay on the floor, in pieces. The side of her head was cut by a sharp instrument. Although there were a few powder burns on her face, Vercoe thought she had not been killed by a gunshot, although she might have been rendered unconscious by it. He thought an axe had caused the cuts he described, but surmised that the blows were delivered after she passed out.

Almost as an afterthought, Vercoe added, "She was pregnant. Seven and a half months gone."

Vercoe also put to rest an initial suspicion that the slayings could have been a murder-suicide, whereby Old Melady killed his wife and then turned the gun on himself. This was nullified when the broken pistol was found to be loaded. It may have been smashed because it had jammed or at least had failed to fire an additional time. Later on, it would be determined that the weapon belonged to Old Melady, and his killers had found and used it. The owner of the axe was presumed to be Old Melady as well, although later investigation concluded that he had probably not carried it inside himself. There would have been no need for him to have the axe in the house because he already had his pistol there for protection.

Once Vercoe had finished his work, the coroner, Coleman, gave permission for family members to set about arranging the burials. Two hastily made caskets were brought from Matthew Robertson's furniture store in Seaforth, the bodies of the deceased were placed inside, and the containers were nailed shut. Then they were set on two tables in what was called the parlour of Old Melady's house, a large, rather formal sitting room that faced the road. A brief, impromptu wake was held, and prayers for the souls of the deceased were said. The following morning, Tuesday, the coffins were placed on a wagon to be transported to the St. Columban church for the funerals. Father James Murphy, the same priest who had married the couple the previous fall, said the funeral Mass. At the conclusion of the services, the remains were buried in the recently acquired parish cemetery on a country side road, half a mile or so southwest of the church. No headstones marked the place then, nor do any today. While there are several family relatives interred in that cemetery, no one knows now where Old Melady and his wife were buried. Perhaps that is just as well.

By the time the coroner had reached the house on Sunday, Tom McGoey, Joseph Nigh, and Jim Kehoe had uncovered a few initial facts about what had happened. They looked closely at the footprints in the kitchen and noticed that the knitted imprint of a sock appeared in several places. These prints were so clear they could even tell that there was a hole in the toe. Other prints seemed to have been made by persons who were barefooted. By nightfall, the blood in the kitchen was completely dry, so the prints remained etched in it. In the course of the next few hours, the marks were checked over and over again.

The three then went to look to see how the killers got into the house. They first examined the kitchen door for pry marks; finding none, they felt that the house must not have been locked the previous night. On the other hand, if the killers had entered somewhere else, they could have committed the murders, unlocked the door from the inside, and simply walked out. In order to check on other possible entry points, the three decided to have a look around outside. McGoey led the way.

A minute or so later, when the three rounded a corner on the east side of the house, they noticed an open cellar window. There, in plain view, just in front of the sill, were several footprints in the wet earth. Nigh leaned over to have a closer look.

Because of all the rain on Saturday morning, the ground was still soft, so the indentations in the clay were quite obvious. There were several prints, made by at least two persons, neither of whom was wearing shoes. The three farmers looked at each other, realizing that they now knew how the killers got inside. And while Nigh and McGoey must have been satisfied with their discovery, we have no way of knowing what emotions James Kehoe must have harboured as he pretended to help in the detective work. Nor do we know if either Nigh or McGoey noticed if their companion was in any way reluctant to assist.

At the time of the murders and for years afterwards, farmhouses in Ontario had basements that were rather similar in design. They were generally constructed with stone and mortar walls and could be entered from outside by way of a dozen or so steps leading down to a wooden door. Because of his deep-seated paranoia, Old Melady would have had this entry locked. For this reason, the killers used the window they were able to open in order to gain access to his house.

Once they were in the cellar, the intruders would have had little trouble reaching the main floor. In Old Melady's house, the kitchen had a trap door in the floor, and the cellar steps led up to this opening. As no bloody footprints were ever found on these steps, it was presumed that after doing their evil deed, the killers exited the house through the door the McGoeys used.

Later on Sunday evening, when the two doctors had done as much as they could in the gathering dusk, they took note of items that were not of a medical nature. This investigation was part of Coleman's role as coroner. His observations of the scene are helpful, even today. Whether he was accompanied by one or more of the police officers is not known. We assume he was.

Coleman said that the house was "tossed upside down." He noticed an empty whiskey bottle on a master bedroom windowsill and a coal oil lamp beside the bed. Because the shade was quite blackened, he felt that the lamp might have been lit for some time and had probably "gone out on its own." Because the house was in darkness before the trio at the woodpile entered, it was later believed one of them lit the lamp when they were searching for the money they wanted. Coleman offered no opinion as to whether the liquor had been consumed by Old Melady or the killers. Nor did he indicate who might have owned it.

Both medical men noticed a large black steamer trunk against a back wall of the bedroom. They found that the catch on the container had been smashed, and several papers inside appeared to have been ransacked. "There were marks of blood and candle grease on the trunk," Coleman observed. The next day, Constable McNamara looked more closely at the container and found candle drippings on some of the papers inside it as well. Because he had no idea what had been in the trunk before the tragedy, he could not tell if anything was actually missing. All he knew for sure was that it looked to have been searched, and that the search seemed to have been rushed, haphazard, or both.

Finally, night came over the scene of horror. The first wave of gawkers and thrill-seekers departed, and the police officers who were there arranged shifts so that the property would be guarded continuously. Family members and a few of their neighbours took turns being present at a makeshift wake on Monday evening, during which time Father Murphy came to offer prayers for the deceased. He did what he could to comfort the distraught, especially Mary McGoey. She had been terribly traumatized when she and her husband had discovered the grisly murder scene.

CHAPTER 7 | THE INVESTIGATION BEGINS

WHILE HENRY VERCOE was doing the autopsies in Old Melady's bedroom on Monday morning, Coleman was endeavouring to put in place the major thrusts of the murder investigation. As coroner, he had not only the proficiency but also the legal mandate to do so. He was assisted in the initial investigation of the crime by the police and others, but there was little doubt as to who was in charge. Everyone deferred to him. In fact, a close reading of the surviving records of the time indicates that the man was so powerful, he was feared by many. He had authority, and he did not hesitate to use it.

The dried footprints found in the blood on the kitchen floor were examined and measured, and Coleman was certain that they had been made by at least two and possibly three persons. Some time was also spent checking for boot tracks, but none were located in the house. Because of this, it was believed that the killers had removed their footwear before they climbed through the cellar window. At one point, a constable discovered a pair of heavy work boots in the basement, but as they were covered with dust and were nowhere near the entry window, it was assumed they had belonged to Old Melady.

The attention of the investigators turned to the haphazard washing of the kitchen floor. No one had any idea why it had been done, although it was thought that the perpetrators must have been trying to hide something. It seemed as if water had been sloshed near the stove, but the effect was really more of a mess than a cleanup. As one of the police officers was on his hands and knees looking closely at the floor streaks, he turned to look at the stove. Here, he made an interesting discovery, and he called one of his colleagues to his side.

In the firebox, near the back, were several charred papers. These were removed for examination, but they were so badly burned, they were unreadable. In fact, most fell apart as soon as they were touched. Both Coleman and the police suspected that the papers likely came from the trunk in the bedroom, but they could not tell for sure. The remnants of what seemed to be a large, partially burned pocket handkerchief were also in the stove. Because the blackened cloth was somewhat damp, they guessed that it, and perhaps a towel, had been used to wipe the floor. The handkerchief bore no hint of why the washing had been done, however.

Readers of this book might wonder why no fingerprints were collected. No thought was ever given to searching for prints at the scene, even though there likely were many in the kitchen, on the weapons in the bedroom, and on the exterior of the trunk where Constable McNamara found the candle grease. This was because fingerprinting as an investigative tool in criminology was then unknown. It would be some twenty years until its usefulness became appreciated.

As soon as the interior of the house, upstairs and down, had been examined, the investigation continued outside. All four cellar windows were checked, but only one had been opened. Constable McNamara turned his attention to the marks there, which Nigh and the others had noticed earlier. By standing back from the window, occasionally kneeling in front of it, and then moving from side to side, the policeman was able to tell that the footprints by the opening led to the house from a southerly direction. They were hard to identify, because they had been somewhat trampled on by the crowds of the previous day. Nevertheless, McNamara was finally able to ascertain that the tracks led from a woodpile, close to the timbers that had been piled in preparation for the barn raising. At the woodpile, he noticed that the tracks changed. There, they became boot marks.

McNamara surmised (correctly, as it was later proved) that the perpetrators of the crime had removed their boots by the woodpile before attempting to get into the house. At a later time, they returned to the woodpile, put their footwear back on, and walked away. Two sets of boot prints led past where the new barn was being built.

It was at this juncture that the investigators got an important break. The heels of one pair of boots left tracks that were quite distinctive. A particular pattern of nails imprinted the soil in a way that was both unusual and obvious, so these marks were easy to spot — particularly so because they had been made in rain-dampened earth. Coleman and Constables McNamara, Grant, and Stephens set out to follow them. Any tracks of a third person going in any other direction were lost in the welter of prints made by the crowds the day before.

Two people who had joined the throng at the house on Sunday afternoon were Tom Donovan and Nicholas Melady, Jr. They walked in from the road together, acted as if they were concerned, and asked what had happened. Both said they had heard there was trouble of some kind. Neither made any attempt to conceal his presence, but both probably felt that if they did not appear, their absence would be noted. As it turned out, their being there brought questions that neither may have expected. Nigh, for one, noticed Nicholas standing just outside the kitchen door with several other men, so Nigh went over and struck up a conversation. He expressed his condolences to Nicholas on the death of his father, but then abruptly asked the young man where he had been the previous night. Nigh was as surprised at the answer as Nicholas had been at the bluntness of the question.

"He gave a bad account of himself," the farmer recalled later. "He said he and Donovan had been drinking, but that he really didn't want to say that. It looked bad." Nigh did not indicate exactly what he meant by his own remark, but it was the first recorded suggestion that Nicholas might have been implicated in the fate of his father. Nigh's exact words may still be found in the records that exist today. Others who were there also wondered about the actions of Nicholas and Tom, neither of whom denied being together the previous night. Tom readily admitted that he had been drinking most of the afternoon and evening, but insisted, rather belligerently, that he had not been drunk. He also went out of his way to explain to anyone who asked that he and Nicholas had been at Dave Donovan's the previous night. So far, Jim's presence with the other two was not mentioned, nor had the police had time to talk to the other drinkers who had been at the Roost in Egmondville. The officers would quickly do so, however, and the fact that Jim Kehoe had been seen leaving the hotel with Tom Donovan would be established beyond a reasonable doubt. Many patrons recalled that the two were quite drunk when they left the place.

Almost every neighbour who came to Old Melady's in the first hours after the murders knew the legal troubles Nicholas had had with his father. For that matter, so did several policemen. One of these, Thomas Stephens, had been in court on another matter when the father and son had quarrelled about land, and he had heard them threaten each other. He had given the matter little thought at the time, but regarded it now as being more significant than it had seemed when it occurred.

Other officers in Seaforth, Goderich, and Stratford had also had dealings with both men. For his part, Tom Donovan, who was a thief, seems to have steered clear of the law in the month or two immediately prior to the killings, but he had been in and out of trouble most of his adult life. And while many of his actions might not have been terribly serious, some showed a decided lack of forethought. For example, three years earlier, when he had been caught wearing a military uniform that he had stolen, he was taken before Justice of the Peace Peter Ramsay to answer to the charge of theft. The accused painted the whole thing as little more than a lark after a night of drunken revelry. The court took a much dimmer view of the matter. Tom was convicted of theft and subsequently went to jail for his actions. Unfortunately, we have no way of knowing if the captain of the Seaforth Volunteer Company ever got his uniform back. He had also been implicated in rather suspect dealings having to do with the ownership of land, but whether he was charged is open to question. Newspapers at the time allude to repeated shenanigans pertinent to the matter, but few were spelled out. Readers of the day would certainly have known what was implied. In fact, most stories painted the man as a drunken, lazy, smart aleck. He was also a bully until challenged. Then he became an instant coward.

As well, it would only have been a matter of time before Jim Kehoe had to appear in court. A month before his death, Old Melady had started eviction procedures against Jim, who undoubtedly would have resisted being moved from the land he leased. In all probability, the heated arguments that the two were already having would have gotten worse, and might well have ended in blows. Old Melady, after all, had never backed down from fighting his son, so a fight with a son-in-law was not totally out of the question. And Jim, even though he was a little man, had apparently never been afraid to take on opponents who were bigger.

One wonders if his wife had married him for that reason. She, too, was a hot-tempered little warrior who had inherited both her father's stubbornness and his drive.

The group of men who followed the tracks from the woodpile found that the task was both easy and difficult, depending on the terrain. At first, the footprints led almost straight south, around the freshly squared barn timbers, through a potato patch, and into an area of slash. At the time, this term referred to acreage where the timber had been cut but the stumps and brush from fallen trees had not been fully cleared. After the wood dried out, it would be piled up and burned. What remained of the stumps would be pulled out by horses and then burned as well, and the cleared land would be cultivated and cropped. Much of the slash was being worked on by Old Melady in the days leading up to his murder.

Not surprisingly, the prints were lost in the slash, but they reappeared just past it where two lengths of wood lay by a rail fence. When the trackers picked up the footprints again in a field of peas, they assumed whomever they were following had knocked the fence rails down when climbing over them. The tracking was easy through the half-grown peas because the soil there was quite moist. The crop was in a field owned by William Fortune, who farmed immediately west of Old Melady.

The trail then led farther south and west, a quarter-mile or more across level land to the banks of the Bayfield River. This area was heavily treed, right to the water's edge; because of the heavy rain two days earlier, the water level was higher than usual, and certainly higher than Coleman and the others expected it would be. They followed the north bank for about two hundred yards, but despite their best efforts, they lost the trail in shoulder-high swale that was almost impenetrable. The fact that the river shore was rock and coarse gravel made tracking even more difficult.

But then, unexpectedly and luckily, the men came to a log lying across a narrow section of the waterway. At one end of the log they discovered the unusual boot marks again in a shallow, muddy depression. The group crossed the river on the log, found more heel marks at the other end of it, and were able to follow these to a line fence that led south towards the next road. They came to that road, crossed it, and from there simply followed another fence that led in the same direction.

By this time, the searchers were pretty sure that the tracks they were following would lead to where Tom and Nicholas said they slept Saturday night. In fact, even though they lost the footprints several times, Coleman and those with him located the marks again by a gate to a pasture just behind Dave Donovan's house. This was on Lot 3, on the north side of what was called Concession VI of the township, some four miles by road from Old Melady's. The coroner wanted to have a look at the house to see if there might be evidence that would be helpful in tracing the killers.

He wasted no time in his quest. There is no indication as to whether he had a warrant to proceed, but as he could authorize searches himself, the lack of written authorization was likely immaterial. The man felt he was on a mission, and picayune legalities were meant to be disregarded when the quest was more important than the rules.

Coleman strode over to the back door, pounded on it a couple of times, and, when he got no answer, told the police officers with him to go in and search the place. The door was never locked, so the men simply entered at will. No one was at home because at the time Dave and Catherine Donovan and their children were at the McGoeys' making funeral arrangements and seeking solace in their time of need. Even though Catherine had often quarrelled bitterly with Old Melady, he was her father, and she was stunned by the awfulness of what had happened. So, for that matter, were her sisters. They had already sent a telegram to their brother Tom in Ohio, telling him of the tragedy and asking him to come home right away. (Later on, Tom's possible involvement in the killings would be a matter of conjecture for some of the police and Crown officials, but surviving records leave no doubt that he was in the United States on the evening of June 6, 1868.)

At the Donovan house, little time was lost in conducting the search. Each officer took an area of the building and checked it. One also had a look through the barn and through an implement shed adjacent to it. Less than five minutes after Constable Grant had entered a ground-floor bedroom off the farmhouse kitchen, he located exactly what Coleman wanted. Grant picked up the items that were there, did a quick check to make sure nothing was overlooked, and left the bedroom.

"I found two pairs of boots and a pair of trousers in the bedroom," he said later. "The trousers and one pair of boots were wet." Grant carried the items outside and handed the pants to Coleman, and then both men began looking closely at the boots. The first thing they noticed was the distinctive nail pattern. There was also caked mud on the soles that resembled mud on the cuffs of the trousers that Coleman held.

But it was neither the mud nor the nail configuration that they would remember most.

"When Grant turned the boots over," Coleman explained, "a reddish liquid ran out of them. I knew it was blood." The liquid puddled in the dust, and a small rivulet ran into a wagon track that led across the yard. Grant held the footwear upturned until all the liquid had been drained.

The two men looked at each other, neither able to hide his surprise at the unexpected ease of their discovery. Then, satisfied that they had what they needed for now, Coleman directed everyone to leave the Donovan household as they'd found it and to return to Old Melady's. They retraced their steps northwards through the fields and along the fence line, and by walking quickly, they made it back before noon. The morning had been a good one.

Nicholas and Tom had been at the Kehoe house that Monday morning, but when they saw Coleman and the police officers return to the crime scene, they walked over. Both were rather quiet, yet they were interested in what Coleman was doing. Tom in particular was visibly surprised when he saw what the policemen carried. When Coleman pointed to the wet boots and asked about them, Tom initially claimed he knew nothing about them, but then reluctantly admitted that they were his. He was equally hesitant about acknowledging the mud-splattered trousers, but eventually said that yes, they belonged to him as well. He did not explain how either item got wet — nor, for that matter, was he asked to do so at the time. Nicholas said the second pair of boots belonged to him and that he had left them at Dave Donovan's when he was there on Saturday night. They were not wet, and when the police had turned them over, they had found nothing inside.

At this juncture, Coleman did not mention to Tom the blood that had been poured out of his boots. Instead, the doctor walked over to the woodpile and began to compare nail marks with the soil indentations that had been found there earlier.

Both he and the police officers quickly satisfied themselves that the footprints had been made by the same footwear. While they were checking the boot marks, Nicholas stood near the house, doing his best to talk nonchalantly with one of the neighbours, but Tom went over to the woodpile and watched the police and the coroner. Although he pretended to be just a casual bystander, it was obvious the young man was consumed with curiosity about the activities he observed. If the lawmen talked to him as they worked, there is no record of what was said.

There was yet another crowd of gawkers at the house, and as the morning wore on, their number steadily grew. Some, whose morbid curiosity got the better of them, managed to bypass the police guards in order to get inside. Others came and went, although several stayed to watch as the coroner conducted a couple of examinations. He finished looking at the boot tracks, made some quick jottings in a notebook he carried, and then ordered the police to bring Nicholas and Tom into the kitchen. A throng of curious onlookers pushed in after them.

When both men were present, Coleman told them to remove their boots. The two looked at each other hesitantly and rather reluctantly did as they were told, largely because they realized that the police would likely do the removing by force if the directive was not followed. The spectators were silent as everyone present craned their necks to see what was about to happen next.

Coleman ordered both Nicholas and Tom to place their feet in the dried prints on the kitchen floor. Neither seemed willing to do so at first, but finally Tom stepped forward, tried to make a joke of the matter, and played to the crowd. There was some muted, rather nervous laughter. Nicholas still hesitated, seemed unsure of himself, and fidgeted nervously. His face grew white, and he sweated profusely. For a moment, it looked as if he was ready to run. Then he looked around the room as if trying to come to terms with what he was being asked to do.

"He looked alarmed and excited," Coleman said later, "hence, I was suspicious of him. Although he pulled off his boots willingly, we had some difficulty making him put his feet in the marks." And no wonder. In Coleman's words, Melady's feet and some of the footprints in the dried blood on the floor "corresponded exactly." Donovan's feet fit precisely into the smaller prints. As there were lots of tracks, there was no need to restrict the comparison to one or two. The police had the men check the imprints several times, in a number of places on the floor. Finally, the process came to an end.

The coroner looked at the men before him and then rapidly made two decisions. He ordered the police officers who were there to arrest Nicholas and Tom for murder and to take them immediately to a secure lock-up in Egmondville. As soon as the accused were removed, he began gathering names for an inquest jury to be empanelled that same evening.

During the afternoon, the doctor and those assisting him scrambled to collect as much information as they could for presentation to the inquest. The coroner did some of the legwork himself; the rest he delegated.

Tom Stephens and Hugh Grant were told to go back to Dave Donovan's and do a more thorough check of the house and gather anything they believed would be beneficial in the murder investigation. This time, they obtained a search warrant issued by Coleman prior to setting out. Stephens also hired a horse and buggy so that the trip could be made easily and in the shortest possible time. In the Huron accounts records, he is listed as billing the county $2 for "horse hire" and $1 for the cost of the warrant. He and Grant were each paid $1.50 for doing the search. Later that same day, Stephens, along with Constable Ebenezer Lusby and others, would mount guard at the Van Egmond house in Egmondville, where the arrested men were first held. All police officers were paid for the hours they worked as guards.

Shortly after Stephens and Grant left for the Donovan home, Coleman and a young policeman named Robert Brett went to the Kehoe residence. The coroner had already determined that Nicholas often visited there, and that very morning he had seen him and Tom Donovan walking from that direction. Now he wondered if either might have left anything behind that would be relevant to the matter at hand. Jim Kehoe as yet did not figure in the murder probe.

Neither Margaret nor Jim Kehoe was present when the coroner arrived, but the children were there, along with thirteen-year-old Katherine Melady, a granddaughter of Old Melady, who was looking after them. She was Nicholas's brother Tom's child, and she was visiting that summer from Ohio, where her mother lived. After Coleman and the policeman had introduced themselves, the teenager readily agreed to let them search the house, and she was quite forthcoming when asked where Nicholas Melady slept when he stayed there, leading the men to a back bedroom and pointing to the bed.

Coleman and Brett did a quick search, opening and closing bureau drawers, turning back the bed covers, and getting on their knees to look under the bed itself. They were particularly interested in a pair of pants they saw hanging on a hook behind the door. When they asked whose trousers they were, Katherine told them they belonged to Nicholas Melady. Coleman stepped across the small room, took the pants down, examined the cuffs, and then checked the pockets carefully. "I put my hand in the pockets," he said later, "and found a pipe and a pocket book." Brett did not handle the garment, but merely watched as the doctor did his work.

Satisfied that there was nothing of importance in the pockets and no mud on the apparel, the doctor hung the pants back on the hook, and he and the policeman left. They did not remove anything from the house because Coleman wanted to have an experienced detective do a more thorough search of the place. At no time, then or later, did he mention anything of significance written in the notepad he had found in the pants pockets. He had been mainly interested in locating the pants themselves.

The lock-up to which Nicholas and Tom were taken was in the basement of the Van Egmond house, the private home of a man named Constant Van Egmond, his wife, Anne, and their family. Van Egmond was a well-known businessman in the county and had also been appointed a magistrate for the area. In the course of his civic role, he dealt with lawbreakers and, from time to time, needed a place to put them. Since there was no jail elsewhere in the community, he had a cell constructed in the basement of his own large house. The lock-up was a small room with brick walls and a low ceiling. It was accessible by a staircase that led down from the ground floor. An outside back door was only a step or two away, so miscreants could be taken inside without being paraded through other parts of the house. The cell was completely enclosed and was not visible from the exterior of the building. A small window with two metal bars enabled prisoners to look towards the stairs and into a tiny area of the basement. Today, even though most of the cell is gone, marks on the foundation of the house indicate exactly where it was, while the wall with the bars still exists. The iron bars, both of which are embedded in the brickwork mortar, are about half an inch thick. Neither looks terribly substantial, but neither can be moved by hand.

This was the place where the two men charged in the bloody orgy of death were first lodged, while the investigation of the crime continued at a feverish pace elsewhere. Already, news of the shocking murders had spread far and wide. The next morning, the story was on the second page of the *New York Times* and on the front of almost every major paper in Canada.

CHAPTER 8 | Arrests and Excitement

BERNARD TRAINER WAS a high-profile detective in Goderich in the 1860s and was generally referred to as the Chief Constable. He had a lot of experience in police work and as a prosecutor in a myriad of cases. He investigated every type of lawbreaking, and was quite successful in doing so. In judicial records of his era, his name appears especially often in cases of assault, threats, and drunk and disorderly behaviour. And there were plenty of those. Goderich, like most small towns at the time, was growing fast, but whatever sophistication it possessed was still in a rudimentary stage.

Trainer reflected the era in which he operated. He was big, rough, tough, and could hold his own in almost any situation. He loved a good fight, and when circumstances warranted, he was not above bending the law to suit his needs. He was in court often, and not always on the side of the law. He had an acute understanding of the mores of his age, and his method of handling brawlers and drunks was almost always confrontational. If his actions got him into trouble, he accepted the punishment and moved on — but kept his job. In 1862, for example, he was charged with conduct unbecoming a police officer when it was deemed that he had used undue force in making an arrest. Because the alleged victim was too scared to come to court to face Trainer, the lawman was acquitted. Two weeks later, he was convicted of assault in another case. He paid the twenty-cent fine — a goodly sum in those days, because his base salary was only one hundred dollars a year. Trainer, however, did earn somewhat more than this for things that would all be part of a police officer's job description today.

Police in Trainer's time were able to supplement their wages by charging the municipality on a case by case basis. They received a particular amount for doing an investigation, a bit more for making an arrest, a small allocation for guarding someone who had been charged, and so on. They did not always get what they wanted, however, and this caused some bitterness and occasional rivalries among officers. After being ordered to work on the Melady murder investigation, Trainer complained because he had to do some work at night and felt that doing so was worth more money. (He was the only officer who made a complaint in this case.) A tight-fisted, arch-conservative group called the Huron County Audit Committee did not agree, so they turned a deaf ear to his request. No extra funds were forthcoming. The policeman appealed his case in writing, but got nowhere. The Audit Committee guarded public funds even more carefully than they did their own money and ignored suggestions that they might have been too stingy at times. In fact, their penny-pinching often meant that some crimes were either not investigated or were pursued only in token fashion.

Trainer went to Seaforth, to the murder site, and elsewhere on the night of Monday, June 8, 1868. In conjunction with Coleman, the Chief Constable was expected to do the necessary investigation and ultimately solve the case — by himself, if necessary. Everyone knew this, and the press often contributed to the understanding. Goderich's *Huron Signal* mentioned that this officer had been assigned to the job and had arrived in Seaforth. "Chief Constable Trainer is down here, doing all he can to assist in the end of justice," trumpeted the paper in its first article on the killings. And although several other policemen were there as well, no others were mentioned or even alluded to in the story. The press loved Trainer. His activities provided lots of colour for their stories, and his descriptions of illegalities were often repeated verbatim in the public prints. He took reporters into his confidence, caroused with them, and often gave them a heads-up when he was about to make an arrest. He was the officer they quoted, and it was as if they decided that anyone else was of lesser status. Trainer also loved to see his name in the papers.

Trainer spent two hours at the crime scene after his arrival. He checked that everything necessary had been looked into and questioned the guards on duty about additional information they might have obtained. Already, rumours about Jim Kehoe's possible involvement were surfacing, particularly when the lawmen heard that he had been with Tom Donovan on Saturday night. At this point, neither Nicholas nor Tom had said anything at all about Jim. However, several people had seen him with Tom at Bummer's Roost and had seen the two leave together. A couple of patrons even said they were pretty sure the two left to go find Nicholas Melady.

Then a neighbour told Trainer about a gun at the Kehoes'.

The Chief Constable reacted quickly to the remark. Within an hour of hearing about a possible firearm, he was at the Kehoe house, only to be told by Margaret Kehoe that Jim had gone to Seaforth for the evening. The policeman explained that he would have to go and look for her husband there and, when he found him, bring him back home. We have no idea how Margaret responded to this remark, or to any of the questions, but we can assume she asked him why he wanted to see her husband. In all probability, however, even if she had asked, Trainer would have refused to explain himself. He did not tell her of the gun rumour.

Half an hour later, the detective found his quarry at the Carmichael, sitting alone at a table in an almost deserted beverage room. All the regulars, he was told, were down at the murder inquest in Egmondville. Jim told Trainer he had decided not to go, but offered no reason why. For his part, Trainer must have wondered about Jim's non-attendance at the most exciting event in town, but he apparently kept whatever suspicions he might have had to himself. He moved quickly to make his intentions known. He ordered Jim to stand, slipped handcuffs on his wrists, and told him he was in a lot of trouble.

"I arrested him in Seaforth on the Monday night," Trainer said a few months later, "and then I took him to his house. It was about eleven o'clock when we got there."

On the way from Seaforth, despite being asked repeatedly, Trainer refused to tell Jim why they were going to his home. It was only after they were driving down the lane into the farmer's yard that the policeman mentioned the reason. "I said I wanted the pistol that was in his house," Trainer later explained.

Jim immediately became quite defensive, and told the officer in no uncertain terms that there was no pistol there. But Trainer had no intention of backing down. Instead, he stood his ground, repeated his request, and became much more insistent in his demand. Jim again told the policeman there was no gun in the house. By this time, both men were shouting at each other in the darkness, while another officer stood back and listened. He did not attempt to intervene.

"I said I must have it," Trainer recalled. He stepped forward, leaving no doubt of his determination. Jim did not move. Finally the standoff ended as the big policeman stood a foot in front of Jim, towering over the much shorter five-foot-seven-inch farmer. Jim decided to cooperate, even though he took his time doing so. If he was afraid, he certainly was not going to show it. He turned away from the policemen, went to a sideboard in the kitchen, and then pulled the large wooden cabinet out from the wall.

"He went behind a cupboard and took out a double-barrelled pistol and handed it to me," Trainer said. "Constable Currie was present," he added, naming his witness to what had just transpired. Currie picked up the kitchen coal oil lamp and held it so that the gun could be examined.

But when Trainer looked at the pistol carefully, he could not hide his disappointment. "It had not been lately discharged," he admitted. The weapon was old, dusty, and covered with cobwebs. It had obviously been behind the piece of furniture for a long time.

Trainer took the gun, however, along with a freshly washed but still damp checked shirt he was told belonged to Nicholas, and then, with Jim in tow, he climbed into the cart he had hired and drove to Egmondville. Currie sat next to Jim, who said nothing on the trip.

A short while later, there were three men facing murder charges in the Van Egmond basement cell.

It did not take the two police officers long to do the second search of the Donovan home. Acting on the coroner's request, and with the warrant he'd signed, constables Stephens and Grant went by horse and buggy back to the residence, arriving in mid-afternoon. While there is no record as to whether anyone was there this time, it would not have mattered. Because they had Coleman's warrant in hand, the two men went inside as soon as they tied their horse.

They systematically combed every inch of the log house: they opened cupboards, upended mattresses, and paid particular attention to the bedroom where the boots and pants had been found that morning. There was a shirt hanging on a hook, and even though they removed the garment, they had no idea whose it was. As they were about to leave the home, after what they felt had been a thorough search of the premises, Grant conferred with his partner; as he did so, he happened to lean against the kitchen stove. Suddenly, it occurred to him that the stove had not really been looked at, so he casually opened the door to the firebox, got down on his knees, and peered inside.

Because it was June, the appliance was cold, but Grant noticed something that seemed to have been recently burned. He looked more closely and drew his colleague's attention to it. Both men put their faces quite close to the firebox, and Stephens took a long iron poker and carefully sifted through a pile of ashes. Some dust was created when he did this, and some half-burned material fell apart. But then the constable thought he saw partly burned fragments of cloth in the heap of grey-black material.

"There were parts of a pair of socks inside, but we could not tell whether they belonged to a man or a boy," Stephens said. "I examined the ashes for traces of the pieces of the cloth, but there was nothing plain to see." He combed through the ashes with great care, but apart from the bits of the socks, there was nothing else in the stove that could be identified.

The men carefully scraped all the ashes to the front of the firebox, then scooped up what charred fragments they could to take with them. Shortly afterwards, they left the house and returned with their findings to Coleman in Egmondville. By the time they caught up with him, he had most of the arrangements in place in order to convene his Coroner's Inquest into the circumstances of the tragic deaths.

The doctor had been extremely busy that Monday afternoon. His first priority was to find a location for the hearing, and he quickly decided that the best site would be the infamous Bummer's Roost. He had already arranged with the proprietor to make use of the beverage room there. The Roost was chosen because it was the largest accommodation readily available in Egmondville, and Coleman was forced to make do with it because he was anxious to get started that evening. Whether the owner of the hotel was pleased to have his place of business commandeered would soon not matter. Because of the widespread interest in the case, space at the Roost proved to be inadequate. After only one session there, the inquest was moved to a larger facility in Seaforth.

The coroner also had to round up an inquest jury. He selected fifteen men from the area, most of whom would have known Old Melady personally or by sight, or at least would have heard of him. Those selected took their unaccustomed responsibilities seriously and conducted themselves extremely well, despite what, for the time, became a rather lengthy procedure. The jury members were William Oldfield, William Shouldice, John Fortune, William Haddan, James Devereaux, John Devereaux, Robert Devereaux, Thomas Devereaux, John Moir, Patrick O'Neil, Peter Carthy, Robert Fortune, a second John Fortune, Thomas Hodgins, and James Lennan. All were upstanding members of the community, and many of their descendants still live in the Seaforth district today.

Whether Coleman expected the number of people who showed up to watch the proceedings is not known. Nevertheless, the room at the Roost was jam-packed and stifling hot an hour before he opened the session. Sweat-soaked spectators stood several-deep around the walls. Some sat on the floor, chatting excitedly as they awaited the start of the hearing. Others crowded at the entrance, hoping to worm their way inside if someone left. Many more stood outside, whispered together, fastened on each new rumour, and gawked at Coleman, the jury, and the police as they arrived. There were horses, some with buggies and wagons and others with saddles, tied to every post for a quarter-mile or more in all directions. Many people came on foot. Most were men, but there were some women and even a few children there. Some of the youngsters in the throng even climbed trees in order to watch the stars of the show make their entrance. Once the adults began whatever they did inside, the kids climbed down and played hide-and-seek.

A reporter for the *Huron Signal* was present, and in his dispatch from the scene, he marvelled at the size of the crowd and the prevailing atmosphere of the night. "The wildest excitement exists in the neighbourhood," he wrote, "and I have no doubt, having elbowed my way out of the inquest room in Egmondville to post this report, that if the murder was clearly fastened upon any individuals, they would be hung to the nearest tree." This writer did not say specifically whether Nicholas and Tom were in attendance, but the *Toronto Globe* implied that they were. In its June 13 story on the killings, the paper stated, "On Monday evening, when the Coroner adjourned the court, he gave Nicholas Melady and Tom Donovan in charge of the peace officers." Jim Kehoe was not mentioned in the dispatch because, as we know, his arrest took place in Seaforth not long after the Egmondville inquest got underway.

The first witness that Coleman called was Tom McGoey. The tall, raw-boned, very nervous farmer explained his relationship to the deceased and told the assembly why he and his wife, Mary, had gone to the home of Nicholas Melady, Sr., on Sunday afternoon. He talked about how quiet the farmhouse was when they arrived and how there did not seem to be anyone at home. In answer to questions put to him by Coleman, he described the murder scene as it was when he and his wife stumbled upon it. He mentioned the upturned furniture, the blood on the kitchen floor, the positioning of the bodies in the hall and bedroom, and the injuries that had been inflicted. Because his testimony was the first direct witness account most of the crowd had heard, those present were profoundly shocked. McGoey recounted the story with reluctance, and there were long pauses as he fought to retain his composure. Everyone there that night could see that he was greatly bothered by what he had observed at the house. For that reason, his testimony served to heighten the impact of everything he said.

The newspaper coverage reflected the sense of the night and the deeds that led to the inquest. The *Hamilton Evening Times*, in an account published on June 10, claimed that "no occurrence has transpired in this district [Huron] for years past which at all approaches this one in the enormity of its cold-blooded brutality and malicious vindictiveness — in fact, it sent a shudder of horror through every heart within miles, and the great excitement which pervades the entire community has seldom had a parallel here." And in truth, the matter so transfixed the local residents that the paper's observation was probably understated. No occurrence in the area had ever affected the populace to such a degree.

Tom McGoey testified slowly, in a near whisper, and at such length that by the time he had answered all the questions put to him, Coleman decided that in view of the hour, adjournment was in order. Although he had only heard from the one witness, he had heard enough for the day. But of more import, he had already made up his mind as to the guilt of Nicholas Melady and Tom Donovan.

That same night, when a reporter from the *Globe* asked for his views on the case, the coroner did not even attempt to state that he would let justice run its course. Instead, he declared that "there was not the possibility of a doubt that they were the murderers." However, despite his jump to judgment, Coleman informed those present that the hearings would, of necessity, continue the next day at Downey's Hall in Seaforth and that the first witness then would be Nicholas Melady. Starting time, he told the crowd, would be 9:00 a.m.

This announcement caused an immediate and sweeping reaction among the spectators. Those who heard it were beside themselves with excitement, and as they poured from the building they repeated to others what had just been announced. In no time, everyone within earshot knew the schedule for the next day and decided they had to be at Downey's. Then they left for their homes, still talking about what they had heard and seen that night, sure they would never witness an event that was more dramatic.

Downey's was on the northeast corner of the main intersection in Seaforth. Because of its location, the hall was easy to find; virtually everyone knew where it was, and many had been in the place. The building was relatively new, and because of its size it had often been used for community functions of all kinds, from political rallies to travelling magic shows to Anglican church services. In 1857, local entrepreneur Tom Downey had bought the vacant corner lot and built his large frame hotel there. He named the place after himself, and the business was profitable from the outset. He advertised regularly in the *Expositor* that the hotel bar sold only the "very best brands of liquors" and that the food available in the dining room was always "the best the market affords." He also prided himself on being the "most attentive" hotel keeper around. Downey was naturally outgoing, gregarious, and hospitable. He knew everyone in town.

But it was neither food and drink nor hospitality that drew the crowd to his establishment at 9:00 on Tuesday morning, June 9. Something far more intriguing was on offer. Ironically, at precisely the same moment the caskets containing his father and stepmother were being taken up the centre aisle for the funeral Mass in St. Columban church, four miles down the Huron Road to the east, Nicholas was being led in handcuffs to the witness box at Downey's Hall. And while we do not know how many were at the church (although it was likely full to capacity), we do know that there was an overflow crowd at the inquest. Undoubtedly, many individuals in the area must have agonized over which function to attend. It is said that a great number, once they had done their duty and buried Old Melady and his wife, hurried to Seaforth to be present at the inquest. Most of these late-comers were disappointed, however. There was such a crush of spectators to enter Downey's that scores had to stand out on the street and wait for any-one who left to relay the news of developments inside. But few left.

Constable Ebenezer Lusby escorted Nicholas to the front of the inquest hall, indicated where he was to stand, and positioned himself a few steps behind and to one side of his charge. The crowd was relatively silent, noting the mood and manner of the tall, dark, good-looking young man in custody. Jury members shuffled uncomfortably in their chairs, and some had trouble even looking at the accused. After all, most of them knew him, per-haps even better than they had known his father. But whether they already thought Nicholas was guilty of murder is not known, despite the coroner's opinions and whatever he might have told the press the night before.

Finally, after shuffling through a number of papers before him, Coleman looked up, cleared his throat, turned to the prisoner, and got right to the point. He asked Nicholas to state his name and then tell the jury where he had been and what he had been doing on Saturday night.

There is no surviving transcript of the testimony at the Melady inquest, even though we know a running record was kept by either Coleman or someone he'd selected for the task. Fortunately, a reasonably detailed summary does exist, so the names of all witnesses, the order in which they were called, and occasional clarifying notes are available. We know how long the entire hearing took, and we know the number of times some witnesses had to be recalled. As well, the press carried state-ment analyses, and many of these exist today. Furthermore, later remarks made by the police, reporters, family members, and others provide a glimpse of the general tone of the procedure. It is thus possible to glean a reasonably accurate idea of just what each witness told the assembly.

But Nicholas did not tell them much. He gave a somewhat rambling, non-committal, deliberately vague description of what he had done and where he had been the previous Saturday. He said he had been working at the Kehoes' during the day and then, after supper that evening, decided he would walk to Bummer's Roost in Egmondville for a drink. About a mile or so before he got there, he came across his brother-in-law, James Kehoe, and Tom Donovan, who were on their way from Seaforth. Because they had some whiskey with them, and they offered to share it, he no longer had any reason to go on to the Roost. Instead, the three decided to go to the Kehoes'. However, shortly before they got there, Tom invited Nicholas to go home with him, so he went.

At no time during his testimony did he mention being at Old Melady's that evening.

In response to further questions from the coroner, Nicholas said that he, Jim, and Tom did walk along the road past Old Melady's, but when they got to the Kehoe place, Jim went in, while he and Tom continued on to the Donovan home. He said the two of them arrived shortly before midnight and remained there all night. Coleman tried again, rephrasing his questions, but got nowhere. Obviously exasperated, he announced a recess, conferred with the police officers present, and decided to make another attempt. During the break, the spectators remained where they were. They knew if they left the room, they would likely not get back inside. Nicholas was recalled, and the interrogation resumed.

This time, the prisoner told the inquest that on Sunday morning, he and Tom got up late, had something to eat, and then decided they would go to Jim's and see what he was going to do that day. However, by the time they got there, Jim had gone to church. As there were then four Sunday Masses at St. Columban, he and Tom decided to go to the last one. In the meantime, as they waited for Jim to return, they chatted, had a nap, and talked to Margaret. They had, he insisted, no reason to do otherwise.

Coleman's frustration was tangible. His questions had produced nothing, and try as he might, he could not get the prisoner to admit to having been at Old Melady's at any time the night of the murders. When the coroner mentioned the footprints on the kitchen floor, the bloody boots, and the pants found at Donovan's, the response never varied. Nicholas said they walked on the road, didn't go near Old Melady's, and didn't have anything to do with the footprints at all. He stuck to his story, repeated it in a number of ways, but in essence, always said the same thing. By the time his testimony ended, some in the crowd actually started to believe him.

Finally, realizing he was getting nowhere, Coleman angrily dismissed the witness and directed that he be returned to the Van Egmond house immediately and be kept under guard at all times. Then he called Tom Donovan to the stand and hoped for something better.

CHAPTER 9 INQUEST: FRUSTRATION AND FAILURE

TO THE CORONER that Tuesday morning in Seaforth, the testimony of Tom Donovan was just as frustrating as Nicholas Melady's had been. And while what he had to say differed in the description of his daytime activities on Saturday, Tom's story of walking on the road, sharing the bottle, and then going home to his brother's was identical to what Nicholas had said. In fact, it was often almost verbatim. Even when Coleman reworded his questions, the answers he got rarely varied.

Constable Stephens brought Tom to the inquest, witnessed his swearing-in, and remained there to guard him. Following the prisoner's long, repetitive, and totally unhelpful contribution to the proceedings, Stephens returned him to the Egmondville cell. Later on, the policeman billed the County of Huron three dollars for his day: one dollar for going to court, one dollar for standing guard over the prisoner, and one dollar to pay for the food Tom ate. All meals for the three prisoners were prepared in the kitchen at Bummer's Roost and then carried about one hundred yards across the dirt street and around to the back door of the Van Egmond house.

Stephens at least had something to show for his time and effort. Coleman and the others at the inquest did not.

Tom Donovan was on the stand three times in all. In his first appearance, he identified himself and then told the jury how he happened to be in Seaforth on the day Old Melady and his wife were killed. He said he had gone to the farm of a neighbour named Chesney that Saturday morning, intending to help sow grass seed. However, because it was too wet for seeding, he went instead to the Hills blacksmith shop in Egmondville. He wanted to see if Hills had finished repairing a broken cultivator that had been there for over a week.

Most of the farmers in the area brought whatever they could not fix themselves to the Hills shop. At any time, there would be two or three customers there dropping things off, waiting for repairs, or picking up equipment that was ready to go. The place had become something of a social gathering spot as well as a thriving business. Often men who had intended to be there for ten minutes would still be there, talking, and hour or more later. That was why Tom Donovan was there when Jim Kehoe came in.

The two had not seen each other for a while, so they chatted for twenty minutes or more. Then, because it was Saturday afternoon and neither was busy, they decided to go to Seaforth and get a drink. They went to the Carmichael at first, but decided to leave there after only a couple of minutes. He did not give any reason why they left, nor was he asked. They went across the street to Walsh's and spent the afternoon drinking there. Later, they returned to Egmondville and stopped in at the Roost. He said they thought about getting some supper, but was not sure if they did. A bit after dark, he and Jim were on their way to Jim's house when they happened to meet Nicholas on the road. They shared a bottle of whiskey with him as they walked, and around that time, he invited Nicholas home for the night. Nicholas accepted, and they parted company with Jim at his laneway.

During his testimony, Tom offered little else for Coleman to use to build his case. He answered the coroner's questions, but took care never to reveal anything of an incriminating nature. Nor did Coleman touch on one matter that might have produced results. He did not ask what the prisoner thought of Old Melady or his new wife. As far as we can tell today, none of the three accused was asked about the relationship. In Nicholas's case, everyone knew he and his father had troubles, but as far as Tom was concerned, any friction was less obvious, so his answer might have helpful for the coroner's purposes. Today we have no way of knowing why he failed to ask each man about the new Mrs. Melady. His failure to do so can certainly be seen as an error in judgment on his part.

At any rate, the coroner grew increasingly irritated as the day wore on. He called two separate afternoon recesses, both of which were brief, and after each tried a different tack with Tom. Nothing worked. The prisoner admitted that the boots found in the bedroom were his, but he didn't know anything about unusual heel marks. When he said he never looked at his heels, a few of his friends in the audience snickered. When

Coleman mentioned pouring the blood from the boots, Tom was taken aback for a moment, but then quickly recovered and claimed that the liquid would have been sweat mixed with dye from the brown leather. He got a laugh from the audience when he went into an impromptu and rather lengthy explanation of how much his feet sweated, and that they had been sweating much more that particular night because of the long walk. On the matter of his whereabouts on Saturday night, he said he had not been at Old Melady's at all, but that he, Nicholas, and Jim had walked on the road and nowhere else. He also testified that he and Nicholas were together from the time they met on the road until they "arrived at David's" later on that evening. He said he had never lost sight of Nicholas at any time during that period. In an answer to a follow-up question from Coleman, Tom stated, categorically, that Nicholas was right beside him all the time and that they had not separated, even briefly.

On a later occasion, these last few words would take on a far greater significance than was realized when they were uttered.

Finally, late in the afternoon, Jim was led into the inquest room. He nodded to several people he recognized, smiled, waved to others, and then, to a large extent, reiterated everything the jury had already heard. He just took a lot longer to do it. In all, he was recalled five times over three days after his first session on the stand, but he never varied from the story — the story the three had obviously concocted as they sat together in the Egmondville cell.

A reporter from the *Guelph Mercury* summed up the testimony in an account published by that paper on June 18: "The prisoners [Melady and Donovan] swore they went straight to David Donovan's house, on Saturday night about 12 o'clock, and were not out until daylight on Sunday morning and they were nowhere else but on the road going there." Much later, on December 15, 1869, the *Stratford Herald*, in a more in-depth wrap-up to the whole matter, pointed out that "the actors in the crime kept their own counsel well and guarded [and] the officers of the law were well-nigh baffled in the efforts to fasten the crime on the proper shoulders."

In essence, what the Crown had so far was incriminating, but circumstantial. No one could be found who had actually observed the killers going into the Melady home, and no one but those responsible had seen

the murder committed. And while Coleman and the police had the footprints in the blood, they had to admit that the feet of many men would
have matched the marks. For these reasons, even as the inquest was being
held, the investigation continued elsewhere.

On Tuesday afternoon, not long after Margaret Kehoe got back from her
father's funeral, Bernard Trainer showed up at the Kehoe residence. He
had another police officer, William Core, with him. When they arrived,
Margaret was busy doing the family washing, but she stopped her work,
asked the men what they wanted, then reluctantly allowed them into the
kitchen. Her hostility towards Trainer was palpable, but she didn't dare
cross him. He had already arrested her husband, who, as she told Trainer,
"had done nothing." She did not intend to give the detective any reason
to take her away as well. She certainly did not trust him.

Trainer got right to the point. He asked for Nicholas Melady's pants,
which he described as black and torn. Trainer knew this because, as he
said later, Nicholas had described them to him "by a tear in the seat
which he said he got while getting out of a wagon."

Margaret knew the pants in question: they were the same ones that
young Katherine Melady said Coleman had been interested in and had
searched the previous afternoon. Unbeknownst to Trainer, Margaret had
also checked the pockets of Nicholas's pants, largely because she was
curious as to why the coroner had done so. "I saw them in my house
before Trainer came," she said later. "I fully searched them after I had heard
the coroner had been there. I found a pipe and a pocket book," she added.

She knew she was under no obligation to tell the officer she had
done the search, so she kept this to herself. She then led the officers into
the room where the pants were hanging. "I pointed out the trousers to
Trainer, and he took them down. They took them outside the door, but
I could not see what they did with them."

Much later, both Trainer and Core explained their actions. "We
found the pants," Trainer said. "They were not wet, and there were no
blood marks on them that I saw. Core was with me, and we found them
together. We examined them in front of the door, in the sunlight. There
was some paper in the pockets and a pipe and some shot."

This was the first mention of any pistol bullets in the pants, even though the pockets had been carefully searched twice before and no shot was there on either occasion. Obviously, the ever-zealous Detective Trainer believed he needed to bolster his case. Presumably, for that reason alone, he had Core there to corroborate the story. The two had gone outside not to conduct the search in better light, but to ensure that they could plant evidence and not be seen doing so. Core proved to be a compliant witness to the deed. Margaret continued her washing while the two men were occupied.

"I was present when we found the trousers," Core explained later, "and I took the shot out of the pocket. Also some yellow paper." Much later, when he was asked what became of the ammunition, Core explained, "I gave the paper and shot to the coroner."

He also turned the pants over to Coleman, along with a hat Trainer had noticed on a wall peg in the Kehoe kitchen. Margaret said the headgear belonged to Nicholas and that it had been in her home for some time.

When Trainer noticed a dark stain on one side of the brim, he made sure he had the hat when he and Core returned to Seaforth. That afternoon, the coroner sent the hat to the University of Toronto, where a chemistry professor named Croft was asked to examine it for traces of human blood. The cloth cap had to be sent away for checking because there was no facility in Huron where such work could be done. Even in Toronto, the testing capabilities were relatively primitive.

The inquest at Downey's continued for several hours on its first day in that location. In addition to the three men charged, a steady parade of others testified, including police officers who had been called to the murder scene, neighbours who said they had heard of the ill feeling between the deceased and his younger son, and area farmers who had had past dealings with Old Melady. None had witnessed the killings.

By the end of the evening, Coleman realized he still lacked conclusive evidence that any one of the accused was involved. In his mind they were, and he had told the *Globe* reporter that they were, but proving it was becoming far more difficult than he'd first imagined. For that reason, he decided to adjourn his inquest until mid-afternoon of the next day. He wanted to use the morning hours to confer with the police, with Doctor Vercoe, and with some of Old Melady's closest neighbours. He also wanted to revisit the murder scene himself. He was sure there had to be something they were all overlooking. To that end, he asked Trainer, Vercoe, and two other men for help. While the reason the two were selected is not known today, it may have been because they volunteered or because they were especially familiar with either the house or the farms adjacent to it. In any event, two farmers from the district, Thomas Gemmell and James McMulkin, were present on Wednesday morning when the Melady home was checked again and the trail of footprints from the woodpile to the river was retraced.

Every room in the house was searched once more, including the rather cold, austere front parlour where the brief wake had been held, as well as the entire cellar, particularly the space immediately below the entry window. The coroner was also interested in checking for full hand prints in the dried blood in the kitchen and bedroom. He felt that if he found any obvious ones, and they matched the hand sizes of the accused, he would have another scrap of evidence at his disposal. However, even though there were several hand prints, all were so smudged they were useless. The coroner was infuriated when he realized this, but he did his best to keep his feelings to himself.

Nothing else turned up in the house, although the coroner ordered Bernard Trainer to take the trunk and the various papers in it from the murder scene bedroom to Goderich. The next day, the detective loaded the trunk on a light wagon; at Seaforth, he met the Goderich train and turned over the precious cargo. Another officer was waiting in Goderich when the train arrived there. Coleman felt there might be something in the large wooden steamer trunk that would be helpful at a future trial, even though the trunk had been more or less overlooked since the killings were discovered. The fact that it could have been tampered with apparently did not matter, or perhaps did not occur to him. When the train arrived in Seaforth, the shipment was merely put into the baggage car with all the other freight. No escort went with it. Nor were the papers inside the trunk removed or secured. The container was not even locked.

Finally, Coleman, Vercoe, Gemmell, and McMulkin, along with Trainer and Constable Hugh Grant, turned their attention to following the footprints. The six men walked slowly, bending over at times to more carefully attempt to find shoe outlines in places where they were barely visible. Three men went on either side of the trail, stopped often to confer with one another, and took pains to double-check in case there were more than two sets of tracks. No others were found. The group spent a lot of time combing the place where the rails from the fence had been knocked down, in case anything might have been dropped there. Again, nothing turned up. The area around the woodpile also came in for increased scrutiny, but to no avail.

The work was hot and back-breaking, but the trail was easy to follow where the soil had been worked. In other places, the tracing became little more than covering the probabilities. The area along the Bayfield River bank was by far the worst. But the place where the river had been forded not only came in for the closest inspection of any place, it also yielded results, if unexpectedly.

Tom Gemmell was hunched over, poking through some long reeds by the water's edge at one end of the log that lay across the stream. As he dropped to one knee to part plant stems to check for tracks, he happened to glance to his left, out over the surface of the water. There, in a little eddy, almost below the crossing log, he noticed what looked to be a small, flat, dark-coloured piece of bark. Because of sunlight glinting on the water, the object was hard to see, and he lost it for a few seconds. When he looked again, he saw the thing a second time and realized it was not bark at all, but a book of some sort. He called Vercoe over and pointed. At first, the doctor was not sure what Gemmell was showing him, but then, looking where Gemmell pointed, he noticed the thing as well. "It was a small account book," Vercoe recalled. "Gemmell found it, just under a piece of timber where one could cross the stream. It was floating, and was wet and a little soiled outside."

By this time, the others had clustered at the spot where Gemmell stood, and all of them could see the object. Gemmell said he would try to go out on the log and get the thing, but cautioned that they keep an eye on it in case it started to float downstream before he got to it. Then he crawled slowly out along the log on his stomach. Once he was over the object in the water, he held on with one hand and with the other reached down and retrieved the notebook as it floated immediately below him.

"It was nearly in the middle of the river," he explained later. "I lifted it out of the water that morning, almost a mile from the deceased's." As somewhat of an afterthought, he added, "Part of the cover was torn off." Later, when Gemmell was testifying at the inquest, Coleman asked him to describe the condition of the book when it was first located. The farmer explained that it was somewhat dirty, from clay stains, possibly, or simply from excessive use. "There was no blood on it." The last remark was an answer to a direct question from the coroner. Then Gemmell volunteered, "When I opened it, I saw names written in it."

Initially, none of the group knew quite what to make of this small, water-soaked ledger. The men passed it around, and each looked at it, some more carefully than others.

"I handed the book to Grant," said Gemmell. "Then he gave it to Doctor Vercoe. I saw it in Doctor Coleman's possession fifteen minutes after it was found."

When he was handed the book, James McMulkin noticed what he first thought was a letter sticking out from inside the back cover. He looked closer, and was amazed to discover that what he saw was not a letter at all. As he explained later, "It was an account, in my writing, rendered to Nicholas Melady, Sr." McMulkin told the others the details of the transaction, which had to do with a rather routine grain purchase the previous year.

Today, a detailed description of the contents of the book and the story of what transpired after it was found are fragmentary at best. There were several names in it, all of which related, in one way or another, to Old Melady's business dealings. It quickly became obvious to the men on the river bank that the book not only belonged to Old Melady but must have been taken from his house at the time of the murder. They also surmised that the ledger had been lost when the perpetrators of the crime crossed the river on the log. This discovery, coupled with the nail marks from Tom Donovan's boots and the bloody footprints at the murder scene, all served to link Tom and Nicholas ever more closely to the killings. The book, after all, had been found along the route Coleman and the others were sure Nicholas and Tom had taken Saturday night.

The inquest resumed in mid-afternoon at Downey's, shortly after Coleman and those who had been with him returned to Seaforth. The first part of the proceedings centred on the finding of the ledger and the identification of it. To that end, James McMulkin gave a deposition, swearing that the account with his name on it was indeed a business dealing he had had with Old Melady. Following McMulkin's testimony, Grant, Gemmell, and Vercoe all took the stand and related their roles in finding the book.

By this time, more than twenty witnesses had given evidence, but none of them had been able to place the three accused at the scene of the crime. This state of affairs was weighing heavier than ever on Coleman, and it seemed at times as if he was making no progress at all. Again and again, he heard from neighbours, relatives, and even casual acquaintances of Old Melady's that they knew of the father-son antipathy. Several mentioned that the deceased was not well liked, that he was a braggart, a drunk, and had a violent temper. Yet even so, Coleman told himself, none of those failings merited murder.

Finally, conscious of the passing of time and almost desperate to prove his case, the coroner remembered the stained hat Trainer had retrieved at Jim Kehoe's. But the hat had already been sent to Toronto, and Coleman knew the results of tests on it would not be available for a few days. Because of this necessary delay, he decided to suspend the inquiry until the hat had been examined and the results were known. He therefore declared an adjournment and said that the inquest would reconvene on Thursday, June 18, at 2:00 p.m. There were only a handful of spectators in the room when he made the announcement.

But the soiled hat was no help to Coleman's cause. The day before the inquiry was to resume, the coroner had a telegram from Toronto. In his message, Professor Croft described his examination of the hat and explained his findings. The mark on the brim, he said, was definitely a bloodstain, but he could not tell whether it was human or animal. When he got this news, Coleman began to fear he might never come up with an airtight key to the case. He could not locate a witness to the deed and could not prove that the three suspects were guilty, but at the same time, he was obliged to carry on.

Several others testified, many of them more than once. In all, thirty-seven individuals took the stand — so many, in fact, that interest waned even more. By the time the inquest wrapped up, there were only a handful of regulars in attendance. Most of them were old men who had nothing else to do with their time. Nevertheless, late on Friday evening, June 19, the coroner charged the jury, who took two hours to return a verdict.

As a consequence of the deliberations, Nicholas and Tom were to be sent to the Goderich Gaol, where they were both to be held on charges of wilful murder. They would then be committed for trial in what the *Toronto Globe*, on March 27, 1869, would call "merely circumstantial evidence." At this point, Jim was released, because there was even less evidence of his culpability.

But his turn would come.

CHAPTER 10 | BEHIND BARS IN GODERICH

POLICE CONSTABLES THOMAS STEPHENS and Ebenezer Lusby delivered Nicholas Melady and Tom Donovan to the Goderich Gaol on Saturday, June 20. On arrival, the two officers stood together until the accused killers climbed down from the wagon that had brought them there. Lusby checked both sets of handcuffs and kept his eyes on the miscreants while his colleague tied the horse to the hitching post and then went and pounded on the oaken door and asked for entry. The ugly bulk of the jail towered above them, and the horse snorted and pawed the ground, as if wanting to be away from this place. For that matter, the two policemen probably felt the same way. No one ever came here for enjoyment.

While the four waited for a response from within the prison, the shadows of noon were short and the sun bathed the trees and grass in front of the jail with a gentle warmth. Because the building stood high on a promontory overlooking the Maitland River Valley, the view to the north and east was dramatic and green and stretched for miles. To the west, the turquoise serenity of Lake Huron reached the horizon, while far below, languid waves lapped the sandy shore. Robins, blue jays, and wrens nested nearby, and high overhead seagulls wheeled, unfettered and free.

But the moment of reverie did not last. There was some muffled conversation from inside, and a disembodied voice asked who was there. Stephens identified himself and stated his business. A minute later, the great door swung wide. The prisoners took one last look around, as if savouring these seconds, then reluctantly stepped into captivity. And while neither knew what he would face behind those granite walls, Nicholas would never walk free outside them again.

A seventy-five-foot-long, dark, gloomy, tunnel-like corridor runs from the outer opening of the jail to an inner door, heavy and secure, encased in stone. The hallway walls are drab grey, cold, clammy, and fourteen feet high. They are rather wide apart at the first door, but cramped and close at the second. The ceiling is concrete, as is the floor, and when Nicholas and Tom were there, the only light came from two small apertures located high in the walls and barred. The entire entranceway is foreboding, claustrophobic, and chilling.

Once their charges were beyond the second door and in the custody of the gaol personnel, the policemen came back outside, untied their horse, and quickly drove away. While they had made the delivery without incident and were now glad to be finished their escort role, their connection with this case was far from over. In the interim, however, the suspects had lost their freedom and were completely secure.

But they were certainly not at ease. In spite of their outward bravado, they were scared, unsure of themselves, and incredibly lonely. For all intents and purposes, this jail might as well have been a thousand miles from Seaforth, from family, friends, and the warmth of home.

While the jailer and his staff completed the initial assessment of the newcomers, the two joked with the guards and pretended to be unper-turbed about the situation they were in, but at the same time they glanced furtively about their new surroundings, like animals in a cage. They found themselves in kind of an anteroom, immediately inside and to one side of the door they had just entered. The area was cramped and drab, the ceil-ing low, and the window grilled. Some pale light filtered through it, but when the two looked through the dirty glass, all they saw was a stone wall. A desk, a couple of battered-looking chairs, and a wooden filing cabinet took up most of the space, with a small weigh scales in one corner. The scales were the same type the two had often used to weigh wheat. What looked to be a ledger of some kind was on the desk, along with a blotter, a small bottle of ink, an assortment of quill pens, and a wooden yardstick.

The new arrivals soon learned that the man in charge here was Edward Campaigne. He was relatively young (aged thirty-six) and handsome, and he seemed to know his job. He took down their names, asked questions, and made several notations in the thick, black-covered book in front of him. The volume, *General Register for the Gaol at Goderich, for the County of Huron*, listed twenty-three categories that had to be completed for each new inmate. Some were to be done immediately; others, such as "Date of Discharge," were meant for later. One wonders if either prisoner gave much thought to this category. Both could see it as they stood beside Campaigne, looking over his shoulder as he filled in the necessary blanks.

Among the required entries were some that were obvious: age, occupation, height, weight, and so on. Others were reflective of the times: could the prisoner read, write, or do both? If the new inmate could read, was his or her ability "Imperfect," "Well," or even "Superior"? In addition, the admitting official was expected to size up the newcomer and make note of whether he or she seemed to be "Temperate" or "Intemperate." Tom and Nicholas were both judged to be the former. It is uncertain today what these categories really meant. A quick perusal of entries for other prisoners shows a wide disparity in this assessment. In fact, in some cases where individuals were sent to the jail for a second or third time, their characters apparently changed. Where they might have been temperate the first time, they became intemperate the second. In at least one instance, the same person changed three times. Because of the discrepancy, one wonders about the abilities of the prison personnel to make snap judgments about the many individuals who appeared before them. In the case of how literate the newcomers were — just how literate were the jailers? How much and how well could they read? Were their assessments reliable? And while we cannot answer such questions, they had to be answered by the guards. These men did their best.

Once the formalities had been looked after, Campaigne, who was what we might call the warden today, gave the new arrivals some wise and reasonable advice. He told them to behave themselves, to stay out of trouble, and to accept their situation. If they did so, they would be treated correctly while under his care. There is no record of their immediate response, although if they continued with the false bravado, they likely pretended to give little heed to what they were being told.

But Campaigne meant what he said. When he died eight years later of typhoid fever at age forty-four, the *Huron Expositor* said, "In his official capacity, he manifested a love of discipline, which, coupled with his warm-heartedness and remarkable strength, maintained excellent order in the jail as well as in its general appointments as in the conduct of the prisoners." It is not surprising that his funeral was a large one, and his expertise was sorely missed when he passed away. His remains are in a cemetery on the eastern outskirts of Goderich, but few who visit the graveyard today have ever heard of him.

Nicholas grew to like Campaigne and also his wife, Catherine. In the weeks and months that followed, he saw both quite often and heard stories about their five little children; he would later thank them for their kindness towards him. Despite the spelling of his surname, the jailer was from Ireland and had been born in Dublin. Even though they shared unpleasant surroundings, Nicholas and his keeper often talked for long periods of time and joked with one another. It was as if their similar ancestry drew them together. Where they were did not matter.

When Campaigne finished talking to Nicholas and Tom, he left the two with guards who told them how the place operated, catalogued their personal possessions, and led them to one of the cellblocks. Presumably, the two were searched and given some kind of medical examination, but no record exists concerning either. Later on, new inmates were all subject to both procedures.

The four cellblocks in Goderich were identical: three cells side by side, with a narrow passageway running in front of them. A somewhat larger space, called a "day room," was located at the end of the passage. Prisoners spent a lot of time there, eating, socializing, complaining, playing cards, smoking, and in general doing anything they could to get through the endless hours of mind-numbing boredom. If their behaviour warranted it, inmates were also permitted exercise periods in the prison yard. Trusted individuals of either sex sometimes used a room on the main floor to fashion things out of wood, to sew, or to repair broken prison equipment. Non-aggressive types contributed manually to the upkeep of the place. Inmates who were judged to be "lunatics" or to be particularly violent were generally restricted to their cells, and sometimes even tethered to a ball and chain secured to the floor. In fact, the last ball and chain used at the institution is still there for visitors to see today. It is a lasting reminder of just how grim the jail was. Straitjackets were sometimes used in order to protect guards when violent prisoners had to be moved from one cellblock to another.

Washing facilities behind bars were decidedly primitive, so outsiders were hired to do laundry on contract. Soiled bedclothes were bundled up, collected, washed, and returned on a regular basis. The County of Huron set the stipend: five cents to wash a sheet, ten cents for a blanket, and fifty cents for each dozen pillow cases. A local man named J.H. Williams came to the jail to shave prisoners who requested his services. During one four-month period, he earned $6.50 for doing this, but surviving records give no indication of how many beards he removed or how much he received for each inmate he dealt with. In its first years of operation, the jail's inmates bathed occasionally in the single bathtub. As late as 1869, the tub was still made of wood. As might be expected, some individuals never really wanted to wash and had to be forced to do so. Not surprisingly, the entire building carried a constant odour.

The jail itself, while imposing when observed from the outside, is not really very large. There are only twelve single cells in all, three in each block. As well, at least one of the blocks, the second floor of the west wing, was reserved for women, although men were housed there at times of overcrowding. There were also four holding cells on the third floor, but these were used sparingly and for short duration.

The small block arrangement allowed for the segregation of prisoners. For example, Tom and Nicholas were housed in the same area because their charge was the same. Local vagrants who happened to be incarcerated because they were down on their luck would generally be located elsewhere. Segregation by sex and crime severity was touted as a reform in their day.

Over the years, several individuals of varying degrees of notoriety found themselves locked up at Goderich. Two of the best known were Jim Donnelly, the patriarch of the clan of the same name, who did time for murder, and Steven Truscott, the fourteen-year-old boy who was convicted of the same offence and sentenced to be hanged in 1959. While both instances were controversial, the latter was a profound injustice. Anyone who has seriously examined the factors behind Truscott's jailing can't help but be appalled by what was done to him. He was locked up with adult criminals, deprived of his youth, and traumatized for life by the experience. In the Donnelly situation, "Old Jim" Donnelly got into a fight at a barn raising near Lucan, a few miles south of Seaforth. He had been drinking heavily, as had his opponent. The drunken brawl ended with a death, and Donnelly was convicted of it. There were lots of contributing factors in the matter, and today the charge would likely have been manslaughter at most. Donnelly was sentenced to be hanged at the Goderich Gaol. Ultimately, however, he was not. The ruling was appealed, but he did serve seven years in Kingston Penitentiary for the crime. Because he was one of the so-called Black Donnelly family, his case was better known than most might have been. Years later, Donnelly and other members of his family were murdered and their bodies burned by a group of self-styled vigilantes, none of whom were ever punished for their actions.

By all accounts, Tom and Nicholas, like most inmates of the time and since, never really adapted to prison life, but they were powerless to do much about it. They existed, if that is the proper description, but all the while they dreamed of being free. They did not admit to their crime — in fact, they denied it behind bars as they had denied it in the days immediately following the murder. Both perjured themselves during the inquest, but lying on the witness stand did not seem to be a serious matter for either. These two, along with Jim Kehoe, lied because they were sure that to do otherwise would have meant certain death at the end of a rope. In this assessment, they were wholly accurate. Now, however, they found themselves waiting and wondering about the progress of the investigation. Whenever a relative or friend from Seaforth came to visit, both inmates asked what the police were doing. In short, the answer was, "Not much."

Trainer's case was going nowhere. In fact, once he succeeded in getting the prime suspects behind bars, he more or less dropped the matter completely, except for a single adventure that summer. Because he was always certain of Jim's involvement in the break-in and murder, he decided to arrest him on suspicion alone, send him to Goderich, and see what would happen. Accordingly, he charged Jim with murder and saw him jailed, but was chagrined because the man was released after a few days because of lack of evidence. In the weeks following this initiative, most of Trainer's involvement in the case ended as he decided to await the outcome of the Fall Assizes of 1868.

The assizes were court sessions held in the spring and fall in the various counties across Ontario. A judge travelled from place to place and presided over whatever cases were to be heard in both civil and criminal matters. The trials were almost always held at the county seat, the administrative capital of the county. Generally, this was also the largest community in the county. In Huron, the sessions were in Goderich.

Most of the time, the items at hand were dealt with very quickly, and even reasonably complicated cases lasted only a couple of hours or, at most, one or two days. In the fall of 1868 in Goderich, the Melady murder trial was expected to take longer than anything else on the docket. It was also the most anticipated, and was scheduled to commence after all other cases had been heard.

The forthcoming trial was the talk of Seaforth, Huron County, and beyond. Interested parties planned to go to Goderich, intending to be in the courtroom to watch and listen. They went by every conveyance possible: by buggy or wagon, on horseback, and on foot. Many took one of the three daily westbound trains from Seaforth. Others came by stagecoach. Some even went the day before and bunked with relatives or friends in order to be in the courthouse when it opened in the morning. All were disappointed.

The Honorable Mr. Justice A. Wilson presided, and in rapid succession he dealt with two cases of larceny and two of forgery before turning to the matter of the Queen vs. Nicholas Melady and Thomas Donovan on the charge of murder. The trial essentially ended before it started. The Crown counsel asked Justice Wilson to put the matter over to the following spring, so that more evidence could be gathered against the two accused. The Crown told Wilson that there had not been sufficient time to do a thorough investigation, and if the matter were to be dealt with right away, both accused would surely be acquitted.

After he heard from the Crown and considered the request for a couple of minutes, Wilson agreed and announced the postponement. Then the crowd in the courtroom, along with the sixteen most essential Crown witnesses present, went back to their homes. Before doing so, however, each of the latter had to put up a two-hundred-dollar bond and promise to appear when next they were called.

The lack of resolution of the case caused an immediate uproar in Goderich and to the far reaches of the county. People complained about the courts, about the shoddy and ineffective police work, about delays in other trials, about the lack of resolve by the coroner and those who answered to him, and about the perception that Old Melady had gotten what he deserved, so his killers would not be pursued with proper diligence.

Finally, the *Goderich Star* editorialized on the case on October 2, pointing a finger in another direction:

> The particulars of this awful murder are pretty well known to our readers, and many of them will no doubt be surprised that the perpetrators of this horrible crime were not brought to trial at the Court of Assizes which opened here on the 22nd. The reasons of such not being the case, is a disgrace, and blame has been thrown on different parties, but only by a few has it been placed on the right shoulders. For some years, the County Council of Huron has been in the habit of appointing what they term an Audit Committee, whose duty is to audit the account for the administration of justice.

The paper then went on to criticize the Audit Committee, and through it the County Council, for being unduly stingy. The Audit Committee was the same panel that would not pay Bernard Trainer extra for night work during the initial stages of the murder investigation. It even went so far as to claim that the members of the committee "would rather see the perpetrators of such a brutal crime go unpunished than give one cent to have the case worked up." No other county in Canada had such a committee, the editorial writer added, because if such a system were universal, "crime would be rampant and criminals allowed to go free."

Finally, in a plea to readers, the *Star* urged all law-abiding citizens not to take it anymore, to tell errant members of County Council to shape up. "It is certainly time the people of this county were fully aroused to a sense of their duty," the paper wrote, "and teach members of the County Council that they cannot trifle with justice as they have been doing. They are sent there to do a certain duty, and unless they do so faithfully and honestly, their place must be taken by those who will."

The *Huron Signal* was equally vocal, although it tempered its criticism of the Audit Committee. "We have nothing in particular to thank the committee for," the paper admitted in an editorial on October 1, "but we cannot blame its members unreasonably." The paper then claimed that "the County of Huron should have offered a reward for the conviction of this outrage, and then it should have taken such steps as would have led to the ferreting out of every tittle of evidence, depending on the government of Ontario to reimburse any extraordinary expenditure." There never was a reward of any kind offered in the Melady murder case.

The *Signal* declared that the real culprit in the delay was not to be found in Huron County. "In our humble opinion, the Ontario Government is seriously to blame in this case." Then it made what sounded like a threat: "The day of reckoning is at hand." The editors did not spell out who was going to do the reckoning, or how it was to be done, but presumably they were suggesting that the government should be defeated at election time.

These editorials seem to have had some effect, and they did express the mood of the community at the time. The plea that something should have been done earlier was also mentioned in a *Toronto Globe* story on March 27, 1869, entitled, "How the Evidence Was Wrought Up." The paper described the inactivity in the period after the inquest and before the assizes began and pointed out that "the matter remained in abeyance." The newspaper continued, "Then the neighbors, fearing that the perpetrators of a heinous crime would escape punishment, petitioned the Attorney General for Ontario for a special detective to endeavor to obtain sufficient facts to bring a case."

Initially, the excuse was the same, that there was no money, but eventually the agitation brought results. The *Globe* wrote, "In accordance with repeated representations, in which motives of economy were assigned as a reason for not undertaking the investigation, Detective Clarke, formerly on the provincial staff ... was dispatched to the scene of the murder."

Today, relatively little is known about Clarke, or about how long he was in Huron County before he made his first move in bringing the guilty to task. We do not know how extensively he had been briefed on the case or, for that matter, how much foreknowledge he had of Huron County politics. We do know, however, that when he got to Goderich, he ignored protests from the members of the Audit Committee and everyone else who crossed his path. The detective knew he had been sent on a mission, and he refused to let the lack of funds at the local level get in his way.

He approached his task with the subtlety of a sledgehammer.

CHAPTER 11 | INVESTIGATIVE FARCE

SHORTLY BEFORE DETECTIVE Clarke agreed to come to Huron to solve the crime, the accused killers applied for bail. Whether either of them actually believed they would be released from jail is debatable; they made the request and waited for it to be acted upon. It is on record today in the Law Society of Upper Canada Great Library at Osgoode Hall in Toronto. In *Reports of Cases* Vol. IV, written by Henry Brown and published by Rowsell in 1869, the prisoners based their demand on two factors: first, that they "were committed to the common gaol of the County of Huron on a charge of murder, before the last assizes for that county, at which Court no indictment was preferred against them," and second, that "upon the depositions which were taken at the coroner's inquest, the case was one of circumstantial evidence only, and amounted to no more than suspicion, which, however strong, would not justify detention."

The request received due consideration by the appropriate officials of the day, but ultimately bail was denied. One of the reasons why it was not granted was the fear that the two might run. Because Nicholas had lived in the United States, he could easily have returned there with Tom in tow. Crossing the border had never been a problem in the past, and would not be now. However, their leaving the country was unlikely — neither man had attempted to flee, especially right after the killings when they had the opportunity to do so. The second reason was that more time was needed to look closer at the evidence already at hand. This was essentially the same rationale for not going ahead with the case at the Fall Assizes. The police were not ready. No airtight case had been built, and in fact, hopes were fading fast that one would be.

We have no way of knowing Clarke's reaction to the denial of bail. Probably he was pleased, but he intended to go ahead and look for additional evidence anyway; whether or not the accused were out was beyond his control. He came into the county, set to work, and, because of his harsh and arbitrary methods, became embroiled in immediate and widespread controversy. At no time did he think to ask for the slightest bit of advice from the locals as to the methods he might employ. He simply charged ahead, and in a matter of a few days he had alienated everyone even remotely connected with the case, as well as those who learned of his actions as reported in the press.

The detective reviewed the evidence that local police had already collected, visited the scene of the crime two or three times, and even retraced the route to the river. Old Melady's house was still essentially unchanged and deserted, but the summer wind and rain had long since obliterated the tracks from the woodpile that Coleman and others had followed. Clarke took all these factors into account, made a show of taking notes wherever he went, but reluctantly concurred that Bernard Trainer had done all he could. Clarke was temporarily stumped, until he decided to turn his attention elsewhere.

He began looking more closely at the Melady family; up until now, only Nicholas had been factored into a potential solution to the problem. Clarke soon learned that Old Melady's children all had a vested interest in his material goods. Nicholas might have been the one antagonized most by his father in the ongoing charade of the Hibbert farm, but virtually all the others had been at odds with him at some time or other. Such a state of affairs might have been tolerable, but only up to the time of the second marriage. At that point, his new wife was in line to inherit some, or perhaps all, of his estate. When she became pregnant with Old Melady's child, his adult sons and daughters felt they might get nothing at all. Indeed, as we have seen, he had threatened to disinherit them all on many occasions. Clarke learned this from several of Old Melady's neighbours, and armed with what they told him, he decided that the entire family was up to no good. He thought it prudent to ascertain what role, if any, the older son and daughters had played in the tragic fate of their father. The best way to do this, he decided, was to put them in jail. Only then would he be able to get at the truth and learn if one or more of them had been involved. For some reason, he thought that if they were jailed, they would start to talk, and when they did, his case would be solved.

Because of the mandate granted him by the Attorney General of the day, no one in authority in Huron seems to have dared quarrel with Clarke's methods. He was in charge, he knew it, and he set out to prove it. He first visited Robert Hays in Seaforth and laid his plans before the Justice of the Peace. Whether Clarke was completely convincing or whether Hays was in awe of the man is not known. In any event, when the detective walked out of Hays' office late in the afternoon on November 19, 1868, he had in hand an arrest warrant for murder for most of the Melady family. At no time, then or later, was Hays criticized for issuing the blanket warrant, although he must have wondered himself if such a mass arrest was either necessary or advisable. He may, in fact, have tried to talk Clarke out of going ahead with the plan, but even if he did question the "big shot detective from Toronto," as Clarke was called by some, he obviously failed to stop the man. The investigator went right to work.

Constables Stephens and Lusby and Detective Trainer were co-opted to assist Clarke in the execution of the order. Accordingly, he hired wagons and horses from a local livery, and the next morning the four policemen set out from Seaforth. They drove south to Egmondville, turned left on the first dirt road to the east, and made their way to Jim Kehoe's. There they had to wait for Jim to finish cleaning a cow stable and then wash up before they charged him and his wife, Margaret, and searched their house (later submitting a bill to the county for two dollars for doing so). With the couple handcuffed together in one of the wagons, they travelled to the Donovan home. The policemen went through every nook and cranny of this residence as well, found nothing, but arrested Catherine and her husband, David Donovan, anyway. The two were ordered onto a second wagon, and the procession moved off. The four young people could barely believe what was happening. No one listened to their protests, and even the police officers they knew refused to explain their actions. The three local officers told the couples to complain to Clarke. When they did, he ignored them.

But there were also complicating factors. The two women who were arrested were breastfeeding at the time, so in each case, the infants they nourished had to go with their mothers. Margaret and Jim's son John James was about a year and a half old, and David and Catherine's baby, Thomas Louis, was barely seven months. Both sets of parents thought the whole ordeal was utter madness and continued to object, but Clarke more or less laughed at their entreaties and continued with his plan. Today, we have no idea who looked after the other Kehoe children while the parents were away, although Katherine Melady may have done so. We also do not know who tended to the livestock that both farmers owned. Joe Nigh may have helped at the Kehoes', but he had plenty of his own farm work to do. Yet whether Clarke took such factors into account is debatable. He had been hired to solve murders, not run farms.

By late afternoon, Thomas and Alice Melady had also been arrested for murder and were taken with the other members of the family. We must assume that brother and sister objected, but they had no choice but to go, despite having been nowhere near Old Melady's when he was killed. Tom had been in Ohio that night and only made it home on the morning of his father's funeral. Alice was at the Donovans' when the murder took place, where she had been since her father remarried.

With his charges in tow, Clarke drove through a cold November rain to the railway station, just off Main Street in Seaforth. Men from the livery came to collect the horses and wagons. A few minutes later, a westbound passenger train pulled in; the police and those arrested all boarded, and a minute or so after that, the train departed for Goderich. Much later, on December 15, 1869, the *Stratford Herald* gave the numbers: "Almost the entire family [was] in jail for the crime — two sons and three daughters of the murdered man, and two sons-in-law. The two married women had infants at the breast." The paper did not count Tom Donovan.

On arrival in Goderich, more horses and wagons had to be rounded up before the trek to prison could get underway. By this time, it was dark, the rain had become mixed with wet snow, and everyone's clothes were dripping wet.

Not surprisingly the situation was chaotic when the four policemen delivered their six adult prisoners and the two babies to the Goderich Gaol. People were yelling, pushing, and shoving, babies were crying because they were cold, wet, overtired, and hungry, and the jail guards were overwhelmed. The gloomy, poorly lit building was crowded before the newcomers even arrived, and some of the inmates already there were hard to handle. This was particularly true of four who were classified as insane. Two were men, two were women. Now, in the women's block there would be five women, two of whom were lunatics, and two babies, all in a space designed for three. The men had a bit more room, but not much.

Not surprisingly, Clarke and his colleagues left as soon as they could.

The initial processing of the newcomers took both time and patience, and Campaigne and his staff coped as best they could. By the flickering light of a coal oil lantern he recorded the information required, while guards weighed the prisoners, checked their height, collected whatever personal belongings they had with them, and then shepherded the men and women to the various cellblocks. A glance at Campaingne's entries indicate that the ages of the adult arrivals ranged from twenty-four to thirty-three, and that apart from one, all were thought to be temperate. Tom Melady's personality was deemed intemperate, probably because he had protested loudly and perhaps physically at the time of his arrest.

The six were issued prison numbers, beginning with 2000 for Alice Melady and running consecutively up to Jim Kehoe, who was given number 2005. When he had been jailed a few weeks earlier, his number had differed. The babies were not numbered.

Physically, the three Melady women probably looked much alike. None were tall. Margaret was five foot, one inch in height and her sisters two inches or so more. All had dark hair, blue eyes, and dark complexions. Their personalities were also rather similar, and all had inherited Old Melady's temperament. They were volatile, strong-willed, and not terribly patient. Nor were they reticent when they familiarized themselves with the conditions of confinement. This was particularly true for the mothers, who suffered much because of the ordeal. They did their best to feed, change, comfort, and amuse their babies, but the circumstances under which they had to do so were terrible.

Now that he had so many of the family where he wanted them, Clarke left word with the guards to pay close attention to cellblock chatter in case any of the newcomers mentioned the murders. And even though Clarke had left the jail immediately after he had taken his new prisoners there, he returned several times in the days that followed and questioned each inmate individually and at great length. He obviously knew they did not want to be locked up, so he pretended to be sympathetic, offering immediate release on condition of a confession — or at least of finger-pointing. He still felt strongly that somebody would talk in order to get out. In fact, he assured anyone who asked that this would happen. He just knew he was right.

But he was wrong. While all family members voiced their opinions of the jail — loudly and often — they kept the cause of their confinement to themselves. They conversed freely with other inmates, but not about anything of substance — and never about the murders. Tom Donovan and Nicholas Melady had been there for weeks now, and neither of them had talked. No one else was going to do so. This stubborn streak served as a kind of buffer against Clarke's obsequious, self-serving entreaties and, if anything, bolstered the resolve of the prisoners to stay silent. Clarke was furious, but he was constrained in what he could now do. In effect, he had played his best card and found that it had been trumped.

Finally, after they had been behind bars for one week, all six prisoners were scheduled to appear before a judicial appointee named Gilbert McMicken, a stipendiary magistrate (or salaried magistrate) who worked out of Windsor, Ontario, and travelled extensively as part of his job. Clarke knew by this time that his pet plan had failed, so he admitted, reluctantly, that he would be forced to let the prisoners go. McMicken would come to Goderich to authorize their release through the courts.

But his arrival was delayed, and since no one else was in a position to rule on the matter on the day in question, all the prisoners had to stay where they were.

In a rather cryptic reference in the *Huron Signal* on December 3, referring back to November 27, the reason for the postponement was mentioned. "The fresh prisoners in the Melady murder case were remanded until next week," ran a small notice in the paper, "in consequence of the absence, through indisposition, of the Stipendiary Magistrate." At the time, no reason for the magistrate's failure to appear was given. There were plenty of rumours around, but few facts. In the meantime, news of the mass jailing had circulated widely. It was a topic of conversation in homes, on the street, and in every beverage room in the county.

Some who heard what had transpired were surprised that so many of the family were behind bars. Others looked upon the incarceration as a necessary evil if the police were ever going to solve the case. Most, however, were shocked by the move, particularly the imprisonment of the young women who had babies at the breast, along with the son who had not even been in the country at the time of the murder. One of those who was particularly disturbed was an individual named K.O. Foote from Goderich, who in all likelihood spoke for many.

After the postponement of the hearing, he wrote a scathing, two-thousand-word letter to the *Huron Signal*, which published it on December 10. The letter left no doubt as to the anger of the writer. He began by mentioning the arrests and the fact that the six were taken before two Justices of the Peace, who asked for evidence as to why the group should be locked up. Foote pointed out that Clarke "stated that the Crown hadn't any evidence against the parties, but he thought they would be able to produce evidence" sometime in the future. No date for the delivery of such proof was ever indicated because Clarke was not sure when that would be. He was, of course, waiting for one or more of the prisoners to talk — and that was not happening.

To Foote, this was shameful: "Presto! The thing's done — a remand to prison for eight days." Then he explained why he was especially angry at the detective and his heavy-handed methods of operating. "Not a fact sworn in yet, either in information or examination. The man Clarke merely thinks there will be evidence …" The sarcastic tone and underlying contempt for court officials and their action runs through the entire letter. The missive is well-written, clearly documented, and devastating in its critique of the judicial system in general and Detective Clarke in particular.

Foote also explained the reason for the remand: the stipendiary magistrate had broken his leg and was not able to come from Windsor to Goderich in order to consider the case. Accordingly, most of the accused had to be left under lock and key. Foote wrote:

> Not a witness was examined, not a fact was stated, upon oath or otherwise, that affected the prisoners. Six prisoners, two of them mothers with children in arms, and leaving families unprovided for at home [in the Kehoe case] are all incarcerated for a period of eight days for further examination. No. Not further examination — not to complete evidence, but to begin to hunt up evidence. The thing would be ludicrous were it not of such a serious nature. It is a good thing to have officials

zealous in the detection of crime and the prosecution of criminals, but it is a very bad thing when the functions of any officials are prostituted in the violation of personal liberty.

If such conduct became the norm, Foote concluded, "liberty will be sent shivering in the cold, and justice will be debauched to serve the ends of corrupt or over-zealous officials."

The letter gave rise to much discussion in the county, and finally cooler heads prevailed in Goderich. Clarke was summarily removed from the case, and a court official in Goderich whose name was not made public, but who had both knowledge of the situation and the necessary authority, interceded for the two nursing mothers. Shortly afterwards, Edward Campaigne came to see them in person and gave them the good news. Both would be released and allowed to go home. However, even though no evidence had turned up, their husbands and Tom and Alice had to stay behind. They remained where they were for some time after Clarke was relieved of his duties. It was as if no one knew quite what to do with them.

But the matter was still in limbo. Two murders had been committed and the two principal suspects were confined, but conclusive evidence against them had not turned up. And because there was still a good deal of public demand in Huron and beyond for the investigation to be concluded, the clamour finally reached John Sandfield Macdonald, the premier of Ontario.

Sandfield, as he was generally called, was a lawyer by profession, with a reputation for being tough-minded, firm, and decisive. As Ontario's first premier, he was used to making things work and getting his way. At fifty-six, he was of an age when he had no time for fools, and he looked upon the situation in Huron as something of a farce. He knew that if he did not bring the matter to a head and obtain some kind of lasting closure, the situation could further deteriorate, and if it did, it would reflect badly on his government. For that reason, he decided to step in and do what he could.

Initially, Sandfield gave a politician's answer, saying that the matter would be looked into, that he had every confidence in the officials in Huron, and that he knew they would come up with a solution that would be acceptable to all concerned. Quietly, however, he sent word to

Gilbert McMicken and ordered him to get the thing resolved. The premier had been well briefed on the case and, in fact, had ignored some earlier requests for help. All along, he probably hoped he would not have to address it, but now he knew he had to appear to be doing something. He was well aware of the letters in the newspapers and the less than subtle opinions that his government could not be relied upon to do anything to help the people who had elected it.

And we have no idea how McMicken felt. The stipendiary magistrate was really on the spot, aware that whatever he did would be scrutinized and second-guessed, not just by the people in Huron County but by his ultimate bosses at Queen's Park in Toronto. Whether his own job was in jeopardy is debatable, but he was in a pressure situation, and he knew it. He gave his word to those above him that he would solve the case. It might take some time, but he would succeed.

McMicken was an interesting character in his own right, and he was to some extent just as bullheaded as Clarke had been. However, he was a politician at heart and was able to use his persuasive skills with positive effect. Fifty-five years old, the Scottish-born magistrate had been in Canada for more than thirty years and already had been a member of the Legislative Assembly in Ontario. In that capacity, he got to know the premier. Later on, McMicken moved to Winnipeg, where at various times he was inspector of the provincial penitentiary, a lands agent who helped immigrants settle the Prairies, and a member of the provincial parliament. He ended his career as the Speaker of the House in the Manitoba Legislature.

In the fall of 1868, he was sent to Huron County. As soon as his broken leg was sufficiently healed and he felt he was well enough to travel, McMicken came to Goderich, interviewed everyone he could who knew anything at all about the murders, and pored over the information available. But despite the passage of time, virtually no new evidence had turned up since Coleman's inquest several months earlier.

In fact, there was now even less. In his haste to solve the crime in the days immediately after it happened, the first investigator, Bernard Trainer, had responded to many demands. He had checked the house, traced footprints, searched homes, and made arrests, all the while living out of a suitcase and travelling often between Seaforth and Goderich.

But he failed to secure some of the evidence he had collected, and some of it had been lost. McMicken soon became aware of this, but it would not become public for some time. Nevertheless, he dealt with the evidence the police still had and then made a decision that, in the months to come, would be both criticized and praised. The *Toronto Globe*, in a story on March 29, 1869, described the sequence of events: "Mr. McMicken, Stipendiary Magistrate ... examined the case [and] placed it at once in the hands of William Smith, and old and tried officer of his own force." Smith arrived in Goderich on December 1.

Smith was now the third chief investigator. His predecessors had done their best, failed, and gone on to other assignments (or, in the case of Clarke, simply disappeared). Whether they harboured any bitterness about being replaced is not known. Nor do we know if Smith either wanted or expected to be involved in the case. However, he soon became generally well-liked in Goderich. He was an older man, innovative, hard-working, and a good listener. He did not put the local police down for their actions, but neither did he shrink from the task at hand. He had been given a job, and he intended to make the best of it. But like the two men before him, his methods of operation were controversial, none more so than the very first decision he made. Even though this move would remain a secret for several months, it was something that was absolutely unheard of at the time: William Smith took a female detective, hired by Gilbert McMicken, and gave her a major role in solving the crime.

CHAPTER 12 | THE ARRIVAL OF THE WOMAN

JANET WAS AN attractive woman. She was also intelligent, resourceful, and daring. She loved a challenge, thrived on intrigue, and was not above using her looks if doing so worked to her advantage. Men found her irresistible.

Always something of a free spirit when she was growing up in the Detroit area where she had been born, she left home early in search of adventure and romance. By the time she was nineteen, she decided both could be found, not in America, but on the other side of the border, in Canada. She left the United States, crossed the Detroit River, and for some unknown reason ended up in the hamlet of Kingsville, Ontario, near Windsor. At the time, Kingsville was little more than a tiny cluster of log cabins. Named in 1843 after Colonel James King, who built the first house there, the place was quiet, isolated, and forgettable. There, she was bored.

She moved a hundred miles or so east to London, where one of her brothers was living at the time. The place was not very big in those days, but at least it was larger than Kingsville. Originally called New London, it was once considered for the location of the capital of Upper Canada. The settlement at the forks of the Thames River became a city in 1855. By all accounts, Janet loved it there. Her activities during this period are no longer known, but during her time in London, the slim, five-foot-three-inch, brown-eyed beauty seems to have gotten into trouble of some sort. She was a wild woman, and we know she changed her name at least twice, first to Mrs. Bond, dropping whatever her maiden name was and adding "Mrs.," although she likely was not actually married. A bit later on, she introduced herself as Mrs. Halton. No one knows anything about a Mr. Halton, if, indeed, he existed at all.

Janet was quite popular in London, and she became well-known. With her easy laugh and husky voice, she was an immediate favourite at house parties, dances, and celebrations of every kind. She never lacked male companionship, and in fact, some of the local gossips claimed she knew every man in town. London was undoubtedly her kind of place, until one day, without giving a specific reason, she told her closest friends she was moving on. There were rumours that she had bedded the wrong man, or perhaps too many of the wrong men, and these activities led to disputes and fights for her favours. At any rate, she left town abruptly. In all likelihood, there were wives who were much relieved.

She returned to the United States, going to live with another brother in Buffalo, New York. Again, she was an active participant in middle-class society. She quickly made new friends, most of whom were men, and was again the most sought-after female guest at every function she attended. But she only stayed in Buffalo for about a year. Then she came back to Canada, continued to travel much more than most women of her day, changed her name yet again, and finally drifted, somewhat aimlessly it appears, across southwestern Ontario to the shores of Lake Huron.

In November 1868, she was living in a small house in a township called Stephen, and by then was clearly married. She now called herself Janet Cooke, but that may or may not have been her husband's surname. We do know that he was a police officer in nearby Goderich and that fall was promoted to the rank of detective.

Apparently Janet was fascinated by his work. Every night she listened intently as her husband told her about what he had done that day. He described the cast of characters he dealt with, the types of crimes he helped solve, the arrests he made, and the attraction that policing had for him. Perhaps because he was new to his rank, the work he was doing was much more interesting than foot patrol around the octagonal "square" or main street in Goderich. As far as we know, Janet loved her husband, was proud of him, and did her best to become a "proper" wife in a small town.

One day, she came to the police station to see him about something, and while she was there she was introduced to a magistrate from out of town. The stranger's name was Gilbert McMicken, and he had just been sent up from Windsor to bring some kind of closure to the Melady murder case. As far as can be determined, he had never met Mrs. Cooke before.

Like every man who had ever seen her, McMicken was immediately drawn to the friendly, twenty-three-year-old wife of the newest detective in town. He admired her spirit, her openness, and her carefree manner. Then, as much by chance as by design, he found himself wondering if she might be of help in solving the case he had been ordered to conclude. He spoke to her about what had just occurred to him, then sat down and discussed it at length with her husband as well. Since both were enthusiastic about the idea, the magistrate offered Janet a job doing police work. She was thrilled, and accepted without hesitation.

It would be unlike anything she had ever done.

Janet Cooke's first assignment would require her to be part actress, part detective, and, for a while, a prisoner in the Goderich Gaol. McMicken would send her there to be numbered and admitted as an inmate, but then she would act as his informant in the case he was trying to solve. The magistrate wanted her to befriend a sister of a man accused of murder and, after she had done so, to elicit from the woman any information she could about the killing. McMicken told Janet he hoped her jail time would be brief, and although he admitted that there was perhaps a certain element of danger involved, he assured her that she would be protected in case of emergency. Because she was relatively new to Goderich, he was sure no one then incarcerated would have any idea who she really was.

McMicken told Janet she would be paid for her detective work at the rate of two dollars a day, payable as soon as she was released — whether successful in the endeavour or not. The jailer would be aware of the ruse, but no one else at the jail would be, at least not initially. She would be booked on the fictitious charge of passing counterfeit money. At the time, counterfeiting was widespread in some places, so no one she would encounter behind bars would be particularly surprised to learn of her crime.

Janet thought the whole idea quite exciting and could hardly wait to give it a try. The fact that she would be locked up twenty-four hours a day, and in truly miserable surroundings, did not seem to be a problem for her. She told McMicken and Smith, who would be her contact and mentor, that she would do the best she could. This venture would be the role of a lifetime. The young woman also liked the old detective immediately and saw in him a father figure she knew she wanted to please. The affection was mutual. Finally, after more discussion and planning, it was decided that Janet would be placed in the jail on Friday morning, December 4. Edward Campaigne explained the prison routine for her and assured her of his personal interest in her well-being.

William Smith spent the two days prior to the entry date coaching his protegé, going over what she might expect, explaining who she would encounter, and sketching the basic facts of the double murder as the police knew them. He told her who the suspects were and recounted the names of those connected with the case that were still behind bars. Alice Melady was now the only female. Smith told Janet that because he was new to the area, he did not know Alice, but had heard that even though she was not very happy about being in prison, she had refused to talk in order to get out. The policeman had been told that in all likelihood, the sister had *some* information about the killings. If only he could get her to divulge it.

Janet's task was to get to know Alice, attempt to bond with her, and gradually draw her out. The two would, according to Detective Smith, be together as often as possible, but not so much so that Alice would become suspicious of her new block mate. Janet was told to be alert at all times, to be observant, and to record what she saw and heard in a small notebook she would hide in her cell. As the old detective escorted her into the Goderich Gaol, he patted her arm for reassurance and told her that her prison name would be Jenny Smith. The name was selected because it was so ordinary; it would not bring undo attention. To Janet, it would only be one more of the many names she had used over the years. She knew she could handle it.

Jenny Smith's introduction to prison life began in the same oddly shaped, roughly triangular anteroom where Nicholas Melady and Tom Donovan had begun their incarceration the previous July. This time, however, the person who performed the introductory routines was Catherine Campaigne, the wife of the jailer; Edward Campaigne filled in the necessary entries in the prison ledger. What he wrote is still on file today, as is the fictitious name and number of the actress inmate. Jenny would be 2122.

Campaigne noted that she was a citizen of the United States, that she was temperate in nature and read well, and that she was married. Her religion was Methodist, and her occupation was listed as "Lady." Making this entry must surely have brought a smile to the jailer's face.

He probably knew something of "Jenny's" background but was gentleman enough not to let on. On the other hand, if he did not know, she was not about to enlighten him. More likely, gossip about the reputation of the woman may have become more discreet, out of respect for the young policeman she had married.

Once the necessary paperwork was finished, the newest inmate was taken to her prison cell. It was next to the one occupied by Alice Melady.

Almost from the outset, Alice was suspicious of the newcomer next to her. She lapsed into silence, while by all accounts Jenny talked rather freely. The initial rush of adrenaline connected with being admitted to prison, coupled with the excitement associated with her new job, probably made her even more chatty than usual. She introduced herself right away, pretended to complain about being jailed, cursed the police, and mentioned the counterfeiting charge that brought her there. She did not give any details of how the supposed charge came about, and Alice did not ask. In fact, Alice did not ask her anything.

Insofar as can be determined from records that cover the next few days, Alice never mentioned being in jail on a murder charge. She continued to keep to herself and to do what she was told, and she rarely spoke. She even avoided the day room most of the time, and rarely ate her meals there. It was as if she preferred to be silent and alone. The *Toronto Globe*, in an article published on March 27, 1869, described Jenny and Alice having the same prison duties and noted that the latter was "a shrewd, keen observer, and during a two week intercourse in which they were together constantly, avoided any reference to the charge on which she was committed."

Alice was not alone in her reaction to the new inmate. The *Huron Expositor*, a week later, went so far as to say, "In consequence of the way in which the case had previously been handled, [Jenny] was very warily received among the relatives of the deceased." The paper claimed that "they at once suspected" the new inmate. Still later, Nicholas even admitted that he had warned his sister to have nothing to do with her block mate. He thought, at first anyway, that the counterfeiting charge was as phoney as the term implied. He was not sure just what to make of the woman; he only knew he did not trust her.

But in time, his opinion would change.

Because of the layout of the Goderich Gaol, an inmate in a cell could see very little. This was particularly true when the doors were made of wood. He could look out through his tiny, barred window, but the view there was just a bit of yard, the outer wall, and a patch of sky. This view must have been terribly bleak during a rainstorm or when the skies were dark and foreboding, particularly in the late fall or in the depths of winter. If he looked through the little slot in his door, he could see nothing on either side, not even the neighbours in his own block. He could observe the corridor wall immediately in front of his door, but not the day room where he and his mates could gather when not locked down.

But once in the somewhat larger, fifteen-foot-long day room, an inmate could look through a small, meal-tray opening and see the central rotunda of the building and the circular stairs that dominated it. The meal slot was about ten inches by four inches in size, so it was not exactly what we might call a picture window. Nevertheless, being able to see into the rotunda was important to the inmates. Because they had nothing else to do, they spent hours watching the comings and goings of jail personnel and other prisoners involved in the routine of incarceration: going for a bath, visiting the sick room, obtaining clean bedclothes. They also saw non-violent, trusted convicts washing the rotunda floor, polishing it, sweeping the stairs, or, during summer days when the building could be more or less ventilated, stripping walls and repainting them. Sometimes inmates who were doing these jobs worked alone. On other occasions, they were paired up. A guard was always present, however, to oversee both the workers and their work. The rotunda was only thirteen feet in diameter, and there were only thirty steps, so the area itself must have been the cleanest in the building. Trusted inmates certainly had plenty of time to make it so.

The afternoon of her arrival, Jenny Smith was assigned maintenance duties with Alice Melady. They had to dust off the banister rails of the circular staircase that connected the three levels of the jail and scrub the main floor of the prison rotunda. The jobs were not difficult, and were more busywork than anything else. The duties enabled the inmates to leave their cells and, as such, broke up the daily routine for them.

The two women worked well together and, by all accounts, did as they were told. However, try as she might, Jenny could never get her block mate to say much. Apart from an occasional reaction to a wolf whistle from a man behind a meal slot, at which both women laughed, Alice was largely silent. The rotunda cleaning could have been finished quickly, but as there was no point in hurrying, the women took their time to do the job. Even scrubbing a floor was better than sitting alone and idle in a cubicle of stone. That evening and those that followed, after she and the other prisoners were returned to the cells and locked there for the night, Jenny was ready to record anything of significance that Alice might have mentioned that day.

However, there was nothing to write.

Finally, Detective Smith, who was to be apprised of any progress in the stratagem, realized the plan wasn't working. Each day he discussed the situation with Gilbert McMicken, but after about a week, they reluctantly concluded that their plan had failed. Now, they had to decide what to do about it. After more consultation, the magistrate agreed to pull the informant out of the jail first, and then to discharge Alice shortly afterwards. Neither woman was told this at the time, although Jenny probably anticipated the move. After all, she knew she was getting nowhere with Alice and likely would not be able to do so regardless of how long they were together. Alice was just too wary to let her guard down. Jenny's job was done.

But then, the unexpected occurred. The morning her release was to take place, Jenny was alone in the women's exercise yard. It was a relatively compact area because there were generally only two or three female prisoners at most, and even then, they rarely went outside. Yards used by men were bigger and somewhat busier.

Like all prisoners in all jails, she walked without thought, back and forth, killing time. It started to snow, and she watched the gathering storm as the trees beyond the wall swayed in the wind. A few leaves in the yard blew in swirls against the side of the cellblock. Finally, after some minutes in the December cold, she was ready to go back inside. To do so, she had to walk past the three cell windows of the lower block, directly below the second-floor women's wing. About twenty feet from the door she would enter, and on the ground under one of the windows, she noticed a piece of brown paper lying on the fresh snow. She was sure the paper had not been there earlier, so out of curiosity, she picked it up.

Doing so had ramifications beyond anything she could ever have imagined. On the small scrap of what seemed to be wrapping paper was a brief, penciled note, apparently scrawled in haste and tossed from a cell. The writing was legible, the message pointed, and the intended recipient, she immediately realized, was herself. There was no one else around.

Jenny held the note, her hands trembling, reading and rereading it. Then she glanced at the nearest cell window and realized she was likely being watched.

Because she was not sure just how to react, she quickly turned around, tucked the note into a pocket, and went inside. Then, deliberately not telling Alice about this development, she returned to her own cell and the privacy she suddenly needed. She was still rereading the message when a guard came to the women's block and told her Detective Smith was there to see her. Jenny got up and followed the guard to the reception area, where the policeman waited. He was about to tell her that her job was finished and that she would soon be released. However, as soon as she knew they were completely alone, Jenny handed him the paper.

The old detective could not hide his surprise. He read the note several times, turning it over and over in his hands, smiling as he did so. He had her explain exactly where she had found the piece of paper and the circumstances surrounding its being on the ground. He wanted to be sure it had not been there for some time, or perhaps had been meant for someone else. When Jenny told him she was absolutely certain the note had been tossed from the window after she was in the exercise yard, the detective was elated. He thanked Jenny for bringing it to him and told her this could be the break they all wanted.

This turn of events was something neither he nor McMicken had even remotely considered. The note, written and signed by Nicholas Melady, began, "Dear Miss — I saw you every day with my sister Alice, and I would like to speak with you." He added that he had noticed the two when they were scrubbing floors together. Obviously, Nicholas had been in the day room, watching and perhaps whispering to his sister as she worked in the rotunda. And even though Alice may not have realized it, her brother had been looking at Jenny as well.

William Smith pondered the new development for several minutes, but he felt he had to discuss it with Gilbert McMicken, and likely Edward

Campaigne as well. Male and female prisoners were never together, so if any significant communication between them was to occur, the jailer would have to be made aware of it. In the meantime, the policeman had to decide what to do with Jenny. Releasing her right now might not be wise, so instead of telling her she was getting out, he asked her if she would stay locked up for a while longer. She told him she would. Then a guard came and escorted her back to her cell. She pretended to complain about the old police officer as she was led away.

That afternoon, the officer talked to McMicken. They went over and over several possible reactions to Nicholas's note, but could not decide how to handle it. There obviously had to be some follow-up, but only if it worked to their advantage. They were still disappointed that nothing had come of the Alice-Jenny association, but they felt now that if the sister would not talk, the brother might. In the meantime, both women stayed where they were. Jenny assured Detective Smith that she would not mention the note to Alice.

Another day passed, and still the magistrate and the officer could not agree on the best scenario. While a blinding snowstorm off Lake Huron blanketed Goderich, the two men huddled together at the police station, totally engrossed in their problem. Finally they decided to ask Edward Campaigne for his advice. As it turned out, doing so only left them with another opinion and even further from a consensus. In essence, as the *Toronto Globe* would say on March 27, 1869, quite understating the matter, Nicholas's note "was a direction that no one anticipated."

In the short term, however, the three decided to monitor the situation and to continue to have the women do duties together. Jenny was told to carry on as before, to listen carefully to whatever Alice might say, and to record all conversations in the notebook. She was also told that, no matter how bad the weather was, she was to go out into the exercise yard every day.

It was Nicholas who broke the impasse. Two days after Jenny picked up the first scrap of paper in the jail yard, she noticed a second one in almost the same spot. At first, she pretended not to see it, but then, on her way inside, she picked it up and headed for the privacy of her cell. Because of Detective Smith's delight in getting the first note, Jenny could barely contain her excitement as she read the new one.

This time, Nicholas repeated his wish to talk to her, but he now seemed much more insistent about doing so. The attitude may have been a reflection of his situation. After all, he had been locked up for many months, and with the exception of an occasional hurried whisper to his sister, he had rarely glimpsed, let alone talked to, a female.

Now, being able to see a woman so close to the window of his cell, albeit on the other side of the bars, must have been more than he could bear. And the fact that Jenny was young and strikingly attractive only made matters worse. Despite his celibate circumstances and the jail rule forbidding communication in any way between prisoners of the opposite sex, he was completely enthralled with the beautiful creature who walked outside.

In fact, Nicholas had fallen in love.

CHAPTER 13 | A LOVE AFFAIR IN PRISON

THE CATALYST IN the murder investigation was the second message from Nicholas. As Jenny walked back into the building and climbed the narrow, cramped back stairs that female prisoners used to get to their own block, she found herself trying to imagine the reaction this time. She was pretty sure she would be asked to respond. She was not exactly sure what she would say, but she knew either Smith or McMicken would tell her. Once more, the prisoner had asked if he could talk to her, nothing more.

As soon as he saw the second note, Smith reacted just the way Jenny expected. He roared with approval and told her that this was it! Now he felt he had nothing to lose if his informant answered. In fact, there was always the chance that Nicholas might mention something in a letter that could be used against him — provided he could be coaxed into writing again. It would be better, Smith believed, to get as much as they could in writing from the prisoner. Later on the notes could be used against him in court. Smith thought that written evidence would be better than oral. Conversations could end up being his word against hers, and they would be less effective in front of a jury. If the Crown had a written admission of murder, the case would be solved. Because of this, and judging from Nicholas's expressed wish to communicate, Smith thought that Jenny could advance the case if she answered the note.

A day or so before the note had been received, Gilbert McMicken had had other legal matters to attend to and had returned to Windsor. As it turned out, the departure was almost a blessing in disguise to William Smith. Even though there was never any real friction between the two, the detective now had the chance to direct the probe in the manner that he alone believed best. He would not have to spend a lot of time negotiating every possible scenario with the magistrate. Doing so, he believed, was often a waste of valuable time, even if it was done with the best of intentions.

The detective took Edward Campaigne into his confidence, of course, and repeated the wish that Jenny stay where she was for another few days. By all accounts, she seems to have welcomed the chance to do so. The intrigue appealed to her, and she now felt she might be able to contribute and show what she could do in her new job. The first thing Smith believed he needed was a greater indication of the prisoner's intentions. He wondered if Nicholas might have more in mind than just a conversation with an attractive young woman. To that end, he asked the jailer how a message from Jenny could be delivered to the accused.

Campaigne considered the request and, after some thought, came up with an idea. He knew that he could not simply ask his guards to start passing notes, because if they did, Nicholas would probably become suspicious. Jail staff members were not supposed to fraternize with inmates, and even the most recent arrival from the courts would probably know that. Anyone in jail for more than a few days certainly would.

Campaigne's advice was to use someone else as a go-between. During the winter, a young boy from Goderich was paid to come to the jail and carry wood from a pile outside in the yard to box stoves throughout the building. The task did not take long, but it was done every day at about the same time. The various doors would be unlocked to let him enter; the youth would drop off baskets of firewood and leave. Because he went to all four cellblocks, he was familiar with every inmate in the place. He sometimes talked to them for a few seconds when he brought the wood in, and he had a passing acquaintance with them all. Because this was the boy's third winter on the job, Campaigne knew him well, trusted him, and was sure he could do double duty as a messenger.

Smith thought the idea was sound and asked several questions about the wood carrier. Among other things, he wanted to know his age, if he had ever been in trouble, and, most of all, if he was reliable. He also asked if the youngster would be able to keep quiet about what he was doing. Campaigne vouched for the boy and said he would meet with him and stress the aspect of secrecy. Then the jailer assisted Smith in crafting a carefully worded message for Jenny to copy. Obviously, whatever they came up with had to be in her handwriting. After all, it was supposed to be her note.

The two paid particular attention to making sure that, above all else, the note hinted that the communication continue. In the message that was ultimately agreed upon, Jenny told Nicholas of her surprise at hearing from him, thanked him for writing to her, and hoped he would write again. She also mentioned that she had talked the wood boy into delivering her answer and suggested the same method of reply. We have no way of knowing whether Nicholas ever suspected the ruse, but in all likelihood, he did not. When Jenny's first words reached him the next day, he was probably too overjoyed to realize that he was about to be entrapped.

Many more letters would follow. Unfortunately, none exist today. We have to rely on newspaper coverage and later court testimony to get the essence of what was in them. Most of the first messages were brief and certainly tentative in nature, with both parties alluding to what might happen between them, neither actually coming out and declaring their hand. In almost every note Nicholas wrote, then and later, he declared his love for this beautiful creature he could only glimpse through iron bars. Gradually, he built his circumscribed world around her, thought of her, dreamed of her, and looked forward to her letters more than he did to the occasional visits from his relatives.

But there were complications. Early on in the correspondence, Alice Melady became aware of what was happening. Because she feared for her brother, and because she could not sit him down and tell him he was being foolish in trusting this stranger in the women's block, she mentioned the matter to Goderich lawyer Wilmot Squier, who, at the time, represented both Alice and her brother. Squier was immediately concerned. He visited Nicholas in jail, told him he had heard about the clandestine messages, and told his client that he should cease what he was doing. Squier had never heard of this Jenny Smith, but he certainly was wary of her. He felt the pen pal arrangement was just too suspicious, and he wanted it stopped immediately.

Strangely, though, considering the possible problems the note exchange could cause, he apparently did not make any inquiries about Jenny, her past, or who she actually was. Had he done so, he would have been quite alarmed. In fact, if Squier had known who Jenny really was, his client might have had a future. In the months to come, Squier was faulted for being ineffective, but in truth, probably nothing he could have said would have dissuaded his client.

DOUBLE TRAP

The fact that Nicholas ignored his sister's caution was of more importance than his ignoring the lawyer's dictum. As a result, he did himself
irreparable harm. He was so enamoured of Jenny, and he wanted to reach
her so badly, that he was willing to take risks to do so. He told her of the
warning. According to a *Huron Expositor* story on April 2, 1869, "The
acquaintance was kept up by letter, the rules of the prison preventing their
being together; but that he was willing to confide in her was evident from
the fact of his shortly afterwards asking her in a letter not to tell anyone
they were corresponding, as his lawyer had warned him to beware of her."
Obviously, Nicholas had reached the point where he intended to forge
ahead in spite of any problem his risk-taking might cause.

At first, Jenny kept the communication with Nicholas noncommit-
tal and light, and according to the same newspaper article, she "never
asked him the cause of his incarceration, preferring to allow such to
come from himself, as showing his complicity in a more direct manner."
In her letters, she told him she cared for him, longed to be with him
someday, and said how much his letters meant to her. At first, she wrote
every couple of days.

But gradually, the frequency of the contact increased, and not just in
letters. Jenny began to spend even more time in the exercise yard. As the
days grew shorter in December, she would go outside, with permission,
and gradually work her way over to the window of Nicholas's cell.
Leaning with her back to the wall outside it, where someone looking
from elsewhere in the jail would not know what she was doing, she
would whisper to him. Soon, the two were spending time each day talking to each other, with Nicholas often standing on the edge of his bunk
in order to get his face close to the narrow opening — and to Jenny.
While she spoke, he could only see the back of her head. Always, however,
just before going back inside, she would turn and smile in his direction.
Then she would be gone, and his heart would melt.

Today, the cell where he was locked up can be readily identified
because its window looks directly outside to the yard where Jenny would
have been, and it is farthest from the day room and the watchful eyes and
ears of suspicious guards. And because the guards would have ordinarily
been out in the prison rotunda, no closer, none would have heard a
thing. A conversation from this location would not have been difficult at

all. As well, in the gathering gloom of late autumn and early winter, when all of these contacts took place, Jenny would have been in more shadow than at any other time of the year, so that her actions would have been somewhat obscured. The bulk of the cellblock wall would have been against the western sky and would have blocked out much of the weak effect of the setting sun, especially in the late afternoon on overcast days. Because there were windows elsewhere in the prison that looked into the women's yard, the wintry shadows were Jenny's best cover. The *Toronto Globe* described the setting in a March 27, 1869, article: "The arrangement of the cells was such that [Jenny], when out in the yard, could speak with him through the grating of his cell. Thus, once a day at least, they could have a conversation in this manner." And there were some days when they conversed more often. In her letters, Jenny would tell Nicholas when she would likely be outside. At such times, he would stay in his cell rather than go to the day room.

It is easy today to understand how the clandestine contacts were carried out. In researching this book, I was able to examine the setting from both Jenny's and Nicholas's positions. From the outside, where Jenny stood, the bottom of the cell window is about six feet from the ground. From inside, it is only five feet. And even though at five feet, three inches in height, Jenny would not actually have been tall enough to be able to look directly into the cell, Nicholas, by standing on his bunk, could have put his face into the window aperture and been very close to her.

Unexpectedly, the contacts came to an abrupt end. Wilmot Squier had occasion to confer with Alice again, and she told the lawyer, with profound disgust, that her brother was still writing to Jenny. Alice had seen the woman with another note, but was cautious enough not to let on to Jenny. Instead, she told Squier to put a stop to the nonsense right away. As a result, for the second time in a week, Squier came to talk with Nicholas. Again, the lawyer warned of the danger of the note-passing and demanded that it stop. He was unaware of the whispered contacts, and as far as we know, Nicholas did not mention them. In all probability, both Alice and Squier would have been extremely alarmed had they known.

One day, Jenny Smith was gone.

A week or so after she disappeared from jail, the reason for the abrupt departure came out. His lawyer had barely left when Nicholas told Jenny in a note about the second warning. She quickly passed the message to Detective Smith, who feared Squier would expose the informant unless her credibility were enhanced. To that end, he had her released immediately, and then set about devising a cover story for doing so. The object of his machinations was Wilmot Squier himself.

Because of subsequent events, it is obvious that the detective contacted and worked closely with Gilbert McMicken in establishing the reason why Jenny was no longer behind bars. Together, the officer and the magistrate went to great lengths to concoct a scenario for her disappearance. And even though what they came up with seems unbelievably far-fetched today, the stratagem actually worked. It depended on timing, luck, and Alice Melady.

In order to explain the abrupt departure of their prisoner from Goderich, Smith and McMicken spread the story that Jenny had escaped when a day room door was improperly locked. She supposedly got out the front door of the jail because a guard mistook her for a visitor who was leaving the building. McMicken informed the Goderich police of the matter, and they in turn issued a widely circulated description of the missing woman. This was done an hour after she was out, in order to ensure that Squier would learn of it as soon as possible.

He did, and because he now knew the woman he had just cautioned Nicholas about was no longer near him, the lawyer rather foolishly put aside all his suspicions concerning her. He had apparently never looked into her background at all.

Once they had Jenny away from the jail, McMicken and Smith launched the next step in their plan. They sent the "missing" Jenny to Stratford on an afternoon train, secured short-term accommodation for her, and kept her out of sight. Soon afterwards, McMicken announced that Alice Melady would be taken to Seaforth to be tried there on the murder charge for which she had been jailed. Whether or not Wilmot Squier had any input in this decision is not known today. On the day of her court appearance, the lawyer took the morning train to Seaforth, made his way up Main Street from the station to Downey's Hall, and was ready to defend his client as soon as the trial got underway. At this juncture, for reasons kept from Squier, McMicken delayed calling the court into session until late morning. He did this to allow the next step of the elaborate escape plan to unfold. Finally, the hearing started.

It ended almost as soon as it began. The stipendiary magistrate stood up, quickly explained the charge against the accused, admitted there was not enough evidence for a conviction, and then, just as quickly, dismissed the case. Judicial records of the time indicate that Alice was discharged on December 23, on the authority of S.M.G. McMicken. She had been in jail for thirty-four days, in what was essentially a witch hunt. Three of the others who had been jailed at the same time, Jim Kehoe, Tom Melady, and Dave Donovan, were all released an hour or so later, but they did not have to go to Seaforth to be discharged. Alice was only there to advance the next step in the "escape" plot and to throw Squier off the scent.

Right about the time Alice was being given her freedom, the noon train from Stratford was arriving at the station in Seaforth with Jenny Smith on board. As previously arranged, Detective Smith met her, hustled her away to a horse and sleigh he had hired that morning, and told her to hide under a mound of buffalo robes that were piled in the back of the conveyance. He told her to stay there, stay quiet, and remain out of sight until he directed otherwise.

Then he raced up Main Street, pulled into the hitching area at the east side of Downey's Hall, and tied his horse. A minute or so later, he bounded up the steps into the building and asked for Gilbert McMicken. At the time, the magistrate was talking to court officials and several reporters who had descended on Seaforth to cover the murder story. Interest in the story had not lessened, even after all the stops, starts, misadventures, and outright incompetence of the investigation.

Smith walked over to the magistrate and, as reported in the *Toronto Globe* the following March 27, in a loud voice "announced that [Jenny Smith] had been arrested while attempting to escape at Sarnia, and was on her way to Goderich." The breathless report was made within earshot of Squier. What Smith did not say was that he was prepared to bring Jenny into the hearing room, in case Squier gave any indication of disbelief. He did not.

Smith and McMicken chatted for five minutes or so, and then the detective left. He took Jenny back to the station, brought her in a rear door, and told her to stay in the baggage room until the next train to Goderich arrived. He said Bernard Trainer would be taking her with him on that train and that she was to pretend she was back in custody. Jenny told Smith she understood, and then settled down to wait for Trainer, whom she already knew.

The *Globe* took up the story from there: "The attorney for the defence, in returning from Seaforth that night, saw [the escapee] in charge of Mr. Trainer, a constable, on the same train, and at once concluded that she had been arrested as stated." Jenny was soon back in her cell, where she pretended to complain about her capture.

Wilmot Squier had been duped. As far as can be determined today, he no longer thought he needed to caution his client about Jenny Smith, and he does not seem to have done so. But dropping his guard was a mistake. Nicholas was overjoyed when Jenny returned. He wrote to her immediately, and soon afterwards got a reply. She also made sure she was outside his cell window every day.

Christmas came and went, and the two continued to pass notes and talk as often as they could. Only Nicholas and Tom were still in prison for Old Melady's murder — and they had no choice. Jenny, on the other hand, willingly spent the festive season behind bars. In doing so, she became the cornerstone in the case that William Smith built. Without her, his efforts would have been in vain. Without her, Nicholas and Tom would probably have been released from jail. All the evidence found at the murder scene and elsewhere would not have been enough for a conviction. Whatever the merits of that evidence, it was still largely circumstantial.

By New Year's Day, the subject matter of the passed notes and their length began to change. Jenny still said relatively little when she wrote, but Nicholas said too much. He had learned, almost at the outset, that she was in jail for passing counterfeit money but had thought the charge was trumped up. Now he was sure it had not been. During a Christmas Eve visit, Wilmot Squier told his client about seeing Jenny on the train on her way back to prison. Nicholas took from this that his lawyer had dropped his suspicions and was consenting to the exchange of letters. Nicholas continued to write.

In all, some sixty notes were passed between the two. In fact, the correspondence gradually became their principal occupation each day. In all likelihood, all of the jail employees had by now stumbled onto what was happening under their noses, but they managed to drop a blanket of silence over their suspicions. Nicholas thought he was hoodwinking everyone, but he was fooling only himself. Each note he wrote was quickly passed along to Detective Smith, who dated it and filed it in the thick dossier he was compiling.

In early January the detective realized it was time he showed some consideration for Jenny. She had been locked up long enough and had moved the case beyond his wildest expectations. First, however, he had her drop hints about her fictitious past and some equally imaginary friendships she had enjoyed prior to being sent to prison. As the *Toronto Globe* would mention on March 27, 1869, Jenny "led her lover to understand that she was in for counterfeiting, and that she was connected with a rich gang." Nicholas knew of the counterfeiting, but not of her associates. The paper described Nicholas's reaction to the mention of Jenny's unsavoury but monied companions: "This led him to the idea that her assistance would be of material avail to him." Up until this juncture, it had not occurred to him that her involvement in counterfeiting could be of help.

Jenny then sent five or six more letters from her cell, all ghost written by Detective Smith. In one of them, she informed Nicholas that her time was up and that she had been told she would be getting out of jail soon. We can only assume she knew he would be devastated by the news, so she went out of her way to ease his concern. She pretended to pledge her abiding love and told him she would be true to him no matter what. While she waited for the happy day of his release, she promised to continue writing.

Nicholas believed her completely and pledged to answer every letter. By doing so, he would quickly tighten the noose around his own neck.

On the expressed order of Gilbert McMicken, Jenny Smith was discharged from Goderich Gaol on January 8, 1869.

The death cell: thick beams, a plank bed, and a window that looked out on a wall.

The church at St. Columban. The funerals for the murdered couple and for Nicholas were held at this church.

The hanging wall. The gallows was built on the top of this wall, with the trapdoor on the outside.

Doorway to death. Five minutes before he was hung, Nicholas stepped through this door and walked to the gallows.

The Van Egmond house. Shortly after they were arrested, the three suspects in the murders were lodged in the basement cell of this house.

Down to the lockup. After the murders, the three accused were taken down these stairs to the cell in the basement of the Van Egmond house.

The window in the wall. The three men arrested after the murders looked through these bars in the basement of the Van Egmond house.

The scene of the murders. The outline marks the stone foundations of the house where the killings were done.

This is where the laneway to the Old Man's house would have been. The house itself was just in front of the tree in the distance.

The original Carmichael hotel, where Old Melady spent part of his last day, was on the main street corner of Seaforth, Ontario. This building is on the site today.

The inquest into the murders was held at Downey's Hall in Seaforth. The building in the picture is on the site where Downey's Hall once stood.

The house where the murders took place was close to the tree in the picture, just up from the bank of the Bayfield River.

The men fleeing after the murders crossed the Bayfield River at this location.

APPROXIMATE LOCATIONS IN 1868

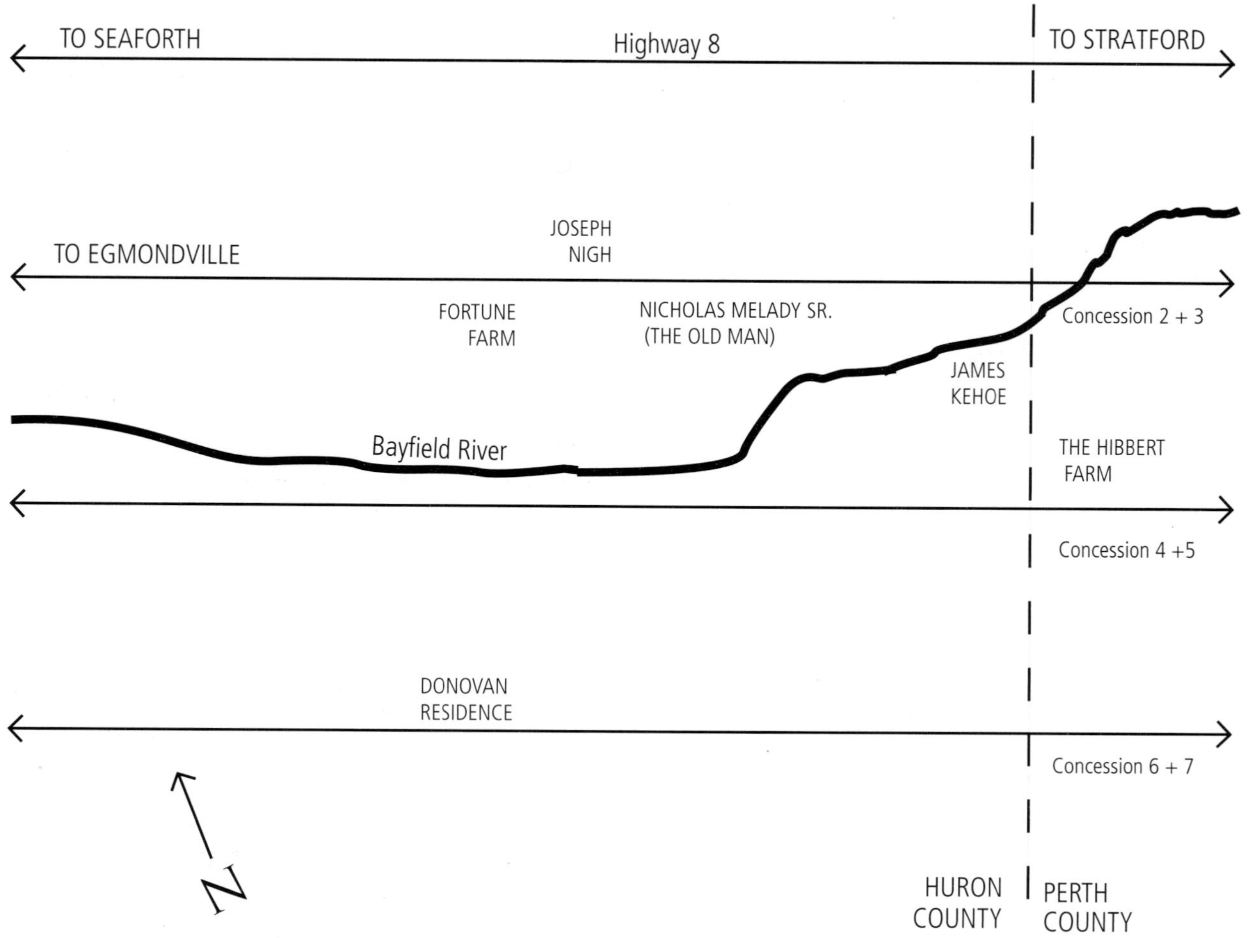

TO STRATFORD

Highway 8

TO SEAFORTH

Concession 2 + 3

JOSEPH NIGH

NICHOLAS MELADY SR. (THE OLD MAN)

JAMES KEHOE

THE HIBBERT FARM

FORTUNE FARM

Concession 4 + 5

TO EGMONDVILLE

Bayfield River

DONOVAN RESIDENCE

Concession 6 + 7

HURON COUNTY | PERTH COUNTY

N

A piece of the rope that was used in the last hanging at this jail in 1911.

This memento was given, by the hangman, to Mr. Owen Geiger, Warden of Huron County who witnessed the hanging and the post-mortem.

Donated by: Ira Geiger

This ghastly exhibit of a piece of rope adorns a wall of the Goderich Gaol today. The rope is identical to the one used to hang Nicholas.

Courtesy John Melady

This was the window inside his cell through which Nicholas whispered to Jenny when she was in the prison yard. (The bed and chair are from a more recent era.)

Courtesy John Melady

This is the cemetery where the hanged man and the murdered couple are buried. None of the three have gravestones.

The Kehoe grave. This large tombstone marks the place in St. James Cemetery in Seaforth where James Kehoe is buried.

The burial site. The two murder victims as well as the hanged man are buried somewhere in this open area of St. Columban Cemetery.

The Goderich courthouse today. The building where the murder trial was held was on this site.

The entrance to the Huron Historic Gaol in Goderich, Ontario. This building opened in 1842, and inmates were housed there until 1972.

Nicholas first saw Jenny through a meal slot in the day room door.

The entrance corridor. Inmates who were brought to the gaol entered it by way of this long, ugly, dark, and dank passageway.

The author standing in front of the cell window where Nicholas and Jenny talked in the time before his trial began.

The rotunda staircase. Nicholas first saw Jenny as she scrubbed the floor below this circular staircase.

Courtesy John Melady

The exercise yard for women at the Goderich Gaol. Jenny and Nicholas whispered together through the cell window at the lower left of the picture.

CHAPTER 14 | THE DEPARTURE OF THE WOMAN

NICHOLAS WAS HEARTBROKEN when Jenny was released from jail. He missed seeing her, talking to her, confiding in her. During the day, he sometimes stood on his bunk and stared into the yard. There he saw the small patch of earth where she had walked and remembered how she had looked, the beauty of her face, the sound of her voice. At night, he dreamed she was nearby: smiling, whispering at his window, pledging her love forever — no matter what the future might bring. He often replayed in his own mind the exquisite and secret pleasure he felt at getting each one of her letters. But now that she had gone, he sometimes feared these would be no more. He was like a man bereaved: lost, lonely, heartsick, and close to despair.

Each day was just like the one before it. The daylight hours dragged. The guards followed their routine. The wood boy came and went. Even he didn't say much now, if he spoke at all. Conversation in the day room seemed more puerile than ever. There were the usual stupid stories, all repetitive, pointless, and boring. The language was always crude, the voices loud, the complaints petty and unceasing. He and Tom Donovan talked every day, but as their frame of reference was in the past, they talked of the past. Occasionally, they wondered what was happening in Seaforth: what their friends were up to, what it would be like to sit in a beverage room, have some drinks, and then walk out as free men — men who could go anywhere they wanted and not just to the day room and back. But when they remembered where they were, thoughts of being free were too hard to bear and they would lapse into silence. They rarely thought of what they had done: of the lives taken, of the family shattered. Like inmates in all jails, they were self-absorbed, feeling sorry for them-selves and remaining unmindful of the consequences of their actions. Any debt to society was not even relevant.

Outside, it got dark early, and a foot of snow covered the ground. The west wind off Lake Huron blew bitter and cold, and the tops of the trees on the other side of the wall were bent and bare. Going out into the yard seemed pointless and unpleasant. And even though he refused to dwell on the reality, Nicholas knew in his heart that his own actions had brought him to this awful place. He was as depressed and unhappy as he had ever been. Time meant nothing anymore.

But the feelings of inmates or the conditions under which they lived were almost never considered by those not in prison. In the real world that was just outside, the citizens of Goderich went about their daily lives, worked, went to school, raised families, and, when they had the time, had fun. They visited friends, played sports, socialized, and attended church. Their lives were not circumscribed by high walls, barred windows, and cold cells that were locked at night. Most towns-people could barely imagine life behind those walls, and they did not want to do so. Like most law-abiding citizens, they had little sympathy for those inside. Anyone who was put in jail deserved to be put in jail, or so most believed.

When they thought of the jail — if they thought of it at all — they assumed all was well. Very few residents of the town or the county had ever been inside the building, for any reason. The few that had been, other than staff and inmates, were those who had come to tour the place a few days before it was officially opened. They had come for two reasons: they were curious, or they wanted to see how their tax dollars had been spent. Most people had never been near the building, and they did not want to be. Their taxes supported the prison, and they elected public officials who were responsible for it. While senior governments of the day made the laws that governed the jail's operation, people elected at the local level made sure it met the standards prescribed. If these standards were minimal, so be it.

The job fell to seven men who were on the county's Gaol and Court House Committee. In 1868, this group (whose surnames are still part of the fabric of Huron County) was composed of the following: Messrs. Creery, Gaunt, Castle, Perkins, Hingston, Snell, and Scott. They went to the prison, inspected the building, talked to the inmates and staff, and submitted a report to the County Council about their findings and recommendations. These men did not hire guards or others who wanted work at the facility, but they did assess potential employees and forward the names of applicants to the attention of the full council. Usually, those who wanted jobs far outnumbered the positions that came open. To some degree, getting work at the jail was regarded as something of a sinecure. Once you had a job there, you were set for life. The paycheque might not have been large, but it was regular.

The committee report covering the last months of 1868 was submitted in January 1869. It dealt with the period when several members of the Melady family were behind bars and was compiled at precisely the time Nicholas was going through his period of depression following Jenny's release. Whether he talked to any of the inspectors when they visited is immaterial, but it is unlikely he ever saw what they wrote.

In their submission, the councillors said that after visiting the jail, they found it to be "clean, comfortable, and in every way satisfactory." And even though the inmates surely must have groused about their living conditions in general, about the food, the overcrowding, or the way they were handled on a day-to-day basis, the official visitors begged to differ, or pretended not to notice. In fact, they said, "the prisoners expressed no dissatisfaction." Such a sweeping statement was likely a whitewash. Committee members told council personnel what they wanted to hear, and the council, in turn, papered over problems before they became public.

The visitors, who were in the jail for two hours or so, did "recommend that some toweling and factory cotton be furnished for the use of prisoners, and also a pair of pants for one of the prisoners, he being quite naked in this respect." This remark indicates that at the time, inmates wore their own clothing and were ordinarily not given prison garb. Such a state of affairs is understandable because people of all ages were locked up together, and little children were sometimes placed behind bars with their impoverished parents. The group also suggested that "a sufficient bathtub be furnished for use of the prisoners." Either the one that had been installed when the place was built had worn out or else a second tub was needed to allow for the increased number of prisoners being held.

The council committee also admitted that they "were grieved to find two insane females ... incarcerated in the Gaol, and as this does not appear to be the proper place to keep lunatics, we would therefore recommend that they be removed to the Asylum at an early date." No doubt Alice Melady would have agreed with the suggestion after having lived with the two for almost five weeks. The visitors made no mention of the males with similar afflictions who were there during the same period. This could have been because there was a bit more room for them, because they were less obviously deranged, or because they were moved before inspection day.

Their report written, the councillors went on to more pressing and, to them, more important matters: road maintenance, culvert repair, and fence line arbitration in a land of flourishing farms. Then the committee men more or less forgot about the jail; having done their duty, they assumed that the public would believe that all was well.

For the most part, they were right. Reports filed in the following few years do not mention any serious problems and do not even allude to possible complaints from prisoners or the public. This state of affairs can be attributed to the fact that the jail was, to a large extent, out of sight and out of mind for most people.

But not for Jenny. One day, Nicholas got a letter from her. She was at home with her husband, just outside of Goderich, but the letter she sent had been posted in Buffalo, New York. She told Nicholas that she was now living there with her brother and that he had mailed the letter for her. In fact, he had, but only after William Smith had forwarded Jenny's letter and asked for it to be sent back into Canada. Smith had decided on this method of communication in order to make sure Nicholas remained unaware of Jenny's real location or identity. He certainly did not want to betray the fact that she was nearby, let alone that she was married and her husband was a police officer.

Again, the scheme worked. Nicholas was overjoyed. It was as if his life had suddenly become more wonderful than he could ever have imagined. He read the words again and again, pictured his lover writing them, and knew he had to respond right away. Within minutes of getting Jenny's note, he asked the guards for an envelope and some paper, and then, in the privacy of his cell, he took his pencil in hand and composed a heartfelt message to the woman he loved. His letter was a forthright indication of both his state of mind and his affection for her. It also encouraged William Smith to insist that the correspondence continue. He still read everything Nicholas wrote, of course, and added this letter to all the others in the prisoner's file. Whether he was particularly amused by the pledge of eternal affection is not known, although the old officer must surely have chortled at some of the things that were said. The policeman must also have been amazed at the naïveté of the prisoner. He wrote with such open and simple trust, obviously never thinking that his letter would be read by anyone other than Jenny. He poured out his heart to her, and later paid dearly for doing so.

"After I commenced to trust you," Nicholas said in the note, "I felt as if I could not do without you. I cannot bear you out of my sight." Then, in a rather ominous hint of foreboding, he added, "I can trust you more than my own friends, for fear they turn on me." Those few words and what they implied must have haunted him in the months to come. Up until this point in his incarceration, he had never hinted that there was any lack of trust in his friends. It was as if being with Tom Donovan every day and Jim Kehoe on occasion had led him to wonder about their intentions and whether the silent solidarity the three had maintained would last.

Then the poor fool continued with what was obviously a concrete reflection of his affection for Jenny. "You are the only one I ever loved," he wrote, and, for the first time in any letter, he added, "If I can get out, we will never part." No doubt William Smith took note of these words.

This statement was a new direction in the love affair, because Nicholas now not only revealed his affection for the woman of his dreams, he put into words the far-fetched idea that he might some-how be free. Prior to this, the most obvious sign that he wanted out had come with his asking for bail, and that had been his lawyer's idea as much as his own. But after that request was denied, he more or less accepted his lot, particularly when Jenny arrived and cheered him daily by her presence and what he thought was her love. Had he not fallen for her, he may well have pursued getting out more forcefully than he had. It was as if, with Jenny there, the centre of his world was beside him, and if he somehow got released, she would have been left behind when he needed her so much.

But now that he had her first letter from outside, Nicholas wondered if Jenny's friends might be able to help him get out so that he could be with her again. During one of the last times they talked at the cell window, she had not only mentioned these friends but had told him they had money. Nicholas had not dwelt on the remark at the time, but he remembered that conversation. It also occurred to him that she had said she had been involved in a counterfeiting gang with her brother. Nicholas believed this tale as well and wondered about the brother's usefulness to him.

For that reason, in his reply he asked about this brother and suggested, as the *Globe* reported on March 27, 1869, that "she should obtain her brother's assistance by money." The underlying idea was that cash required for any reason would simply be printed. Moreover, the actual amount would be unimportant, because any sum could be made available. The purpose, as the newspaper explained, would be "to bribe the jury at [his] trial, and buy up evidence." In addition, Nicholas also asked if it would be possible for him to join the gang. Even William Smith must have been taken by surprise by the suggestion of bribery, and even more so by the question that followed it.

Jenny responded to the query in her next letter. She told Nicholas that she had always assumed he would be welcome to join, but added that she had asked her brother in order to be sure. The brother supposedly said he would be happy to have a new gang member, so Jenny added that detail to the letter. As always, William Smith was the writer, and again he had the letter sent from Buffalo so that there would be American stamps on the envelope. We have no way of knowing how Nicholas reacted to the news, but probably he was buoyed by it. He seems to have believed that as a gang member, he could somehow get out of jail because he would have help.

From this time forward, Nicholas's messages began to change. The *Huron Expositor* alluded to this shift in emphasis in an April 2, 1869, story: "Gradually his letters became more detailed, and, at last, commenced to hint, and then to detail broadly, the cause of his incarceration, his connection with the crime, and the manner in which it had been committed. In one [letter] he states that one good circumstance in his favour was that he changed his pants immediately after the murder." While he might not have actually admitted that he was involved in the killings, he implied that he was. He also told Jenny in another note that he wished he could send her "some nice things" as gifts, but whatever he might have sent had been in a trunk that Dave Donovan had burned. He went on to say that the trunk "contained evidence," but did not say in what direction the evidence pointed, or what it was. All of these comments ended up in his file, and later they would be used against him in court. No doubt Detective Smith was pleased with the way the correspondence was going.

The letters continued as regularly as the mail carriers could deliver them. They all contained the most profound expressions of love, longing, and Nicholas's hope that somehow, togetherness might someday be possible.

"I have never seen one that I loved more," he told her in a letter in mid-February. "Believe me Jenny; I will love you until I draw my last breath. You are the only one I ever loved, and if I can get out, we will never part." This message also contained his first mention of marriage, but with an added and utterly foolish twist: "We will get married and you will show me how to make the counterfeit money, and I know lots of places where we can pass it off." One wonders at this remark. Was the man living in a dream world, or was he basically so uncaring that he had no misgivings whatsoever about cheating those who got stuck with his fake funds?

And then, although the murder was not mentioned in so many words, he told her, "No one saw me do it, and if they bring evidence against me, you can buy it off." Here again, he seems to have been prepared to go to any extreme in order to get out of his predicament.

Detective Smith was ecstatic when this admission arrived. It was, and would remain, one of the strongest links to the deaths. And the fact that Nicholas penned these thoughts shows his complete trust in Jenny. He never seems to have had any suspicion that what he put down on paper would be seen by anyone else. It also indicated that he was grasping at straws, trying to find any way he could to get out. Whether his prime motivation was to get away with murder or to be with his lover could be debated endlessly. The obvious answer is that he wanted both.

In another letter, Nicholas specifically mentioned Tom Donovan, if only in passing. This comment had a connection to a prior message, but now, according to the *Huron Expositor* on April 2, Nicholas "said he felt pretty sure no one saw him. He was led … to understand that some man was going to swear that he saw him and Donovan going and coming from the house that night, but with her assistance, could be bought off."

This reference would lead to the "mysterious witness" aspect of the case, and would be alluded to in the months to come. At the time the letter was written, however, it was a strong and direct link to Tom Donovan's involvement, and would ultimately have a major bearing on his future actions.

The Spring Assizes opened in Goderich on March 23, 1869. Once again, the murder of Old Melady and his wife was the most serious matter to be dealt with, and interest in it ran high. The trial involving the Queen vs. Nicholas Melady and Thomas Donovan was scheduled to begin at 9:30 a.m. on March 25, the third day of the sessions. Cases heard during the first couple of days were relatively minor in nature, and few spectators bothered to show up. However, the attendance was much different when the two accused killers were brought into the courtroom that Thursday morning.

"There was a tremendous crush in the lobbies and on the staircases of the courthouse, of parties desirous to hear the opening of the Melady murder case. The courthouse was densely crowded long before the time of opening had arrived," the *Globe* reported in their story published the next day. The *Huron Expositor* said, "every part of the courthouse was densely crowded." And no wonder. The curious descended on Goderich in droves. This trial would have everything: violence, money, greed, and revenge. And all these existed even before the love affair between Nicholas and Jenny came to light. The sexual aspect of the case would become the titillating denouement in the courtroom drama that would follow.

The killings had shocked the county, and virtually no adult in the area would have been unaware of them. The murder victims were well known, and the shoddy police investigation had enraged the locals. (Later on, when even more investigative incompetence came out, the effect would be amplified.) These factors, coupled with what today would be called a media feeding frenzy, ensured that news of the crime was widespread. The matter had reached the highest levels. The premier of the province had tried to keep out of the fray, but even he had been drawn into it — and people in Huron knew that. Newspaper readers all across Canada and in the United States were aware of the killings, as were lawyers, clerics, medical men, and law enforcement officials, because so many of them had direct input into the case.

As always, the assizes had been scheduled far in advance; papers of the day made mention of the cases that would be heard and the name of the judge who would be presiding. In this instance, the trials were before Mr. Justice John Wilson, a no-nonsense jurist who ran his court by the book. He had a reputation of being fair, and he refused to tolerate court-room theatrics. The newspapers also named the Crown attorney, the defence lawyers, and all the members of what was known as the grand jury. This panel, which has now been abolished in Canada, was respon-sible for evaluating cases that were to come to trial. Its job was, in effect, to double-check the file on the crime and to decide whether or not there were reasonable grounds for proceeding to trial. If there was cause, the grand jury submitted what was called a "true bill" to the court. Following this presentation, a second jury was chosen for serious crimes.

On the first morning of the assizes, Judge Wilson addressed the grand jury members, all of whom were men, and told them what they might expect once the various trials began. He pointed out that infractions of a relatively minor nature would be addressed to begin with, and then three serious matters — murder, manslaughter, and arson — would follow. He stressed his expectations for the group and impressed upon them the seriousness of the legal proceedings they had been chosen to help carry out.

Most of the grand jury members were at their first trial, and each was determined to do his best. All were nervous, and the judge knew that. In an attempt to put them at ease, he assured them of his assistance, when warranted, and thanked them in advance for their civic participation.

Six cases were dealt with the first day, and five on the second. Finally, on the third morning, the long-anticipated murder trial was about to get underway.

But to the surprise of virtually everyone in the courthouse, and very quickly far beyond it as well, the proceedings came to an abrupt and unexpected end.

In less than two hours, the spectators were all back on the street.

CHAPTER 15 | THE TRIAL THAT WENT NOWHERE

WHEN JUDGE WILSON was ready to begin the murder trial, Nicholas Melady, Jr., and Thomas Donovan were led into the courtroom in Goderich, placed in the dock, and told to remain standing while the clerk read the indictment against them. Both were nervous and embarrassed, yet when they looked out at the packed room, they smiled and nodded to friends who dotted the benches near the front. The crowd, which had been rather noisy up until that point, grew silent and listened to the charge. It said, in part, that the two, "on the 6th day of June, 1868, at the Township of Tuckersmith did feloniously and of their malice aforethought kill and murder one Nicholas Melady." Each was asked to respond, and both pleaded not guilty. Then they and the spectators took their places and prepared to watch the spectacle unfold.

Once their pleas were recorded, Crown attorney Christopher Robinson informed the court that he wished to have the prisoners challenge prospective jurors together. He had decided to do so, he said, because this would be more efficient than having individual challenges; it would still result in a fair trial, and it would not waste the court's time. Robinson really did this, however, to cover up a glaring fault in his own handling of the case — something for which he would soon be sorry.

Defence counsel R.A. Harrison, who was taking the case for Wilmot Squier, jumped to his feet, objected to what the Crown had said, and asked that the accused be allowed to challenge prospective jurymen separately. Mr. Justice Wilson considered the matter for a couple of minutes, sided with the defence, and said he would allow each of the accused to reject up to twenty potential jurors. No reason had to be given for anyone rejected. Then His Honour advised the clerk to get the procedure underway.

The selection began, and many in the crowd began to act as if they were at a sporting event. They applauded, cheered, or both when someone they knew came before the defence lawyer. Judge Wilson was forced to restore order several times.

The first man challenged was William Walters. He was rejected by Harrison on behalf of Nicholas Melady. The crowd cheered, and Wilson slammed his gavel and yelled for order. He then told the raucous crowd that he would clear the room unless there was order. This seemed to work for a while because the spectators were relatively quiet for the next few examinations. The second potential juror was James Aikenhead. The man stood and was so nervous it was as if he were on trial rather than the two accused. Harrison rejected him, acting for Tom Donovan. Aikenhead slunk away and disappeared at the back of the crowd. Then Harrison rejected Thomas Grey on behalf of Melady, Robert Davis for Donovan — and so on. There was more cheering, followed by additional gavel pounding.

One after the other, the men who had been called for jury duty entered the court and just as quickly were rejected for first one and then the other accused. None were being accepted. After a few minutes of this, it occurred to the clerk of the court that there was soon going to be a serious problem. By then, Harrison had rejected the first thirty-five candidates, so the clerk jumped up, dashed across the room, and began to whisper animatedly to Judge Wilson. Wilson looked at the discomfited clerk and questioned him, and the clerk was seen to nod several times.

Judge Wilson indicated that the Crown should approach the bench. The three men conferred for some minutes; at first, everyone present watched in relative silence, wondering what was going on. But gradually the packed crowd began to grow restive. They whispered, as if mimicking the officials at the front of the room. Then there was muted conversation, and finally shouts of "Hurry up! Get going!" and the like. Judge Wilson again called for order and finally told the assembly that the clerk would explain the delay. The hubbub ceased.

The clerk turned to the throng before him and announced that the potential jury pool that had been present was now largely depleted and that only a handful of men were waiting to appear. He pointed out that as a complicating factor, some of those who were called up had had to be excused earlier that morning for medical and other reasons. Now, only five men remained on the list. Since twelve jurors were needed for the trial, the stalemate was critical. Tom and Nicholas listened and then broke into broad smiles. Their supporters in the crowd looked on in disbelief at first, then nudged each other and whispered. When they realized the implications of the problem, they laughed, hooted, and even shouted encouragement to the accused.

The *Stratford Herald*, in an article on December 15 that year, carried a reporter's version of what had happened. "As each prisoner was entitled to twenty peremptory challenges, and as there were but forty-eight men summoned, the panel was exhausted before a jury could be empanelled." A potential solution was suggested, but just as quickly tossed out. Judge Wilson offered to let Harrison choose men from the crowd, but the newspaper added, "The prisoners decided not to take a jury from the spectators, so the case was transversed [sic] to the fall assizes in 1869." When Wilson made the offer, there were shouts of "Take me, take me," intermingled with grandstanding, whistles, and much laughter.

Finally, in the words of the *Huron Expositor* on April 2, "His Lordship ordered the prisoners to be remanded to jail, and announced that the Sheriff would be directed to summon seventy-two jurors instead of the ordinary forty-eight." The gales of laughter were now at the expense of the clerk and the Crown. Judge Wilson stormed from the courtroom, obviously angry, looking as if he could not believe the incompetence he had just witnessed. The entire morning had been an utter waste of his time.

Surprisingly, few in the crowd seemed dismayed at the morning's turn of events. "The prisoners were removed," reported the *Globe* on March 26, "amid much congratulations on the part of their friends. There was great excitement in court when the result was announced, numbers having come evidently to enjoy a first-class sensation."

The crowd poured out of the courtroom, reached for their smokes, and passed around more than one flask. There was lots of laughter and good humour, despite the seriousness of the occasion. As they were led away, both prisoners jostled and joked with those they knew. Several friends came over, slapped the two on the back, and congratulated them on their supposed good fortune.

A short while later, Nicholas Melady and Tom Donovan were back in their cells.

In surviving records, there appears to have been little overt criticism of the defence lawyer's methods. But even though what he did was legal and had the blessing of the assize judge, the deliberate rejection of so many potential jurors was somewhat unusual, even for the time. Nevertheless, Harrison had a valid reason for doing what he did. His actions came about because of the questionable police and legal manoeuvrings that had plagued the case from the beginning. This time, Christopher Robinson in particular was to blame, and he knew it. He had tried to cover his actions by his insistence on the joint challenge recommendation. As soon as he was faced with the shortage of jurors, he would have realized his machinations would be exposed. The depletion of the jury pool was merely the most obvious flaw in the Crown's action.

The Crown attorney had obtained information pertinent to the case that had been kept from the defence, and in so doing, had failed to provide the necessary disclosure. This matter, more than the lack of jurors, was the deeper problem. The *Globe* mentioned what had been withheld on March 27, although ultimately the paper would be severely reprimanded by the court for doing so.

After commenting on the rejection of the jurors, the paper said, "This course arose from the fact that the prosecution had secured confessions and admissions which were unknown to the defence till a few days before the Assizes opened. The manner in which these were obtained, their nature, and the extent to which they incriminate the accused, are facts which would have been submitted in evidence had the trial proceeded." Then the paper recounted much of what Christopher Robinson had kept from the defence, particularly the matter of the correspondence between Nicholas and Jenny. The Crown attorney, in the parlance of the time, had attempted to "pull a fast one" and had been caught in the act.

In the weeks and months that led up to the aborted trial of Tom Donovan and Nicholas Melady, their companion in crime was in and out of jail several times. Jim Kehoe was arrested shortly after the murders and locked up in the Van Egmond basement and, later, in the Goderich Gaol. Despite the best efforts of Bernard Trainer to keep him there, he was released on his own recognizance during the summer of 1868. Trainer was furious when he heard of the release but was powerless to do anything about it. He did not have enough proof of wrongdoing to keep Jim behind bars.

Jim did what he could to catch up on necessary farm work, but after being out for only a couple of weeks he was jailed again in the early fall, then re-released within days. At the time Detective Clarke rounded up most of the Melady family, he was jailed again. Two days before Christmas, Gilbert McMicken let him out, but then turned around and had him arrested again on December 30. He was let go on January 6, 1869. Each time he was taken back to jail, he was given a new number but, generally, his old cell. Eventually, he knew it as well as he knew his own home. He came back so many times that even the guards and the jailer himself welcomed him like an old friend.

One of the newspapers in a nearby town verged on the sarcastic when they reported on the repeated arrests. On April 9, 1869, the *Mitchell Advocate* mentioned that Jim had been jailed and then had been "nine times remanded and enlarged on his own recognizance." The number of jailings was exaggerated, but the essence of the story was not. In fact, it alluded to a problem this prisoner would face for some time.

The paper explained that, while incarcerated, inmates "are in the habit of talking about the cause of their imprisonment, and Kehoe let out enough to a fellow prisoner to implicate himself." The paper may have known what Kehoe had confided to others during the many times he was locked up, but did not publish it. The editor claimed to have made this decision because "the publication of evidence likely to be produced at court, whether calculated or not, has a tendency to prejudice some people against the prisoner." This was a thinly veiled criticism of two other papers, one the *Toronto Globe* and the second a local publication.

Apparently Jim's comments about the night of the murder were quoted in a newspaper printed in Clinton, a town just west of Seaforth. Unfortunately, the paper, called *The New Era*, no longer exists, nor do microfilmed copies of it. There are only two issues in the Archives of Ontario, but disappointingly, there is nothing in either that concerns this case.

The *Advocate* then added that "one of the greatest complaints Nicholas Melady had to make is the many articles written about the affair, by parties who knew little about it." The Mitchell weekly went on to castigate the *Globe*, which, in its October 12 edition, published "an article which had not one tittle of truth in it." In fact, the *Globe* had juxtaposed some names, but the essence of the story was accurate. Of course, the mix-up in names was more obvious in the region the *Advocate* circulated, where everyone knew everyone else. There also seems to have been some resentment because the big-city papers continued to cover the murder story. The local organs felt that they were being pushed aside by outsiders who did not know the facts, the people involved, or the sensibilities of smaller communities.

Even though it was a serious incident, at least to Jim, the manner of his arrest on March 26 was a matter of lasting amusement for many of his friends and others who heard of it. The story was told and retold, embellished with time, and served as an example of how not to avoid arrest. The joke was on Jim, but he got as much enjoyment out of describing what happened as others.

That Friday morning, the same day as the Goderich trial, he was out in the barnyard at his farm, fixing the wheel of a wagon. He was all alone. The day was sunny, the snow was almost gone, and the water level in the nearby Bayfield River ran high. The first robins were back from their winter in the south and were busily building new nests. The sap was flowing in the maple trees, and those who were making syrup that spring were happy with the volume of the run. There had been many of the sunny, cold days that syrup makers love.

Kehoe had his head down and his back to the river as he concentrated on the task at hand. He was enjoying the day and had deliberately not gone to Goderich for the trial. He had lots of work to do and had decided he might be wise to keep a low profile. What happened in that courtroom would go on for two or three days. If he wanted to sit in on any of it, there would be plenty of time to do so. For the most part, though, the farther he was from Goderich and anything to do with the law, the better he felt.

Just then, his wife, Margaret, came to the back door of the house and shouted at him. He didn't hear her at first, but when she caught his attention, she told him to go and hide because Constable Stephens was coming. Although Margaret had seen Stephens on the road, she only assumed that he was coming to their place.

Because of everything that had happened in the last few months, Jim also felt instinctively that any officer's visit would mean another arrest. If that was the case, the wagon would not be fixed, nor would anything else get done around the farm. He stood up, glanced over his shoulder to the west, and immediately recognized Stephens's black mare, trotting briskly along the road from Seaforth.

When Kehoe first saw the horse and buggy, the policeman was on the other side of the river, perhaps four hundred yards away. Ordinarily, it would take him only a minute or two to close the gap, but a few days earlier, spring flooding had caused some shifting to the nearest of the two wooden bridges at a corner near the farm, and Jim knew his visitor would have to come to the corner, then almost stop before picking his way across the damaged right of way. The farm entrance was little more than fifty yards from there, but his house and barn were about one hundred yards down the laneway. There just might be time to hide. As far as Jim could tell, Stephens did not seem to be looking anywhere but ahead.

The farmer didn't hesitate. He raced over to the barn, slammed the stable door behind him, dashed down a passageway between half a dozen milking cows, and ran up some stairs to the second floor. Once there he climbed a ladder into a mow, quickly burrowed into the mound of hay that was there, and pulled as much of it as he could down over himself. In no time, he was completely concealed. He remained there, stock still, barely daring to breathe, his heart pounding. Outside, he heard Thomas Stephens drive into the yard.

Stephens pulled his horse to a stop, hooked the reins around a fence post, and then walked purposefully towards the kitchen door of the Kehoe home. He knew his way; he had been here often enough. A scruffy-looking farm dog appeared out of nowhere, barked a couple of times, and then ran around the house and out of sight.

Margaret heard the policeman's first couple of knocks, but she deliberately avoided answering them. If she could gain a few more seconds for Jim to hide, all the better.

After he had pounded on the door for a third time, it opened, and Stephens was greeted, coldly, by the young housewife. He told her he had a warrant for James Kehoe's arrest on a charge of murder, signed by Justice of the Peace C. Crabb, at Goderich. Margaret Kehoe stared back and, in order to prolong the delay for her husband's sake, asked to see the warrant. The policeman obliged. At the same time, he asked if her husband was in the house, and if he was not, where he could be found. She took her time examining the document in her hands, then handed it back.

Margaret told the officer that Jim was not there, and that she did not know when he would be back. She even offered to let him come in and look around. She stood back from the door, allowing the policeman to see beyond her. Stephens told her he did not think it would be necessary to look through the house this time, but that he would be checking the barn instead. Then he turned on his heel and walked towards the stable. Once inside, he shouted several times, saying he knew the farmer was there somewhere and that he might as well give himself up. Margaret came out onto the back doorstep, listened, and wondered how well her husband was hidden.

We cannot tell today how long it took Thomas Stephens to check the barn, but we know that his search was a success. He looked through the stable, ducked low to check that his quarry had not crouched behind some standing cattle, and then went to the second floor. Jim heard the policeman's footsteps as he walked towards the hay mow.

"He said he saw me coming," the policeman said later, "and I found him concealed in a hay loft." Stephens ordered his man to come down out of his hiding place and gave him time to say a quick good-bye at the house, and shortly thereafter, the two left for Seaforth. There, the policeman bought two tickets, and together they boarded the westbound 2:22 p.m. train that took them to Goderich. Initially,

Jim had protested his arrest, but eventually, apart from a few comments when they were sitting together on the train, he seemed to be resigned to returning to jail. It was as if he expected to be back there again.

Jim, who on this occasion became prisoner number 2233, was in time to have supper in a dayroom with his co-accused, whose trials had been cancelled that morning. The three talked well into the night, laughing about the unexpected debacle in the courtroom; Jim regaled his listeners with his story of hiding in the hay. Ultimately the day had been a bad one for him, but good for them — at least in the short term.

Somewhere, a cell door slammed, and then there was only snoring.

There are no definitive records concerning what happened to Old Melady's house in the first few weeks after he and his wife were murdered. There seems to have been a period when it stood empty, but all indications point to a subsequent cleaning of the place by family members, and perhaps others as well. It is probable that Alice returned to what, after all, had once been her home. Her older brother Tom may have moved in for a while, and if so, his daughter Katherine likely came from the Kehoes' to be with her father. We are certain that one or more of the family lived there in the fall of 1869, and the names of both Alice and Katherine appear on the 1871 census. No additional information could be located concerning Katherine's siblings, if any, or her mother, although the woman was likely in the United States.

Not surprisingly, perhaps, Old Melady had not made a will, so the allocation of his house, the land where it was located, his other farms, and his possessions all had to be looked after by lawyers. The division of the estate quickly became a legal quagmire, and it was years before everything was settled. Even the county registry files for the one farm where he died are complex, and at times almost impossible to understand. Sometimes, three or four family members are listed jointly, and these often change, for reasons that are now unclear. Then there are lot sizes that vary, registry numbers that seem contradictory, and even question marks written on original documents. Sometimes it appears as if those in charge of keeping the records were confused as to what was going on at any given time. Occasionally the dates listed seem out of order, and others are completely missing. Some are so faint, they are scarcely readable.

There were so many inheritors, creditors, and opportunists that Wilmot Squier and others in his firm who did the legal work on the file must have sometimes bemoaned the fact that they ever took it on. Time and time again, Squier's name appears on the records of property transactions, and just as often as the designated individual when parcels of land were held in trust.

One entry is particularly intriguing. In the 1890s a William Aberhart is listed as owning the Melady home farm. We know Aberhart had a son of the same name who was born in 1878 and who spent his formative years growing up in the area. Young Aberhart completed his secondary education in Seaforth, taught school in the vicinity, and ultimately went to western Canada. There, in 1935, he became the first Social Credit premier of Alberta. It is possible, therefore, that the future politician may well have lived for a time in the house where one of Canada's most notorious murders took place. Admittedly, this is conjecture, but it is of interest.

Shortly after the murder, we have to presume that Jim Kehoe, when he was not in jail, Dave Donovan, Tom McGoey, and perhaps Joseph Nigh worked the land and, in effect, ran the farm. It has always been common for rural residents to help in time of need. Many farmers who have fallen on difficult circumstances have been assisted by neighbours who ploughed fields, harvested crops, and fed animals when there was no one else to do so. Later on, the names of the four individuals mentioned here can be found on the property transfer lists pertaining to the estate. Eventually, they all would own sections of the land.

The surprising results of the 1869 Spring Assizes gradually became yesterday's news across Huron. Summer came, and with it, all the warm-weather activities that commanded attention. Work went on, of course, in factory and farm, but there were games: baseball, soccer, even cricket, along with activities such as swimming, horseshoe pitching, and fishing. Newspapers of the day refer to the state of the crops, the visits of politicians, the vagaries of the weather, and the usual tales of runaway horses, farm accidents, and house fires. Then there were the scores of advertisements for everything from bunion cures to custom-made coffins.

People visited, danced, held barn-raising bees, attended weddings, and took part in shivarees, the latter at times when the newlyweds hoped they would be left alone. This custom involved calling on the bride and groom a week or so after the wedding, generally after they had gone to bed. An integral part of the visit involved banging pots and pans, blowing whistles, or ringing bells, all of which were intended as part of a raucous welcome to the community. Generally, someone in the shivaree party had a fiddle, and when the new husband and wife were finally dragged out of bed by the revelers, the instrument was played and drinks were poured.

Often, the good times lasted until dawn. Then the party stragglers, exhausted and hung over, headed for home as the sun rose over the bush.

But the people of Huron certainly did not have to attend a shivaree in order to find a place or an occasion to drink. There was lots of alcohol around, and much was consumed. On December 17, 1869, for instance, the *Globe* mentioned that Seaforth had a population of fifteen hundred, and no less than "sixteen whiskey shops, or one for every ninety-three and three-fourths people." Most of the surrounding towns and villages boasted similar numbers. No wonder the Temperance Movement came into being, although at times those involved in it must have felt they were fighting a losing battle.

Temperance organizations started in Canada as early as 1827, and originally their goal was to have alcohol used in moderation. Gradually, however, this aim became more pronounced, and eventually they championed banning all alcohol in any form. This in turn led to the Canada Temperance Act of 1878. For years afterwards, the sale and use of intoxicating beverages was reflective of the era and of changes in society.

Finally, September came: the days were not quite as long, the nights were cooler, and the first hint of fall colour came to the leaves. In Seaforth, school-aged children, both Protestant and Roman Catholic, returned to their slates and readers. They were taught together, in a new brick school that opened on the corner of Church and James Streets. Land for the building had been acquired two years earlier, when town fathers realized that the one-room schools of the past were not adequate for their growing municipality. Some two hundred youngsters now attended. Outside of town, most of the grain crops had been harvested, and soon ploughing for the next spring would be well underway.

In no time, the Fall Assizes would begin. The summer might have passed, but the closure to the most sensational murder case the county had ever known had not. The interrupted trial would now resume, and before it ended, a swirl of controversy would envelope the community and shock and titillate the sensibilities of anyone remotely interested in the rule of law.

CHAPTER 16 | A SECOND BETRAYAL

THE LOVE AFFAIR between Nicholas and Jenny came to an abrupt end a few days before the assizes in the spring. In letter after letter, the prisoner had continued to pledge his eternal devotion to the dearest, most beautiful woman he had ever known. She had reciprocated on a daily basis while she was in jail; on a less regular, but frequent, basis after her release. Nicholas knew in his heart that she loved him and would always be there for him. For that reason, his letters had gradually become more passionate and, because of his abiding trust in Jenny, more self-accusatory. And while he never specifically said he was involved in the killings, he came precariously close to doing so. In several notes, he also alluded to the actions of Tom Donovan and Jim Kehoe, but always with emphasis on his belief that no one saw any one of the three of them at the murder scene. Despite some talk of a mysterious witness to the deed, none ever materialized. In fact, the rumour of a shadowy figure who prowled at night and watched the murder being committed was almost certainly a story planted by Bernard Trainer, with the hope that at least one of the three accused would hear of the witness, panic, and subsequently confess.

Because he was severely constrained by the need to have everything ready for the spring trial, Detective Smith was forced to terminate the correspondence earlier than he wished, and certainly earlier than he would have if time had not been a factor. He was always sure that, given another two or three weeks, and as many letters, Nicholas would have let Jenny know more about the night of the murder. He had become so enamoured with her and dependent upon her that if she had asked outright what happened that night, he would have told her, or so Smith believed. Nicholas's desire to get out of jail, to be with Jenny, and possibly to run away and marry her consumed his every fibre and his every moment. The old detective was also sure the prisoner would have told his lover about the actions of his co-accused, thereby cementing the case against both of them as well. Already, a rumour picked up by a jail guard had Nicholas shooting Old Melady, while at roughly the same time Jim and Tom murdered his wife, even though they were so drunk neither really remembered much about doing so. However, this sequence of events would remain a rumour, no matter how plausible it might have sounded. Another theory had Tom shooting Old Melady, and Nicholas and Jim killing his wife. However, because full disclosure had to be made to the defence attorney in the spring, further admissions through letters would never be made. Neither the police nor the Crown would risk another delayed trial because *they* had not complied with the law.

William Smith realized Jenny's pivotal role in the investigation was, of necessity, coming to an end. He had her come to the office he used in the Goderich police station, and together they discussed every aspect of the case, right from the beginning. The officer wanted to be absolutely sure, in his own mind, that there was not one scrap of information Nicholas had related to Jenny that she had either forgotten to mention or dismissed simply because she thought it of no use.

Finally, satisfied that together they had done all they could, Smith told Jenny her job was done, thanked her for her wonderful work, and referred her to Gilbert McMicken for her daily two-dollar prison pay. McMicken settled quickly, but ultimately the taxpayers of Huron were accountable. From then on, Jenny Smith ceased to exist. She called herself Janet Cooke during the trial that followed.

We have no idea how Nicholas reacted at first to what he later considered a complete betrayal. He sent one last letter, which William Smith filed, but ceased the correspondence when Wilmot Squier told him to do so, just after the lawyer had received the Crown's disclosure. Nicholas was shattered by the revelations, but this time did what he was told. However, the damage had already been done. He had written so many letters to Jenny, had talked to her so often, that he must have been unsure how much she now knew. At the same time, however, he was certain he had never told her he was one of the killers. Later on, in another context, he would affirm that.

But Gilbert McMicken and William Smith had most of what they wanted, and everything they felt they could get from Nicholas. From then on, it would be up to Crown attorney Christopher Robinson to exploit it.

Once he had all of Nicholas's letters together, Smith went over them with care, traced the pattern of admission in those that contained even the slightest kernel of evidence, and then set those aside for use in court. Some of the notes were especially pertinent to the matter at hand; others were less so. Among the former were those that mentioned or hinted at the participation in the murder by Tom Donovan and Jim Kehoe. Smith gave these his undivided attention — for a reason he had not really considered earlier in the investigation. Now that he knew more about the three accused, he decided to try an age-old method of breaking the case: he would try to get one of them to turn against the other two. For that purpose, he deliberately selected the weakest of the three.

That was Tom Donovan.

After the aborted trial in the spring of 1869, and before the assizes that fall, William Smith had almost six months to pursue his plan of action. The three suspects remained in jail in Goderich, and the longer they were kept there, the more they hated the place. Smith knew that, and he decided to deprive them of one measure of satisfaction they had had. Until now, all three had been in the same cellblock, side by side. Insofar as it was possible, they settled in and did not cause trouble in the jail because they were together and had the luxury of shared misery. Now, however, Smith decided to split the trio up, hoping to learn something from at least one of the three that would assist in the murder probe. If they were alone, he felt one of them might find it less risky to break their self-imposed silence. As long as they were together, they stuck together — in their stories and in their silence about what had really happened the night of the murders.

The specific methods he used to get at the truth are not known, but the general approach that was followed is relatively certain. After some weeks of separation from one another, during which time the three prisoners were watched for their reactions to being apart and for anything they might let slip, Smith decided to put the rest of his plan into action. From time to time, he or one of the other detectives removed Tom Donovan from his cell and took him to a room where he could be questioned in private (this may have been in the reception room of the jail or even in what passed for the infirmary). Little by little, the investigating officers dropped hints as to how much they knew of his actions on the night of the killings. Much of what they said was a bluff, but Tom did not know that.

Initially, he was told in no uncertain terms that he was the killer, that Nicholas and Jim had been there that night but had not participated. He denied this, of course, and reiterated his inquest account of being with Jim, meeting Nicholas, and never leaving the road. His interrogators then reminded him of the tracks to the river, the unusual heel marks, and the bloody footprints that matched his on the kitchen floor. As he had admitted so many months before, Tom said the boots were his, but that he knew nothing else. He stuck to the story for several weeks. So long, in fact, that Smith began to wonder if he would ever break the man.

But one day, the police showed the prisoner one of the letters Nicholas had written to Jenny. And while the note said nothing of consequence, other than reaffirming unending love, it did mention Tom in passing. Tom knew about Nicholas's fascination with Jenny, and he was well aware of the clandestine correspondence. It is probable that he would have known that Nicholas had talked to Jenny through his cell window. For that matter, he had likely heard the two of them whispering together. After all, he had spent most of his prison time in the very next cell.

Tom was again asked about the night of the murder, but just as forcefully as in the past he denied knowing anything at all about it. The police then pointed out to him that he was mentioned in several more of the letters and that he might as well clear his conscience and admit his role in the tragedy. He had been at Old Melady's. He had been in the kitchen. He had tracked blood all over the place, and later blood was poured out of his boots. The police asked him how he explained all this.

Again, Tom claimed he knew nothing about what had happened. But he began to wonder and worry about other things Nicholas might have said in those letters. The police not only hinted at other revelations, they told him there were more — many more. Then Tom was left alone, with plenty of private time to ponder. More days passed, and his concerns grew.

Finally, about two weeks before the murder trial was set to begin, the questioning began again. Every day, and often more than once, Tom was called from his cell, brought to the interrogation room, and asked to explain his actions on the night of the murder. On those occasions when he said little, the police said more. They reminded him that his name was in a lot of the letters and that he was incriminated in them. He was shown a second note, allowed to read it himself, and saw first-hand Nicholas's comments about the mysterious witness who had supposedly seen him and Tom entering and leaving Old Melady's house. The fact that Nicholas thought that such a person, if there was one, could be bought off with counterfeit money did little to allay Tom's fears. Obviously, he noted, Nicholas must feel there actually could have been a witness. Tom knew he had seen no one, but he had been drinking heavily that night, so he could have failed to notice anyone else around.

The police then pointed out to the prisoner that the trial would soon start, and all of the things they knew, coupled with the letters, would send him to his death. He would be strung up in front of a crowd that would point to him on the gallows and laugh and joke as he died. All his friends would be there, and they would really enjoy the show. When it was over, they would go somewhere and get drunk and talk about him. The police offered him a chance to get off and avoid all that if he simply helped them out.

We have no way of knowing exactly when Tom began to seriously consider the proposal. The police no doubt told him that if he turned Queen's Evidence (testified for the Crown) he would not end up dying at the end of a rope. They likely explained that some kind of a prison sentence would be imposed but that he would not be executed. If he was given time in a jail, his friends could come and visit him there. Would he not like that?

Tom listened, but still refused to co-operate. He spent many hours alone in his cell, thinking, agonizing over what he should do. When he could no longer live with his indecision, he made the mistake of asking a fellow inmate for advice. This, he soon learned, was a foolish move. He might as well have written his problem on a sign and posted it in the prison rotunda. In no time, that fact that he was even thinking of switching sides and helping the police was known by everyone in the building.

On another floor of another cellblock, Jim Kehoe heard the story. At first, he dismissed the possibility that Tom would even consider such a thing. Had not the three of them sworn never to deviate from the agreed-upon version of what happened that night, no matter what the circumstances? For that reason, Jim initially defended Tom and said the rumour was only that, a rumour started by the police. He told anyone who would listen that he, Nicholas, and Tom were all innocent, that none of them had ever left the road, that they had not been near Old Melady's, and that there was no one on earth who could prove anything to the contrary. When he was told about the so-called mysterious witness, he laughed. That was just another story the police made up. He didn't believe it for a minute.

But the rumour about Tom switching sides did not go away. In fact, it became common knowledge throughout the jail. Outwardly, at least, Jim still refused to believe it.

One morning, a week before the start of the Fall Assizes, he was sound asleep in his cell when a fellow prisoner, a man named Hugh McLaren, called him to the day room. Edward Campaigne was there, and he wanted to talk to Jim in private. The jailer took the prisoner out into the rotunda and then to one of the rooms where Tom had been interrogated so often. McLaren gave little thought to why the jailer wanted to see Jim, but an hour later when he was brought back, McLaren noticed that his block mate was terribly upset. "He paced back and forth, excitedly," McLaren recalled later. "When I asked him what ailed him, he said, 'Tom Donovan has turned Queen's Evidence.'" Campaigne had given him the word.

Jim Kehoe had been absolutely stunned by the revelation. He continued to pace from his cell to the day room and back. As he did so, he grew more agitated and unsure of where he now stood. If Tom was going to testify for the Crown, he would likely get off. And that being the case, his own fate was precarious. He did not know what Tom had actually said, but anything was too much. Because the solidarity agreed upon had broken down, Kehoe began to panic, wondering if he should switch sides as well. Tom must have decided that that was the only way out. Then Nicholas could take the blame for everything that had happened at Old Melady's that night. Jim found himself wondering if that was the best way.

For his part, Tom's decision to switch allegiance was ultimately triggered by one specific letter in which his brother had been mentioned. In it, Nicholas explained to Jenny that Dave Donovan had burned a trunk that contained evidence. That was why Nicholas said he had no gifts for her. When Tom read this, he was completely convinced that the police knew far more than he realized — enough, perhaps, to convict them all. And because that was probably the case, he finally decided to co-operate. If doing so sent Jim and Nicholas to the scaffold, then that was the price that had to be paid. He intended to look out for himself. The deal the police offered to save his own life was more important than his two friends.

As far as Detective Smith was concerned, Tom Donovan's about-face, even though welcome, was still quite problematic. The old officer had dealt with similar situations too often in the past, and he knew from experience that an agreement made was not necessarily an agreement kept. He had sat in countless courtrooms and listened with barely concealed fury as witnesses who had promised co-operation retracted statements when they were put on the stand. For that reason, he did not know whether he could rely on Tom, yet at the same time he felt he had to use him to bolster the Crown's case. Several newspaper articles that appeared later on attest to the doubts the police had in accepting Tom's help. They did not trust him, and initially, at least, they were not sure how best to involve him. Getting help from a man they were sure was a cold-blooded killer might not be worthwhile in the long run.

In the lead-up to the trial, they spent many hours with Tom, going over and over his story, adjusting it when necessary, rehearsing him so that the points he would have to make were done in the most efficacious way. Some statements would cry out for clarification; others would seem incredible, even scarcely believable. In essence, Tom would have to get up on the witness stand, take the oath to tell the truth, and then lie.

During all this time, we have no specific knowledge of how Nicholas was coping. Initially, the rumour of Tom's change of heart must have seemed too far-fetched. But as it spread through the prison, Nicholas would have been unable to dismiss it. In no time, news of the development was common knowledge outside the jail as well, to the extent that it was reported in both local and national newspapers before the trial even commenced. And the papers did not attempt to fudge their reporting. They said Tom would be testifying against his co-accused.

To Nicholas, Tom's action was a second betrayal. And while he never really got over losing Jenny, later forgiving but not forgetting her, he had long suspected that Tom Donovan or Jim Kehoe, or both, would turn against him. In fact, he had mentioned such a fear in a letter to Jenny. Now he would have to turn to his lawyer for help. There was no one else.

Even though Wilmot Squier handled his share of cases involving petty law-breaking miscreants, his expertise was primarily in small-town commercial and real estate work, not criminal matters. But now, faced with one of the most high-profile murder cases imaginable, he knew he needed help — lots of help. To that end, he had approached a lawyer named R.A. Harrison before the Spring Assizes and obtained his services. Now that the fall sessions were about to begin, he convinced Harrison to come back to Goderich, this time for the duration of the proceedings. Squier agreed to be at his side in order to offer advice and provide background information, but Harrison would be handling the defence.

Robert Alexander Harrison was a brilliant man. Born in Montreal and educated at Upper Canada College and the University of Toronto, the thirty-six-year-old lawyer had been practising law for fourteen years. He spent five of these as a federal civil servant, then entered politics, and at the time of the Melady trial he was a sitting member of the House of Commons, representing the riding of West Toronto. Some six years after that, he would be appointed Chief Justice of Ontario, a post he held until his death from overwork on November 1, 1878. Twice married and a published author and editor in his spare time, he was undoubtedly one of the finest defence attorneys around. His performance at the upcoming trial would enhance that reputation.

The Crown prosecutor was equally renowned. Christopher Robinson was five years older than the counsel for the defence. Toronto born, he too had graduated from Upper Canada College and the University of Toronto. The father of three sons and a daughter, he would be involved in some of the most important trials in the land. Like his counterpart across the courtroom, Robinson wrote and edited numerous papers on legal matters. He ultimately became such a high-profile member of the profession that he loved that he was offered a knighthood for it. The honour was declined. Robinson died in the fall of 1905, in the city where he was born.

Although these adversaries at the trial were well-known at the time as specialists in their field, the man on the bench had a reputation that was equally formidable. His Honour Sir John Hawkins Hagarty was born and educated in Dublin, Ireland. The son of a lawyer, the young man immigrated to Canada and took up residence in Toronto in 1835, and was called to the bar the following year. He quickly rose through the ranks of his chosen vocation until, like Robert Harrison, he became, on May 6, 1884, Chief Justice for the Province of Ontario. An active member of the Church of England, he married a doctor's daughter, and in his spare time, he wrote poetry. When first offered a knighthood, Hagarty declined the honour. Later he accepted it on the occasion of Queen Victoria's Diamond Jubilee in 1897. For a period during his career he taught law at the University of Toronto, and in 1855 he received an honourary doctorate from the same institution. He was fifty-three years old when the Fall Assizes for the County of Huron began in 1869.

All in all, the three senior members of the judiciary at the Melady trial were among the most exalted in the country. Now, they were about to put their skills to use in a Goderich courtroom.

CHAPTER 17 | To Lie on Cue

THE MELADY MURDER trial opened at 9:00 a.m. on Thursday, September 16, 1869, the fourth day of the Fall Assizes in Huron County. There were seventy-two potential jurors on hand, and despite twenty challenges from the defence and one from the Crown, twelve men were selected, and the most important step towards closure to the case began at last. Fifteen months had passed since the killings had occurred.

The venue for the proceedings was the beautiful, tree-shaded court-house in the centre of downtown Goderich. In a way, this setting was particularly appropriate. Many aspects of the trial would prove to be controversial, and so was the building where it was held.

The central section of the large, two-storey, grey stone courthouse was essentially square in shape, with smaller balancing wings on either side. The architectural firm Mellish, Morell and Russell did the design work, and when it opened in 1856, the structure was said to be one of the finest looking public buildings in Upper Canada. However, the fact that it was located within the tract of octagonal park land in the middle of town was decried by some.

Years earlier, the property where the court stood had been deeded to the municipality as a market location, and it was to remain so in perpetuity. Just at the time the new building was really taking shape, a small group of vocal agitators who wanted their market retained sued the town to achieve their ends. They did not want to compromise, and insisted instead that what had been erected be torn down, the construction material taken away, and the land returned to its original purpose. In their demands the complainants refused to even consider the cost of reversing course. At the close of the hearing that followed, the judge who took the case concurred with the protest group. As soon as the judicial ruling was announced, the workmen on the site picked up their tools and left the property. For weeks the project lay dormant: it was neither a courthouse nor a market. In fact, it was just a shell of a building surrounded by the usual piles of lumber and assorted detritus of a construction site. This state of affairs satisfied no one.

Fortunately, in time, cooler heads prevailed, but officials with the provincial government in Toronto had to step in, overturn the judge's decision, and order the building completed. The construction continued, and finally the work was done.

The new edifice was grand in scope, with high windows, great vaulted ceilings, and polished floors. Once the grading was done and the necessary lawns and trees planted, the building was appreciated by the vast majority of ratepayers. They strolled on the grounds, held social gatherings of various sorts there, and took pride in showing the magnificent place to visitors from out of town. Postcards depicting the edifice circulated widely. The courthouse would go on to serve Huron County for almost one hundred years, until it was destroyed by fire in 1954. Sadly, it was replaced with a much less attractive building done in modern classical style. Even though a few people may not have liked the old structure, a lot hated the new. But this was far in the future for those involved with the assizes of September 1869.

The murder trial had been anticipated for months, and interest in it was widespread. As had happened in the short-lived spring session, people flocked to attend. They came in every conveyance imaginable, regardless of the difficulties that getting there entailed. Anyone who arrived by train had it easy, particularly those who travelled from Seaforth. The *Expositor* announced on September 10 that "a special passenger train" would be going from Seaforth to Goderich "for the accommodation of persons attending court." On board were trial witnesses, relatives of the deceased and the charged, and scores of curious people who simply felt they had to be there. Many went because they were nosey; many more went for entertainment. To them, this court case was the highlight of their autumn season. They would remember it and talk of it for years.

Many people came to Goderich on wagons, buggies, and horseback, but just as many walked. They might have had long treks, but even then, they were probably better off than some who came by stage. Stagecoach travel in Huron was a tough way to travel at the best of times, and not just because of the roads. This was particularly true on a route called the Seaforth and Wroxeter line, which brought travellers into Seaforth from the north. One rider became so fed up with such trips that he wrote about them for the *Expositor*. His letter was published on August 19, 1870, but the description was quite applicable at the time of the trial when many used that stage to get to the train in Seaforth. One wonders how they ever got to the station in time.

The disgruntled patron complained about the late starts: "Two hours frequently elapse before the stagecoach is ready. Then the passengers get in, and if there are more of them than one carriage can accommodate, another hour or so is spent hunting up an extra rig." Once underway, the riders always encountered other problems. "The taverns along the road are neither few nor far between, and at each of these the driver dismounts to liquor up and replenish his pipe," he complained. The writer then began to warm to his subject: "Passengers are continually subject to insolence and abuse. Proprietor and driver both appear to be actuated by the same principle, and that is that all the passengers are captive rogues." The correspondent even touched on a subject that, all these years later, is as controversial as ever: "The driver smokes incessantly, and in an open carriage of course, the smoke goes directly into the eyes of the passengers. I have seen remonstrances against the practice made on behalf of the ladies, treated with contempt." He finished, "I suppose a stage proprietor has a right to charge what he likes, but I don't see what right he has to keep back your change if you happen to hand him a bill in payment of your fare. Yet I have seen a polite request for correct change met with downright insult, and the passenger told in an insolent way, to take what he was offered or walk." No wonder many did just that.

The courtroom was packed, and people stood around the walls long before the business at hand commenced. Many in the crowd wanted to be there to watch the jury selection before the trial really got underway — the modern equivalent, perhaps, being present for the warm-up skate before the start of a professional hockey game. In the courtroom that day were many who had enjoyed the debacle at the Spring Assizes and who possibly hoped for more of the same now. Before the start of proceedings, there was a lot of laughter, jockeying for the best view, and greeting of old friends.

This time, the jury selection was completed with relative dispatch, and that alone seemed to have a calming effect on the crowd. Within an hour, the following male ratepayers from Huron County took their places in the jury box: John Dixon, James Elder, Francis Meyer, two men named John Broadfoot, George Brown, Henry Lawlor, John Porter, Thomas Bell, John Bailey, Thomas Mason, and Josiah Butt.

By then, Nicholas and Tom had been brought, handcuffed, in two light wagons from the jail to the court. They were transported separately because, as Nicholas knew of Tom's decision to turn Queen's Evidence, their police escorts wanted to head off possible confrontation between the two. The two wagons pulled to within a few feet of the jail door, the passengers were loaded, and the procession to court began. The drivers went from the jail south along Victoria Street (or what is Highway 21 today), turned right onto Newgate, and went to a rear door of the courthouse. It was somewhat ironic that this grim, half-mile journey passed along Newgate Street, because at the time, the notorious prison of the same name was a place where criminals were hanged in London, England. Charles Dickens, arguably the most popular novelist of the day, had made Newgate known across the English-speaking world, but it is doubtful either of the men in handcuffs would have made the connection.

On this morning of the first day of the trial, the crowd in the courtroom continued to be rather subdued. This was not just attributable to the seriousness of the occasion and to the quickness of the jury selection; it also had to do with the stern and businesslike demeanour of the man on the bench. Judge John Hawkins Hagarty exuded authority, and every spectator sensed that. They sat in relative silence when Nicholas and Tom were led into the room, were directed to the prisoner's tables, and took their seats.

At that point, Crown attorney Christopher Robinson rose to his feet, turned to the bench, and requested that, because Thomas Donovan would henceforth be testifying for the Crown, he be excused. Judge Hagarty concurred, and Tom was led to a witness waiting area elsewhere in the building. During the time in the courtroom, he had not looked at Nicholas at any time, even though they were only a few feet apart. After 465 days behind bars, Tom was almost a free man.

Robinson then began his address to the court. As reported in the *Expositor* coverage of September 17, 1869, the lawyer "touched feelingly on the case of which the prisoner was charged. Murder in any sense is terrible, but the murder of a parent is perhaps the most terrible conceivable. The counsel said he would not enter into the details, but briefly related the circumstances." In reading the reporter's account, it is hard to tell if he was pleased or disappointed that more details were not forthcoming.

The Crown then answered the widely asked question of why Nicholas was charged with the single killing. Robinson explained that this was because "there could be no doubt but that the same person guilty of this, was also guilty of the murder of Ellen Melady." The lawyer elaborated slightly, but in essence let the explanation stand.

Those assembled in the room seemed satisfied. A murmur swept the crowd, but it was followed almost immediately by silence.

A minute or so later, Robinson called his first witness, James Williams. A tall man with a weathered face and a slight stoop was directed to the witness box. Williams told the court that he was a carpenter, and in response to the Crown's question concerning the matter at hand, explained that at the time of the murder, he had been overseeing the construction of a barn for Nicholas Melady, Sr. He said he had seen the deceased that Saturday, not long before his death. He added that Melady looked well then, as did his wife. He had talked to both that same day.

In response to a question from defence attorney Robert Harrison, Williams said that Old Melady was reported to be rich, but that he, Williams, had no idea where he hid his money.

The Crown then called Thomas McGoey.

There was absolute silence from the spectators as the farmer was brought into the room. Virtually everyone present knew that this was the man who had discovered the murders, and they wanted to hear, first-hand, every grisly detail of what he had seen. Many in the crowd had been there when McGoey had testified at the inquest so long ago, but they wanted to hear everything all over again. They leaned forward, listening with rapt attention, not wanting to miss a word. For his part, the witness was as nervous on the stand at the trial as he had been when he had answered Coleman's questions during the first night of the inquest at Bummer's Roost. And while the crowd he had faced that night was large, many more people hung on his every word today. The poor man trembled as he took the oath to tell the truth, the whole truth, and nothing but the truth. Even his promise was hard to hear. It was barely a whisper.

Old Melady's son-in-law explained why he and his wife had gone to the house that Sunday afternoon. He told the court that, when there did not seem to be anyone around as they drove in, he wondered if he had gotten the days mixed up and that perhaps they were to come the following Sunday. Then he told the court of entering the house and of the terrible things they had seen there. As he spoke, McGoey gasped for breath, his whisper became softer, and every so often he had to be told to speak louder. It was as if he was reliving every moment of that fateful Sunday afternoon in June. Testifying was a torture indeed.

The crowd was transfixed. By the time Robinson finished leading McGoey through his testimony, the spectators, both those in attendance for the first time and those who had heard it before, seemed pleased that they had made it a point to be present. McGoey made two unexpected comments concerning Old Melady's new wife. He told the court that he had been blamed for introducing the murdered couple. He did not say who blamed him, but in any event he insisted that such a rumour was wrong. In answer to one of several follow-up questions from the Crown, McGoey also mentioned that he recalled a comment Nicholas had made that had been a bit of a surprise when it was uttered. The farmer knew Nicholas was referring to his father's intention to remarry when he said, "He won't bring another woman here." McGoey testified that he was alone with Nicholas when the statement was made. He did not say where they were at the time. The jury took note of the remark.

The witness left the stand, his ordeal over.

A minute or so later, Joseph Nigh was sworn in. Nigh told the court that he had learned of the deaths when the McGoeys came in that Sunday afternoon. He told of going to the house with McGoey, and then described a scene that was unforgettable. To a large extent, Nigh's testimony was much like McGoey's; both had seen three weapons on the floor: a club, an axe, and a broken revolver.

Christopher Robinson turned to a table behind him, picked up an axe that was lying there, and asked Nigh if it was the same tool he had seen that day. Robinson held the item up so the witness could examine it.

"It looks like the same one," Nigh answered. "Melady had an axe."

Robinson then held up the object that Nigh had called a club. It was a badly discoloured leg from a broken kitchen chair. After he had looked at it with more care than he had taken in checking the axe, Nigh said that the chair leg looked like the same piece of wood he had seen near Ellen Melady's body, but that he couldn't be sure. He also told the Crown that he had seen what he termed a "box" across the bedroom, but he had not examined it. For that reason, he said he was not sure if anything had been stolen out of it. The box was actually the trunk that at the time had been against the back wall of the bedroom.

Robinson then led the witness through a fairly comprehensive explanation of what happened later that day and the next. Spectators and jurors all listened with obvious interest. It was as if they all imagined themselves enmeshed in the atmosphere that had prevailed at the scene of the crime.

Nigh said that after viewing the victims and realizing the extent of the problem, he sent for the coroner and for Jim Kehoe. The coroner got there very quickly, the witness recalled, but Jim came "after a while." Nigh was not asked why he thought Jim took so long to come from his house, a mere five minutes or so away.

The Crown attorney asked Nigh if he had seen the accused later on in the afternoon, the same day the bodies were found. Nigh testified that he had, at Old Melady's, and that he had talked to Nicholas for a brief time as they stood outside at the back of the house. He told of asking the prisoner where he was the night before. "He said he and Donovan had been drinking," Nigh said, but he had gotten the impression Nicholas did not want to talk much about it. Nigh then said, "He gave a bad account of himself." Nigh did not explain in more detail what this comment really meant, and the Crown attorney did not ask.

At this point, defence counsel Harrison asked his first question of Nigh.

"How long did you know the accused?" he asked.

"For eight or ten years," the witness responded.

"Describe the relationship between the deceased and the accused," the lawyer said.

Nigh explained that he was aware of the fact that the father and son were not on good terms at times, and that because of this, the prisoner had gone to live in the United States on occasion. In response to the defence attorney's question about the character of the accused, Nigh responded, "I can say nothing bad against the prisoner." Harrison turned to his client just as Nicholas looked up. Their eyes met in a kind of unspoken, shared reaction to what had just been said.

Nigh stepped down.

The next witness was Henry Liddell Vercoe. The twenty-nine-year-old, English-born physician had performed the autopsies on the murder victims. In answer to the Crown's question about his background, the doctor explained that he had come to Canada with his parents as a child and that he had grown up in Elgin County. His degree in medicine was from McGill University in Montreal. Upon graduation, he practised in Sparta, Ontario, but had moved to Egmondville three years earlier.

The well-liked young doctor, who sometimes looked as ill as those he treated and who would die of cancer at forty-five, described the post-mortem examinations he had done on the bodies of Nicholas Melady, Sr., and Ellen Melady on the morning of June 8, 1868.

Vercoe's observations were at times quite gruesome in nature, and many spectators were both shocked and revolted, but none turned a deaf ear to anything that was said. In fact, most leaned forward and listened carefully so they would not miss a word.

After Vercoe mentioned the three slugs he had removed from the male deceased's brain, the items themselves were produced in court and identified by the witness. When these were placed on a table at the front of the courtroom, some spectators craned so far forward to see, they almost fell out of their seats. Gasps from the crowd came after the young doctor described the wounds of the two deceased. He was sure, he said, that the gunshot wound suffered by Old Melady would have killed him instantly and that "there would have been no struggle after it." Vercoe said he observed powder burns on his face, and from that he deduced that the "shot must have been very close." In his testimony, Vercoe implied that Old Melady had put up a fight prior to being shot. He was also in his bare feet.

The witness then described the many gruesome wounds suffered by Ellen Melady. He said he found a few powder marks on her face, and that while he noticed a gunshot wound on her forehead, he felt such a shot would have only rendered her unconscious. He testified that she had likely been killed by a blow from a broken chair that had lain nearby, and that a cut across her ear probably came from an axe. Both the chair part and the axe were produced and identified. Again the spectators strained to see. A few near the back stood to get a better look. No one left the courtroom.

The physician was asked if any of the wounds he saw could have been self-inflicted.

He responded with a single word: "Impossible."

The testimony then shifted to matters that were not of a medical nature. Vercoe told of helping to track the killers, along with Coleman and others. He mentioned that a notebook had been found in the river, but said little about it. Nor was he asked what its significance, if any, might have been. Just before getting down from the stand, he said that he had been present when Nicholas placed his foot in the tracks on the kitchen floor. The size "corresponded exactly as far as we could see." The physician was then permitted to return to Seaforth and his medical practice.

Following Vercoe's testimony, Judge Hagarty declared a dinner (lunch) recess. The court clerk intoned, "All rise!" and those present stood as His Honour made his exit. Almost immediately, a loud buzz of conversation filled the courtroom as the accused was led out. At this juncture, some in the crowd decided to go and get food at one of the nearby hotels, but before leaving they asked those who stayed behind to "save the seat" for the afternoon session. In many cases, spectators who went first ate quickly so that they could return and switch places with friends who were still inside. None wanted to miss the afternoon proceedings, mainly because of a rumour that gained credence as it was repeated.

Tom Donovan would be called next.

Nicholas Melady sat in silence as he watched his friend Tom Donovan enter the courtroom. It took only a couple of minutes for the witness to be sworn in. During his entire testimony, Tom studiously avoided making eye contact with the accused. He looked at whoever was questioning him, then at his hands, the floor, and occasionally at the members of the jury. He was very nervous, and it showed.

Christopher Robinson got to his feet, walked over to where Tom waited, and asked the witness to state his name and then to tell the court about the events of Saturday, June 6, 1868, as they had to do with him.

The room suddenly became quieter than at any time so far. Everyone wondered just what the witness might say — now that he was testifying for the Crown.

Tom launched into a description of what he had done that day, where he had gone, and with whom. Most of the first part of his testimony was taken up with going to Egmondville, drinking in Seaforth with his brother, Dave, and Jim Kehoe, and then leaving Bummer's Roost and encountering Nicholas Melady on the road. All this was precisely the story told at the inquest several months earlier. At no time during this recitation did he hesitate or fail to clarify anything he was asked.

From that point on, however, the account changed dramatically, and the witness became much less sure of himself. He paused for seconds at a time, coughed, cleared his throat, and looked as if he were trying to remember the lines of a prepared script. He told the court how he, Nicholas, and Jim "crossed the fields over to the barn." He did not say, nor was he asked, why they did not simply walk down the lane to the same place. This was at Old Melady's, he explained when he was asked to be more specific.

They went there, he continued, in order to see how the framing was progressing on the new barn that was being built. He was not asked how much of the new construction they expected to see in the darkness. Understandably, perhaps, the Crown might not have gained anything by making the query, but surprisingly, the defence did not broach the matter either.

They then sat down beside a woodpile, he said, but Jim and Nicholas both walked away and left him alone, Jim going in the direction of his home and Nicholas towards Old Melady's house. Tom said he just stayed where he was and watched them go. From where he was sitting, both destinations would have been in the same direction, but the witness did not mention this. However, he did say that during the time he was sitting there, he took his boots off. He did not tell the court if his friends did likewise.

Later on, when defence counsel Harrison asked why he removed his boots, he pondered for the longest time, and then finally explained, "I wished to be ready to run." This was stated reluctantly, observed an *Expositor* reporter who was there. There was a ripple of laughter throughout the courtroom. Harrison then asked why he wanted to be ready to run.

"I got ready to run because I thought the framers were coming out of the house, and I thought they might think I was doing mischief there," Tom said. A few more people in the crowd snickered as this was said. The defence lawyer let Tom's remark hang in the air. He said he would not ask the witness to explain why the framers would be coming out of the house to work in the dark. Many in the room laughed outright at this conclusion. Tom's face got red, and he studied his hands so intently that it was as if he had never noticed them before that moment.

The next part of Tom's testimony was confused, contradictory, and fragmentary, so the Crown devoted much care to leading the witness through his explanation. Most of the answers he gave were no more than three or four words each.

Tom said that as he sat in the dark he heard a noise at the house, and possibly someone talking. Then he claimed that he continued to sit where he was until he heard a shot. The transcript of his testimony covering the next few minutes is as follows; these utterances were more of less linked together by prompting from the Crown. When viewed in their entirety, they resemble a youngster's early attempts at reading aloud. There were often long pauses between sentences, as if Tom was not quite sure what to say next. "I heard a noise down at the house … I then heard a shot and a first noise … I heard someone speak and then noise … I jumped up … I ran to the house … I ran to the door at the kitchen … It was open … I ran in a step."

Then Tom testified that he saw Nicholas with something in his hand, and Old Melady lying near the bedroom door. At this point, Tom said he did not know what Nicholas had in his hand. He did remember his own feelings, however, and what he did. "I was excited … I ran out the door … As I ran, I saw Kehoe coming along the road leading to his place. This was about ten to fifteen minutes from the time he started. Kehoe said, 'What's up?' and then went into the house. He said, 'Oh Nicholas, what have you done?' Then Kehoe returned. I was outside the door … Then Kehoe said he thought he had better go home, and he went." Tom explained that he remained outside the door, but "looked in two or three times." Finally, he said, Nicholas came out after about half an hour.

Tom mentioned three other significant items, all of which occurred, he said, while they were at the house: he saw Nicholas putting some papers into his pocket; he saw Nicholas break a gun; and Nicholas told him to stay quiet about everything.

Harrison cross-examined the witness on these points, but also raised other items. First of all, he asked Tom if he had said he ran "a step" into the kitchen.

Donovan concurred. He did not explain exactly how he was able to run "a step." The defence lawyer looked on, incredulous.

Then Harrison asked where he left his boots.

After another interminable pause, Tom sheepishly admitted that he couldn't remember that. However, he said he knew for sure that he had been wearing socks. Harrison followed this by asking how, if he only went a step into the kitchen, his footprints were "all over the kitchen floor?" There was another long pause, some throat-clearing, and then continued silence. The witness looked decidedly uncomfortable, until he finally admitted that he had no explanation for the discrepancy.

Harrison's next query concerned the fact that Tom had told the inquest that Nicholas Melady had never been out of his sight on the night of the murder.

"Did you tell the truth at the inquest?" Harrison asked, his voice sounding nonchalant and his manner non-threatening.

"Yes," Donovan replied, obviously relieved because he could answer so readily and with certainty.

"And Nicholas was never out of your sight?"

"No," the witness responded.

"And now you tell us that he *was* out of your sight?" the lawyer continued.

"Yes."

"So which version is correct?" Harrison's voice was loud, cold, and clipped. Tom knew he had been trapped. He fidgeted, avoided the lawyer's eyes, mumbled something under his breath, and then finally told the court which version of the story he intended to use now.

"This one," Donovan replied. A murmur of reaction came from the crowd. One or two people laughed, and the judge pounded his gavel.

Harrison did not bother to pursue the line of questioning but went off on another matter. He asked Tom if it was dark in the house.

Tom said it was. The answer came readily, as if it was easy to state the obvious.

"Was there a light on?" the lawyer asked.

"No," Tom replied. Again the response was straightforward and definitive.

Then Harrison asked where Nicholas was standing when he was putting papers into his pocket.

Donovan paused briefly, as if trying to picture the scene in his mind.

"Back in the front hall, near the stairs," he replied.

The defence lawyer explained to the court that the staircase was not only across the kitchen, but several steps beyond it, well past the bedroom where the bodies lay.

"If the house was dark, how could you see the accused putting papers into his pocket?"

"There was a light on," Donovan answered quickly, as if he had completely forgotten that only two or three minutes earlier he had said exactly the opposite.

Then Harrison waved a copy of Donovan's inquest statement for the jury to see, and as he did so, he walked closer and told them they would have to decide which of the conflicting stories to believe.

There was laughter in the courtroom. Again Judge Hagarty asked for order.

Before leaving the stand, Tom told the court about going to his brother's for the night, but he could not remember how they got there. "I was so confused, I can't speak of the road we went," he said in response to the Crown's question about the route followed. He also testified that when they were crossing the river, Nicholas crossed on the log. This was a quarter of a mile from Old Melady's house. A minute or so later, he said he fell in the river at the same place Nicholas crossed on the log. This time, he said the location was "a mile from the deceased's."

He said Nicholas wore black trousers that night and a black cap, while his own pants were grey.

Tom's boots were held up for the court to see, but rather surprisingly, no questions were asked by either the Crown or defence about the blood that had been in them. Tom also told of sleeping at his brother Dave's, and then, the next morning, going to Jim Kehoe's. In answer to the Crown's question, he admitted that he had been drinking the night of the murder, "but was not drunk."

Just before stepping down, the witness identified, for the Crown, a deposition he made and signed for Goderich Justice of the Peace, Joshua Calloway, Jr. The document read: "This is the statement of Thomas Donovan, made this eighteenth day of March, 1869, in relation to the murder of Nicholas Melady and Ellen Melady (his wife). I believe that Thomas Melady, Alice Melady, and Mrs. Kehoe are aware of the murder of Nicholas Melady and Ellen Melady (his wife); and further, that I know that Nicholas Melady was the murderer, or one of the murderers."

Justice of the Peace Calloway had then added: "Taken and subscribed before me at Goderich this 18th day of March, 1869. Joshua Calloway Jr. J.P."

After Tom Donovan left the courtroom, several individuals who were able to contribute in lesser ways to the Crown's case were paraded before the jury. One of these told of seeing Jim Kehoe and Tom Donovan leaving Bummer's Roost, another of recognizing Nicholas and Tom walking towards Dave Donovan's home at dawn. Police officer Michael McNamara told of his arrival at the murder scene and what he did there. Katherine Melady, Old Melady's granddaughter who had been staying at the Kehoes', testified that Jim came in late on the night of the murder. Justice of the Peace Robert Hays told of seeing Old Melady at the Carmichael and of his dealings with both Nicholas, Sr. and Nicholas, Jr. Rather surprisingly, he told the jury, "I thought very little of the deceased." On the other hand, he said, "The prisoner had good characteristics."

By the time the witness who followed Hays was through on the stand, Nicholas would need every one of these "good characteristics."

And they would not be enough.

When the court clerk stood and called Janet Cooke, spectators in the Goderich courtroom watched with barely concealed anticipation.

190

CHAPTER 18 | THE TESTIMONY OF THE WOMAN

TWO HOURS BEFORE her testimony began at the murder trial, Janet Cooke came to the courthouse and met in a small witness room with Detective William Smith. The old detective wanted time with the young woman in order to go over everything she would say on the stand. He knew her testimony would be vital, and if she did not do a good job, the accused would walk. If that happened, months of hard work would be wasted, and the taxpaying public would be even more critical of the police work in this dragged-out investigation.

The officer told Janet the types of questions the defence would ask and the general approach that would likely be used. He stressed that she be herself and answer to the best of her ability whatever was asked. He also warned her to be wary of leading or hypothetical questions. He suggested she keep her answers as brief as possible and not stray from her topic. He also advised her to remember that the jury would be evaluating everything in her testimony, so if she could win them over, they would be more inclined to accept what she said.

Finally, just before she was called to testify, he reminded her that she knew far more about the accused and what he had told her than any defence lawyer ever would. The police officer said he had every confidence in her, and he knew she would do well. Janet smiled, thanked him, and promised that she would do her best. They shook hands, and she went into the courtroom to give the performance of a lifetime.

Few of the spectators at the trial had ever seen Mrs. Cooke. For that reason, as soon as the court clerk intoned her name, they became profoundly attentive and, almost as one, turned to watch the door through which "the woman" would enter.

Janet did not disappoint.

She walked erect and businesslike, straight to the witness stand, and in a clear, earthy voice, gave her name and her promise to tell the truth, the whole truth, and nothing but the truth. Then she glanced around the room, smiled graciously despite her nervousness, and prepared to answer any question put to her.

She did not look at the accused.

So far, the crowd seemed impressed. There were a lot of muted whispers and, from the males in the room in particular, an unspoken acknowledgement of her natural appeal and sexuality. Even the members of the jury — all men — did not attempt to conceal their reactions. Without realizing they were doing so, they sat up straight, swept their eyes over her face and figure, and prepared to hang on her every word. After years of dealing with and pleasing men, she was well aware of her effect on them, and now she was prepared to do what she could to influence these twelve strangers. If her words and actions turned them against and vilified the prisoner she had pretended to love, then that was the way it would be. She had been given a job, had done her best, and now intended to ensure that her efforts were a success. If a man died because of what she said on this day, then that was the price of her testimony. That, she told herself, was reality. She understood that and knew she could live with it. She had assured Detective Smith that whatever the future brought, she would be fine.

Newspapers that covered the trial mentioned Nicholas occasionally but did not dwell on his reactions to things said in the courtroom. From time to time, they noted how attentive he was; at other times, how seemingly bored; at others, how upset. But apart from a look of utter incredulity that crossed his face several times during Tom Donovan's testimony, his demeanour most of the time was outwardly, if artificially, rather calm.

When the woman he called his Jenny was on the stand, however, his eyes rarely left her face. Even though she could — and would — send him to his death, he never got over her. From time to time, he made notes and then passed them to his counsel. On other occasions, he leaned over and whispered to Robert Harrison, and as often lent an attentive ear when the lawyer did likewise. Occasionally, the accused read a newspaper when some of the more boring, technical matters were discussed, but never during Janet's time in the room. He loved her with every fibre of his being, and now he watched her closely, as if willing her to acknowledge him in some way, any way.

But she never returned his gaze.

We have no way of knowing if avoiding it was advice given by her mentor. William Smith had grown to know and like Janet, but he was also aware of her feelings towards Nicholas. He knew that despite being close to and seeing the prisoner on a daily basis while in jail, she had not fallen in love with him, but had found him to be pleasant, good-looking, and solicitous of her well-being. And though she had steeled herself against loving him, she did like him a lot. She also realized that he was somewhat naïve — far more so than most of the men she had known. That was why he had been so completely fooled by her words and actions.

Crown attorney Christopher Robinson began by asking the witness to tell the court about herself. He did so as a lead-up to having her testify about her time in Goderich Gaol and after, but he wanted the jury to know a little about her first.

She said that she was an American, born and raised in Michigan, but for three of the last four years had been living in Canada. She told of going to New York State for one year, but because life was not what she thought it would be there, she had returned to Canada. She had resided briefly in other towns in southern Ontario, but in due course had made her way to Goderich.

She went on to explain that she had been employed as a detective at the Goderich jail, and that her job there was temporary. She mentioned that her husband was a police officer, but they often did not see each other regularly because he worked so much. For that matter, she had not seen him now for a few days. She said that his surname was not hers, but was not asked to explain what it was. She and her husband did not have children. Later on, in his submission to the court, Harrison implied that the woman's marriage was not especially solid. However, because she had been excused from the witness stand long before the remark was made, she did not have the chance to respond to the insinuation.

After most of the preliminaries were over, Robinson asked his witness to explain how she had become involved in the case before the court.

The question seemed to be of particular interest to the accused. He sat with rapt attention, learning for the first time the particular circumstances that had ultimately led to their paths crossing. He had never known about her life in Goderich but had accepted the cover story of the counterfeiting. When the case had broken months earlier, Wilmot Squier had explained to Nicholas who "Jenny" was, but at the time, even Squier did not know she had a husband, let alone that he was a police officer. Strangely, the lawyer had not asked much about her, even after he learned that she had been a plant in the prison.

Janet also explained to the court the reason she became involved in the murder probe in the first place. McMicken had hired her, she said, for two dollars a day to try to find out what Alice Melady knew. The contact with the accused arose only after he wrote a note to her. She had not expected to meet him at all, let alone correspond with him and talk to him.

Harrison, during his cross-examination asked sarcastically if she got her two dollars in blood money.

"I have been paid in full," Janet replied.

When he heard this, Judge Hawkins carefully recorded the answer in the procedural record he kept as the murder trial progressed. His notes, in his own handwriting, can still be seen in his Bench Books, located in the Ontario Archives in Toronto.

Once he was satisfied that the jury knew why the witness had taken the job at the jail, Robinson turned to the circumstances of Janet's dealings with the accused. She began by explaining that even though she and Alice had never argued, they were far from close, and in fact Alice was, for the most part, cold and distant. Janet explained that she had let Detective Smith know that the prisoner's sister would not talk about the case at all. She had told Smith that she was willing to keep on trying to get information out of the sister, but that nothing would likely be forthcoming. The surprise came when the brother sent the first note.

Then Robinson asked her to pause for a moment while he turned to the exhibit table, picked up a manila folder, and extracted a small piece of brown paper from it.

"Is this the note that he sent you?" the lawyer asked.

Janet looked at it carefully, acknowledged that it was, and, responding to another question, told of finding the message in the exercise yard. She said she read it then, but later gave it to Smith. She was not asked to describe her feelings on getting the note. "I did not answer the first," she added, "but he wrote again, and I replied."

Robinson turned away, went back to the exhibit table, and drew several more papers from the folder. All had been numbered and filed in the sequence in which they had been received. He brought them to the witness, held them up one by one, and asked her to identify each in turn. Since sixty notes in total had been written, merely identifying these pages took some time. After they had all been accounted for and she had finished looking at the last, Janet said, "Yes, those are the letters I received from the prisoner."

For his part, the accused betrayed an emotion he had not exhibited at the trial thus far. His face was flushed, obviously with embarrassment, because these were love letters he had written. Never had he imagined they would be read by anyone other than Jenny. He now knew that the police officers and court officials had likely all seen them, and because of this revelation, he seemed to actually squirm with mortification.

But there was more to come.

Christopher Robinson proceeded to read the letters aloud. Janet listened; Nicholas listened; the crowd listened — and laughed, sometimes uproariously. For that reason, not long afterwards, the matter was mentioned in the *Huron Expositor*. In an editorial on Friday, October 22, the paper criticized the reading of the notes, calling the act of doing so a kind of public torture:

> We wonder that the society for the prevention of cruelty to animals has never got up an agitation against the practice of reading old love letters in Courts of Law. Compared with this exquisite and prolonged torture of fickle humanity, what is bull baiting or cock fighting, what is plucking off the feathers of live poultry, or skinning of live eels? What other elaborate anguish, in fact, can be named in the same breath?
>
> The wretched defendant must writhe at these entertaining passages. They seemed so eloquent and true when they gushed from the passionate pen, with no destination imagined for them but to be read with bright eyes, kissed by ruby lips, and hidden away in the secret safety of a beating bosom.
>
> Now however, as [the Crown attorney] mouths them for the court, glaring with forensic joy at all the flowery bits and fond underlinings, each word becomes a torment, a Nemesis; a terror. It used to be nice to fancy them, carefully folded and numbered, tied with a dainty piece of ribbon in a true

love-knot, and put away, if not just as we have imagined, at least in the private apartment of "her" desk for occasional delicious study. To see them thus ferociously docketed for legal warfare, bound about with horrible red tape, and produced one by one, while a snigger runs around the court, and a jurisprudential chuckle echoes up and down the bar — that must be anguish, despair, madness itself.

Nevertheless, the letters were read, and not just once. Later on in the judicial summary addresses, they were brought out again, this time by the defence.

Robinson asked his witness to tell the court how long she was in the jail, and once there, how she got to know the accused as well as she did.

"I was there for about a month, in total," she explained. "I went in on a counterfeiting charge. I suppose the purpose was known to the jail authorities, but I never saw the warrant myself."

Then she related the circumstances under which the correspondence with the prisoner was conducted. She told the court about being in the prison yard and of finding the first couple of notes beneath the window of the cell where the accused was at the time. She went on to explain how the correspondence was conducted.

"The boy who brought the wood to my ward, brought the letters," she testified. "I also started to talk to the prisoner about the charges against him." She mentioned the location of the accused's cell and the position of the window through which they talked. She said she could stand outside it and whisper and he could hear her. He did not have to leave his cell to answer.

As she said this, Janet smiled conspiratorially, drank a sip of water from a glass in front of her, and glanced around the room. Then she set the glass back down, clasped her hands in front of her, and waited, smiling and patient, for the Crown's next question.

Spectators in the packed room kept a dutiful silence, and the jury members leaned forward in anticipation of what the next revelations might be. Nicholas looked on, as before, as if wondering himself just what she might say now. The witness revelled in the attention. It was as if she were posing for a roomful of portrait artists.

"Go on," Robinson directed, quickly bringing the seriousness of the situation to the fore.

"We often talked," she said. "I spoke to him through his cell window, during the day, and also in the evening. The conversations became more important." At this point, Janet stopped, ensured that she had the undivided attention of the jury, and added, "Finally he detailed the charge against him."

There was an audible gasp of surprise from the overflow crowd. Nicholas flinched and swallowed hard, but his gaze never left his lover's face. No doubt he wondered what was coming next.

"The night before I left the jail, he said that if I ever told anyone all the things he had told me, he would be convicted for sure. But he said he knew he could trust me," she added.

A ripple of conversation swept the courtroom, but died away as quickly as it began. A few of the jurors looked at each other. The remark was interpreted by most as indicative of the gullibility of the accused. His face flushed.

Christopher Robinson asked his witness to explain what she meant.

"Well, he said the crime was committed about twelve o'clock, and he said he was guilty, but that he felt there was a means of getting clear. He said he would be all right if no one saw them coming from the deceased's house. Then no one could bring evidence against them. About an hour or two before I left, he said his only hope of getting out was for me to get him five hundred dollars to buy evidence." Janet went on to explain that the prisoner wanted her to get the money to bribe jury members. "He also said one of his lawyers had a man engaged to swear he was in a different place on the Saturday night."

This revelation caused an immediate and prolonged reaction from Nicholas's legal team. Not only had they not heard of it before, it had not been mentioned in any of the letters, and in reality it was a blatant falsehood. Nicholas had never at any time indicated that his lawyers were to bribe anyone. Robert Harrison jumped to his feet and protested the allegation vociferously. The way in which the witness had mentioned the bribe by a lawyer reflected on him personally, and he was having none of it. Harrison assured the court such a stratagem never happened. Finally, as soon as Harrison completed his protest, the testimony continued. Janet then went on to other matters that the prisoner had supposedly confided in her.

"He told me David Donovan would help in any way her could," she explained. "He told me that David would throw a revolver over the jail wall, and if he could not get away any other way, he would use it. He also told me that if all else failed, he could put the blame for the murders on McGoey and his wife."

Whether the prisoner actually said these things is open to question. There is no record today that would lead us to believe there was much truth in any of them. Tom McGoey was not recalled to the stand and questioned as to whether he ever thought his brother-in-law would say such a thing. His wife, Nicholas's own sister, did not testify at all. There had been minor conflicts between Nicholas and the McGoeys, but in general, Nicholas had always been on good terms with both. And even though Dave Donovan appeared as a character witness for the accused, the Crown never asked him about the gun story at all. If it had been true, it is likely Christopher Robinson would have used it in order to further solidify his case. Had the prisoner intended to use a gun in a jailbreak, surely such an action would have been interpreted as an admission of guilt in the murders themselves.

In all likelihood, Janet Cooke said what she did in order to further ingratiate herself with the jurors. She was the star of the day, and by going out of her way to fabricate evidence, she enhanced her importance in the entire trial. She loved being the centre of attraction, and as long as she was on the stand, she intended to play that role. She looked at the jurors often, smiled at them, and played to their sensitivities. She knew they liked her, and most of the time it seemed as if she were putting on a performance for them. She also told how, once she got the prisoner to fall for her, she moved to cement their relationship. "I presented him with several small presents in jail," she said, smiling demurely, almost whispering to the juror closest to her.

The Crown did not ask what these gifts were, and Janet did not elaborate. She told the jurors that the prisoner had given her a photograph of himself, but that she got rid of it quickly because she did not want it at all. "Mr. McMicken has it now," she added, with an air of mock disdain. Harrison seems to have disregarded this statement. He did not even bother to ask McMicken if such a photo existed.

After her testimony for the Crown, the witness was cross-examined, briefly and inconsequentially, and then allowed to step down. Because of the overall impact of everything Janet had said, Harrison elected to make his most telling statements against her in his final address to the court, rather than now, at the close of her testimony. He knew, instinctively, that anything said against the woman now would be largely disregarded by the enthralled jurors.

Nicholas sat in silence and watched as the woman he loved left the witness stand, smiled at the twelve jurors she had held in the palm of her hand, and walked from the room. He never saw her again.

The courtroom seemed to lose its lustre when Janet left. The jurors, in particular, looked as though they had to force themselves back to reality, to remind themselves that they were in the middle of a murder trial, and that it was a serious affair. Because Janet and Tom were the two most important witnesses that would be heard, the testimony of others who followed was somewhat anti-climactic. Nevertheless, there were still holes in the Crown's case, and Christopher Robinson set about filling them as quickly as he could.

His next witnesses were Constable Hugh Grant and Coroner T.T. Coleman. Much of what these men had to say was complementary; what one forgot to mention, the other recalled. They told of following the foot-prints to the river and then to the Donovan home, and of locating both the wet pair of trousers and the boots with blood inside. The articles were held up in court and identified, first by Grant and then by Coleman.

"The boots were very wet," Grant testified, "and later Thomas Donovan told me they were his. They compared exactly with the nail marks and the tracks. I gave the boots to the coroner."

For his part, Coleman mentioned the blood poured out of the boots, and elaborated somewhat on the trousers found at Donovan's. "They were wet to the knees," he said under oath, "and there was new blood on them. We also found a wet shirt there, and it looked as though someone had attempted to wash it." He identified the shirt when it was held up in the courtroom, but did not indicate who he thought might have owned it — or washed it.

Then Robinson led Coleman to the crime scene. "The kitchen floor was covered with blood tracks," the doctor told the court, "and water seemed to have thrown over it. The footprints were quite plain. It seemed as if in some of them, the toes escaped from the stockings." His wording caused slight laughter among the spectators.

Robinson asked the coroner to tell the court about comparing the footprints. "I put the prisoner's foot in the tracks," Coleman explained. "He pulled off his boots willingly, but we had some difficulty making him put his feet in the marks. He looked alarmed and excited." Robinson asked how the prisoner's feet and the size of the tracks compared. Coleman said they "corresponded exactly."

Just before the coroner left the witness stand, Robinson asked if he was acquainted with the accused. Coleman looked over at Nicholas and replied, "Yes, I have known him a long time."

After Coleman had left the room, two men who might have been called minor players in the murder drama were sworn in, heard, and rather quickly excused. The first was an express agent from Seaforth. Caleb H. Cull told the court that it was he who sent a hat to Professor Croft at the University of Toronto. "I remember sending it down by express," Cull testified. "It was sealed in my presence by Doctor Coleman."

Cull was followed to the witness stand by Croft himself. "On the thirteenth of June, the hat was sent to me by express," he testified. "It came as a secure parcel, and carried Doctor Coleman's seal." The man identified the headgear for the court.

Robinson asked the chemistry professor what studies he had made on the hat. "I examined it for stains," he replied, "and there were three on it. I cut one of them off in order to check it more closely, and even though it was dried blood for sure, I could not say if it was human."

"How long have you been a chemistry professor?" Robinson inquired.

"For twenty-nine years," the man replied. He then stepped down. Harrison did not question him, nor, surprisingly, did he cross-examine Coleman.

The controversial finding of the gunshot pellets in the pocket of the accused took almost an hour of the court's time late in the afternoon on the first day of the trial. Detective Bernard Trainer was on the stand when the subject first arose.

The Crown attorney held up a pair of black pants and asked Trainer to identify them. He said they belonged to Nicholas Melady, Jr. "I found them at Kehoe's," the policeman stated. "They hung on the back of a bedroom door. Mrs. Kehoe told me they did not belong to her husband, and the accused identified them for me by a tear in the seat. He said he was getting out of a wagon when they got ripped."

Robinson asked the officer to tell the court what he had found in one of the pockets.

"Core was with me," Trainer replied, referring to fellow policeman William Core. "We found the pants together, and then we examined them in front of the door, in the sunlight. They were not wet, and there were no blood marks on them that I saw, but we found some shot in one of the pockets. There was also a pipe and some paper."

Trainer was excused, and Constable Core was asked to take the stand. "Yes, I was there when we found the trousers," the policeman testified. "I took the shot out of the pocket. There was also some yellow paper."

"Where are those things now?" Robinson asked.

"I gave the paper and the shot to the coroner," Core answered.

By this time the jurymen were starting to get restless at the repetitive testimony. They looked around, seemed to lose interest, and slouched in their seats. Two of the men looked as if they were falling asleep. Because of the warm September afternoon and the capacity crowd, the courtroom was hot and the air was stagnant, and the legal procedures were monotonous.

But when Coleman was called back to the stand, the spectators seemed to revive. The forty-one-year-old doctor was a dynamic character in his own right, and he had the ability to become the centre of attention no matter where he was. A native of Tralee, Ireland, Coleman was a natural raconteur, but he could be direct and uncompromising in his opinions. Because he had not been in the courtroom when Trainer and Core testified, he had not heard them mention the shot found in the pocket at Kehoe's. As soon as he was back in the witness box, the Crown asked about the pants mentioned by the two policemen.

"Yes, I went to Kehoe's on the Monday, I think it was," Coleman testified. "I found the trousers there and I searched them."

Coleman was asked what he found in the pockets.

"I found a pipe and a pocket book."

"Did you find any shot in the trousers?" Robinson asked.

"No," Coleman answered.

"You are certain?" Robinson asked.

"There was a pipe and a pocket book," the coroner replied crisply, "there was no shot there!" His voice became louder.

The doctor, who at the time was also commanding officer of the Huron Battalion, a county army regiment, stood ramrod straight, a picture of a military colonel. When he said there was no shot in the pockets, there was no shot in the pockets. His words brooked no argument.

The Crown attorney turned his back to the witness, walked to the exhibit table, and picked up an envelope containing the ammunition. He asked Coleman about it. "This was the shot that Trainer produced," the witness declared with finality. The doctor did not specifically state that the policeman had planted the evidence. He did, however, imply as much.

Coleman was excused.

The concluding part of the Crown's case concerned the account book found in the Bayfield River at the time of the tracking done by Coleman and Vercoe, Tom Gemmell, James McMulkin, and police officers Grant and Trainer. Both Gemmell and McMulkin told the court about finding the book, and both said they had identified it at the inquest.

Gemmell testified that he was the one who had lifted it from the water. "I saw it with the coroner fifteen minutes after I found it," he stated, "but I cannot say who gave it to the coroner. I originally handed it to Grant." When Constable Grant was called to the stand, he said he gave the book to Vercoe, and he believed Vercoe gave it to Coleman.

But whatever the order of examination, the notebook ended up with Detective Trainer.

Then he lost it.

Bernard Trainer was recalled. "I can't swear where I got the note-book," the policeman testified. "The coroner gave me a lot of books and papers at the murder scene, and a trunk that was there. I brought them all to Goderich."

"Where was the trunk stored?" Robinson asked.

"At the jail," said Trainer.

"Was the trunk locked?"

The witness looked decidedly uncomfortable. He started to say something, then paused, and finally admitted, "No, it was not. It was up at the jail since the last assizes."

"Was the notebook in the trunk?" asked Robinson.

"Yes," replied Trainer. "I think so."

"And you have no idea where it is now?"

"No."

The defence did not pursue the matter.

While its loss did not do irreparable harm to the Crown's case, the missing book was nonetheless important in establishing that the murderers had been in Old Melady's house on the night he was killed. The notebook, the footprints in the kitchen, and the bloody boots at Dave Donovan's were part of the thread that tied the investigation together.

The *Huron Expositor* reporter, in his account of the matter on September 17, explained that even though the missing item "had been identified at the inquest, it was not to be found." That being the case, the reporter added, "one strong link in the evidence was lost."

Eleven witnesses for the defence were called at the trial of the Queen vs. Nicholas Melady. Almost all of them were ineffectual. Three were police officers who ended up arguing about one of their numbers who was drunk during the investigation at the murder scene.

Another witness was named John Curry. He told the court he kept a saloon in Seaforth, and he had personally witnessed Nicholas Melady, Sr., with a lot of cash. "He did not take much care of his money," the hotel owner recalled. "He would show it in the barroom and would boast of it." The implication of the testimony was that Old Melady could have been robbed by anyone, as the defence attorney then alleged.

Leopold Van Egmond testified in his role as a gunsmith, but what he said was of more help to Jim than it was to Nicholas. Van Egmond merely stated that the gun Trainer had confiscated at the Kehoe residence had not been recently fired.

One man got on the stand and said that witnesses could be mistaken. Then he stepped down. Today, there is nothing in the records of the trial that explains exactly who the individual was, or even why he was called.

Dave Donovan, his wife, and Alice Melady all testified as to the approximate time Nicholas and Tom arrived home. Their comments were contradictory and vague. None seemed to know the time, or if they did, they were not prepared to tell the court.

Two other witnesses made significant remarks, but ultimately neither would do much for the accused. The first was Margaret Kehoe. She talked about the pair of pants that she, the coroner, and Trainer had searched. In her testimony, she agreed with Coleman. There was no ammunition in the pockets when she checked them. Then she strongly implied that Trainer had taken the trousers outside so that he could plant evidence.

One final bit of information was brought to the attention of the court. A woman named Margaret Miller, a sister of Tom and Dave Donovan's, testified about her knowledge of Old Melady. She repeated the widely held observation that he was not careful with his money, and that when he got drunk, he became argumentative. She went on to say, "Old Melady feared for his life about two months before his death."

Harrison asked how she knew that.

"We invited him and his wife to our house," Miller explained, "but he told us he could not come."

"Why could he not come?" defence lawyer Harrison asked.

"He said he could not go out because he was afraid," Miller answered.

"What was he afraid of?" Harrison continued.

"He was afraid that a man from Tecumseth named Lester would take his life. I know from my own knowledge that he was threatened."

"Did you mention this at the inquest?"

"No."

"Why not?"

"Because I wasn't asked."

Harrison dropped the matter.

Finally, the last witness had been heard, the last scraps of condemnatory and defence arguments were made, and the final item of information was incorporated into the record of the trial. Now it would be up to three men to summarize what had transpired: the Crown attorney, the defence attorney, and the judge. Once they finished, the fate of the defendant would be handed to twelve men who never wanted to have such a terrible responsibility.

CHAPTER 19 | CLOSING ARGUMENTS

THE CLOSING ARGUMENTS at the Melady murder trial were among the most powerful ever made in a Canadian court of law. And no wonder. The three men involved, Judge John Hawkins Hagarty, Crown attorney Christopher Robinson, and defence attorney Robert Harrison, are widely regarded as giants in the history of criminal jurisprudence in this country. Two became Chief Justices for the Province of Ontario. Two were offered knighthoods. One was a widely respected and influential member of parliament. All three wrote extensively about their chosen profession, and they were routinely consulted in matters of legal interpretation. All were highly educated, and all were brilliant.

In their concluding statements to this trial, they left us with clear, balanced, and carefully crafted treatises concerning the guilt or innocence of the man being tried. None of the three was unduly flamboyant, yet all were reasonable men, sure of themselves, and convinced of the essential worth and strength of the law. The controversial and lacklustre investigation of the crime was balanced by what, in Melady's case, was a just and warranted conclusion. And although the same thing cannot be said about the ultimate fate of his accomplices, the blame for the matter cannot be attributed to the three jurists who dealt with Nicholas. He had a fair trial, and its result was not unexpected.

The final arguments began with the defence attorney's address to the court at noon on Friday, September 17. His summation, along with those of the Crown and the judge, were covered widely, but, understandably, with particular prominence in the *Huron Expositor*. That paper devoted extensive space to the trial in the September 24, 1869, edition. Much of the reporting was a verbatim account of courtroom procedures.

"May it please your Lordship, and gentlemen of the Jury," began Robert Harrison as he stood before the court and bowed to His Honour.

"I have to congratulate you on the termination of this tedious trial and the approaching close of the proceedings. Upon the decision you give depends on the life or death of the prisoner at the Bar. You are to arrive at the conclusion that he is 'guilty' or 'not guilty.' Some members of the Press have injudiciously written about this case, which is most disreputable. I ask you, gentlemen of the Jury, if you have formed an opinion from what you have heard or read, to disregard it from your mind. No doubt a great and atrocious crime has been committed in our midst. People in their anxiety to detect crime are apt to distort or magnify facts, likely to lead men astray. This anxiety has existed since this fatal occurrence took place. When once a man is suspected, he is watched and dogged; inference upon inference is drawn from every circumstance.

"The evidence has been of two kinds, circumstantial and positive. Take from the evidence of a man who is an accomplice; of a woman of many aliases, and of biased constables, and what have you? Constables, detectives, and others who trace crime, and give evidence with an eye to interest. They go to work to bag their game, and if they don't bag their game, they are discharged. The testimony of those who testify for money should be received with extreme caution. Reflect on the danger of relying on this," Harrison said. As he made these remarks, one wonders if any jury members thought back to Janet Cooke's testimony. When she was before them, they had hung on her every word. Now, listening to Harrison, were they in any way swayed by him from the opinions they held?

The defence attorney elaborated on his views of Tom Donovan's testimony and pointed out to the jury that they should be wary "of persons who are connected with crime, who have told untruths when it involves the life of a human being." Harrison paused, then cut to the heart of what Tom had said. In so doing, he strongly suggested that Nicholas's friend was a liar. "Facts can't lie, but witnesses can lie, can distort, and can exaggerate. The Crown has got to prove more than suspicion; it has to establish guilt. There are such doubts and difficulties in this case that it would be unsafe for you to give a verdict of 'guilty.'"

Then Harrison made pertinent observations that had not been given much attention during the earlier portions of the trial. "This man had money," he said in reference to Old Melady, "and would scatter it about when drunk. Before he died, he produced a roll of bills containing about five hundred dollars, and a second roll nearly as large. He was a quarrelsome man, a drinking man. The motive for the murder was robbery. But there was no trace of money on the prisoner, no trace of bank notes. The wife was murdered on the principle that dead men tell no tales." He continued, "The Crown says that the prisoner at the Bar is the guilty one; guilty of the most terrible murder that a man can be, the murder of his father, the man who gave him being." Harrison dropped his voice to little more than a whisper, pointed at Nicholas, and asked the jury members who were listening intently, "Gentlemen, look at that man. Do you suppose him capable of so horrible a crime as patricide? Would he have remained in this country one day? Did he go? No! Hounded by his neighbours, made to put his feet in his father's blood, what wonder if he was nervous? You must be ready to swear he is guilty, suspicion won't do."

He continued, "Suppose you had only Thomas Donovan's story in this case. What is that story? He says he heard a noise; he took off his boots, prepared to run. When he was asked why he took off his boots, you saw his tremor. He could not tell why he took off his boots, and then could not tell where he put them. He took them off and walked to the house. He stayed there for three quarters of an hour to an hour, and then walked home."

The defence attorney then looked down at a sheaf of papers in his hand, and explained that he was now going to ask his audience to think back to the inquest, and Tom Donovan's recorded testimony given at that time.

"Thomas Donovan took an oath before the coroner," Harrison reminded the jury. "Is it possible to take an oath if one has lied? If he lied before, he may lie now. A perjurer is not the man to be depended upon in a case of life and death. Thomas Donovan's oath at the inquest is corroborated. He swore then that he and the prisoner went to David Donovan's house, and never parted company. Yesterday, he swore they parted company. He says he sat on the timber while Nicholas went towards the house. Yesterday he says they did part. Here is perjury."

Then Harrison cut to the grain of his presentation insofar as Tom Donovan was concerned. The defence lawyer walked across the room to the exhibit table, tossed the transcript of the inquest on top of a pile of other papers, collected his thoughts, and came back to the jury box. He planted his feet wide apart, and in a loud voice that dripped with sarcasm repeated his last sentence and then explained it.

"Here is perjury!" he thundered. "Donovan comes to court with a rope around his neck and asks the Crown not to tighten it. He does not *care* whose life is forfeited if he saves his own. Contrast his evidence at the inquest, when there was no rope around his neck; no gallows before his eyes. Is not the probability of truth on the side of the oath at the inquest weightier than the probability of truth yesterday?" he asked. "Are you prepared to believe his oath at the inquest, or his oath yesterday? Looking at his oath against his oath, it is not safe to take his evidence when life is involved." Harrison had gradually worked himself up to the declaration that would ring through the courthouse halls and follow Tom Donovan for years afterwards. The lawyer referred to Tom as a "coward, who turned squeamish, afraid of the trial." Harrison continued, "Either he was not at the murder, or he did it himself. Supposing he was there, who did it? These tracks are Donovan's. He who knew the Old Man had money; he who had no regular home, was not a steady worker, is he not likely to be a guilty man? Having compared his history, his prevarication, and his oath, against his oath, I ask you, what reliance can you place on his testimony?"

At this point, Harrison paused, walked over to his desk, and quickly glanced over some of the notations he had made during Janet Cooke's time on the stand. He rearranged two or three of the yellow lined papers in front of him and then set out to tear her testimony to shreds. In choosing to deal with Tom first, it had been obvious that the lawyer regarded the man's account as more damaging to his client, but he knew what Mrs. Cooke had to say was almost as critical. In the words that followed, he painted her in the most negative light possible.

"Now gentlemen," he began, addressing the twelve men who had been so enraptured with Janet and had treasured her every word, "let us now consider the next witness, Mrs. Cooke, Mrs. Bond, Mrs. Smith, Mrs. Halton and several other aliases. Taking all things together, her conduct is most disreputable, a disgrace to her sex, sent to jail to entrap Alice Melady, and then attract a man to love her, to lead him to the gallows. What cannot be done by moral means should not be done by strategy. Though this evidence is admissible, the machinery is disreputable. To send a woman into a cell with all the arts and smiles of Cupid, with all the fascinating charms and witchery of her sex, to betray with letters, love, and kisses this confiding, generous, truthful, and honest man." Harrison pointed to Nicholas as these words were said, as if to remind the jury that the trial was about the man who sat before them; the man who was wronged by the machinations of a beautiful woman. "By putting on all her wiles, smiles and curls, she drew him out, like a snake. Believing this woman who promised to procure him some money to bribe jury and witness, believing her to be an angel sent to deliver him, he was betrayed by a hireling, trafficking her love for two dollars a day." Harrison almost spat these words, as if what they represented was beneath contempt.

The jurors watched and listened, but they did not react. Harrison realized this, but if it bothered him, he did not let on. He went to the exhibit table, took a few seconds to select the ones he wanted, then, with a handful of Nicholas's letters, came back to the jury.

As the twelve men sat in silence, Harrison read to them — read parts of the same notes they had already heard, but now stressed the writer's pining for Jenny, not the snatches of confession the Crown had highlighted earlier. "'God knows I am innocent,'" he read from one. Then he repeated the words. "'God knows I am innocent,' says the prisoner in one of his letters to that deceitful woman. A letter full of love, honour, and honesty."

Harrison pointed to Nicholas, then turned back to the jury. "There is the man, gentlemen of the Jury. There is the truthful, confiding, innocent man who calls God to witness his innocence, and there *she* comes, the base counterfeiter, offering bribes, vowing fidelity to the man who wrote those manly, honest, honourable letters. Suppose it is true, he wanted her to bribe," said Harrison, "is it evidence of guilt? Is it consistent with innocence, to fabricate evidence in peculiar circumstances? She says she was discharged in December, but she goes back again to write down his every expression. Now we have him heart and soul. In the early part of January she gets the long looked-for confession. When she got the confession of guilt, she kept up the deceit. The leech when gorged with blood, drops off. After *she* leaves the prison she keeps up the disguise, mailing the letters in Buffalo, wishing him good health, and sending the prisoner a 'kiss,' a Judas kiss. The human leech still sucks his blood, and betrays his life. A pretty face and a dishonest woman!"

Once he had finished most of what he had to say about Tom and Janet, Harrison turned to other, lesser factors that had been part of the murder investigation. He dealt with these individually, and in so doing presented extenuating circumstances that he felt the jury should consider. In effect, he was explaining how unreliable the circumstantial evidence was.

As his lawyer addressed the jury, Nicholas listened with care, watching both the twelve men who would decide his fate and the man who was labouring so hard to plant seeds of doubt in ground that was obviously arid. Some jury members looked as though they just wanted to get the whole thing over with. One man in the front made a big production of checking the time on his pocket watch. And all twelve were hungry, because Judge Hagarty had informed the court that no meal break would be taken before the submissions ended.

"The prisoner bears a good character, not likely to commit so heinous a crime. We have heard of threats; many a threat is made as idle wind, no sooner made than forgotten. A threat must be a recent one; a persistent and continuous one. What is the threat the prisoner is charged with? He said the father should not bring another woman home. A very common and natural thing, for grown-up persons to object to their aged parent marrying. Now I don't want to say anything bad about the Old Man. Nobody said anything good of him. But after giving this boy a lease, he sought to destroy it," Harrison said.

"The man who found the burnt stockings in the stove at David Donovan's could not tell whether they belonged to a boy or a man, so they proved nothing. The detective had to admit that the book found in the river was lost. The shot was put in the pocket by one interested, a detective. The coroner searches the pockets and finds a pipe. Mrs. Kehoe searches and finds a pipe. Trainer searches the pockets, so often searched, and finds the shot. As for the boots; they show you they are Donovan's boots. Then the barefoot tracks; there is no peculiarity about them, for in many million men, many would be the same. Professor Croft found blood on the hat. Does that prove it was Melady's blood? Suspicion rests on the prisoner. If a handkerchief is found with blood, is it Melady's blood?" he concluded.

Once or twice during this submission, a few of the jurors looked as though they were considering some of these factors for the first time. Occasionally an individual nodded in apparent agreement with what the defence was saying. The man with the pocket watch was not impressed, and he took pains to show it, but all the others were reasonably attentive. We have no way of telling how Harrison read his audience, but he gave his all in his conclusion, and the spectators in the room sensed the importance of what they were about to hear.

"Gentlemen of the Jury," he stated, "I do my best at all times for my client, but with you rests the greater responsibility. I have shown you how the evidence is unreliable. I have shown you how the prisoner is surrounded by enemies, suspicious and detecting, but I would rather be Melady, a prisoner in that box, than Donovan a free man. Melady says 'I am a young man, a world before me; don't send me so soon after my father.' Gentlemen of the Jury, pause before you send this young man to eternity — on the evidence of a female detective, and a perjured accomplice. God gave him his life. You can take it away, but don't take it away with a doubt in your mind."

Then the attorney walked back to his desk and sat down in a silent courtroom.

The reporter for the *Expositor* told his readers what he thought of the Crown attorney's address, and then reproduced much of it: "This was a calm, deliberate speech defending the detective system, and placing the evidence before the jury, in a plain, explicit style."

Robinson addressed Judge Hagarty and the jury, and then began his summation with words of praise for the defence. "My Lord and Gentlemen," he said, his voice booming to the farthest reaches of the chamber. "It is a satisfaction that the prisoner has had such an able defence, so strongly and forcibly put. I ask you, with my learned friend, to clear your minds of all you have ever heard or read on this subject, for a gross injustice has been done to the prisoner."

As he said this, he asked the court clerk to hand him a copy of the *Globe* that was on a desk a few steps away. Robinson held the paper up and drew the jury's attention to a story about the double murder that had run the previous spring. "Whoever published this article deserves the severest punishment; deserves the censure of every man. But I have implicit confidence in your justice and rest the case with you, conscious that judgement will be done." In the story Robinson pointed out, the newspaper had strongly implied that Nicholas was guilty and had even published Tom Donovan's affidavit saying so. Whether or not it had any significant effect on the jury is impossible to determine.

The Crown attorney then defended the methods used in the investigation of the murder. "I differ from my learned friend," Robinson explained to the jury. "He said it was morally wrong to use secret detectives, but on me rests the responsibility of using stratagems. Crime is generally done in secret, and secrecy must be used to bring murderers to justice. Inducements of pardon must be held out to accomplices to divulge the secret crimes of their confederates. Many a murderer is brought to justice, many a gang of robbers brought to punishment by means of detectives. I believe the great object of servants of the Crown is to secure evidence to punish the guilty and protect society. I would rather see the prisoner walk out of that box a free man than shake the confidence in the administration of justice," he declared.

"Let us look at the evidence. There is Mrs. Cooke. Are we not justified in receiving her evidence? We did not send her to ask Nicholas Melady for a confession. *He* commenced the correspondence. Does it not look like God's Providence; a discourse, so unexpected and unlooked for to occur?" he asked.

Then Robinson dealt, head on, with the matter of entrapment — one of the major criticisms of the Crown's handling of the case. Defence attorney Harrison looked up, listened carefully, and waited to learn just how the Crown intended to deal with the matter. Nicholas paid equally careful attention.

"We do not think it would be right to place her there to entrap him," Robinson admitted, "but when *he* comes to her, when *he* commenced it, should we not accept it?" The question was left with an implied affirmative.

"Would my learned friend tell you, in his seat in Parliament, to do away with the detective system? [The reference pertained to the fact that at the time, Robert Harrison was the sitting member for the West

Toronto riding in the House of Commons.] If there is one system better than another, it is the employment of detectives. You must be careful and cautious in receiving her evidence," Robinson said Mrs. Cooke, "but whether she is honest or not, the letters are there. No one can deny them, and if you draw a wrong inference, on you rests the responsibility."

The Crown attorney then turned his attention to Tom Donovan. What the jurist would say seemed of particular importance to the accused. He put aside the *Globe* story that his lawyer had handed him and listened more closely, curious as to what the Crown would actually make of his former friend's testimony. Robinson's initial remark was somewhat unexpected, but what followed it was predictable.

"No doubt you must receive Donovan's confession with caution," he began, "but if we disbelieve accomplices, we discourage criminals from divulging the secret history of their confederates in crime. The exposure keeps them in dread of each other. And though we despise the informer, and loathe his occupation, we must receive his evidence when corroborated by other circumstances. If we disbelieve accomplices and discourage those who give information, we remove the power we have over criminals. It is the means by which the greatest crimes on record are discovered.

"We find that before the murder, the deceased had law with the prisoner, in Stratford, about land. The Old Man lived on the worst terms with his family. We are not inquiring now whether Donovan is guilty or not, whether he told the whole truth or not at the inquest. It is an undoubted fact that Donovan was there. There are Donovan's boot tracks and the nails in his boot tracks. If they were both there that night, and the prisoner can't prove otherwise, it is consistent with probability that Donovan told the truth. I shall not use eloquence, for the Crown need not resort to such means to find a cause against the prisoner, or influence a jury. Just the same right as a person has to receive a fair trial; just the same right the public has to be protected.

"I have listened in vain for the prisoner's Defence to explain his own whereabouts on that Saturday night. Do you think it is possible that Donovan was there and the prisoner not? If you can acquit him, consistent with evidence, give him the benefit of your doubt. If not, painful as it is, you must find him guilty.

"My learned friend tells you that the prisoner is candid, honourable, and just. Can it be that a person who would bribe witnesses is honourable, or just? Would not an honourable man go to his grave with his innocence, in fact his soul unsullied rather than tarnish his reputation by bribery? My learned friend says that fabrication of evidence and admission of guilt has been drawn from him, and portrays him as innocence itself. Do you think that is the character of the prisoner at the bar?

"Your position, gentlemen, is one of responsibility. There are cases when men have suffered wrong. Men have been hanged on the suspicion of murder, when the supposed murdered man returned. But we know Melady, Senior is dead."

In his concluding remarks, Christopher Robinson summarized the case for the Crown, and told the jury members to do their duty. His words were succinct, eloquent, and powerful. "Examine the evidence carefully," he said to the twelve men who sat before him, "but if you have a reasonable doubt, acquit him." Then he asked one critical question that had never been answered by the Defence. "If Donovan was there on the evening of the sixth of June, where was the prisoner? The Crown has spared no pain to ferret out the criminal," Robinson continued. "The Crown has offered no reward, held out no enticement, but used all legitimate means through an efficient detective to bring the guilty to justice. If we have failed, the Crown has failed honourably. I ask you, gentlemen of the jury, to find a verdict that will justify your conscience, satisfy the public, and do justice to the prisoner."

Then Robinson bowed to the bench and walked back to his table.

For some moments, there was an air of spent silence in the Goderich courtroom. The midday sun shone through the high windows, and tiny dust motes hung in the air, caught momentarily in the shafts of light. Robinson poured a glass of water from a pitcher that stood amid the papers before him. When the glass was empty, he put it down and started to collate the notes that he had used. As he did so, the spectators watched, as if they too understood that a Crown attorney's materials were supposed to be in order.

All eyes turned to the judge. "His Lordship charged the jury, reading the evidence and commenting on the strong and weak points of prosecution and defence, amid profound silence," the *Expositor* reported.

"Gentlemen of the Jury," Judge Hagarty began, "Thomas Donovan and Nicholas Melady were charged jointly with the crime of murder in the indictment, yet only Nicholas Melady was tried. Apart from Thomas Donovan's evidence, and the female detective's, the other evidence would break down.

"The Coroner found no shot in the prisoner's trousers, therefore there is some doubt about it. If Donovan's testimony is believed, then you have no doubt as to the prisoner's guilt. If you accept his evidence as true, then there can be no doubt. The jury should not receive the evidence of an accomplice without it being corroborated.

"Had Donovan held his tongue, there is not a shadow of a doubt that the prisoner would be free. Else there was no evidence against him. Thomas Donovan tells you that he and the prisoner were there, on the day in question. If Thomas Donovan's story is correct, he took no part in it, and knew nothing of the crime. If Tomas Donovan has made up the story, why risk his own safety? Why did he not confess fifteen months ago?

"Why Donovan made the admission is a mystery to me. He made no attempt to fly. Either he thought there was a heavier case against him than there was, or his statement is true."

Judge Hagarty then dealt with the controversial employment of the female detective. His reasoning was succinct and informative, and both the Crown and defence attorneys took notes on what he had to say. He mentioned both men in his statement.

"Mr. Harrison spoke severely against the woman, and even Mr. Robinson indicated that ordinarily, gathering evidence in such a way should be avoided. But without the use of secret detectives, most crimes would go unpunished. Gang after gang of burglars are detected by accomplices, turning informer. Without informers, murders done in secret would go unpunished. It is a necessary evil.

"This woman went to jail under a false warrant for counterfeiting. Letters and presents passed between the two of them. She says they talked together, but whether you believe this or not, there are the letters. The prisoner, after pleading innocence, writes to her and incriminates himself. If this man in his folly said he would bribe witnesses, it does not necessarily prove him guilty. You are not trying the prisoner for bribery.

215

"Whatever your verdict will be, the prisoner must say he had a patient hearing. Every human means has been used to find out the perpetrators of this horrible crime, and we have heard all sides as rational men."

His Honour informed the jury that they should come to one of three conclusions at the end of their deliberations. They could find the prisoner guilty, not guilty, or, in what was called the Scotch verdict, not proven. Then the judge summarized the viewpoints and delivered a caution. "If you believe Thomas Donovan," Hagarty pointed out, "there is no moral doubt of Melady's guilt. However when you go into your room, if you have reasonable doubt, give the prisoner its benefit. But if you feel that the evidence is conclusive, it is your duty to find him guilty."

The jury retired at two o'clock in the afternoon.

The jury at Nicholas Melady's trial deliberated for seven hours and twenty minutes. At 9:00 p.m., they sent a message to Judge Hagarty and asked for guidance in a matter of technical law. Shortly afterwards, they informed him that they had made a decision. Then they filed back into the courtroom with the verdict.

CHAPTER 20 | THE TRIAL WITHIN THE TRIAL

INCREDIBLE AS IT may seem today, in the relatively short time the jury for Nicholas Melady, Jr. deliberated in an anteroom, another complete trial took place in the Goderich courtroom. This time, it was "The Queen vs. James Kehoe for the Murder of Nicholas Melady." The proceedings began at 2:15 in the afternoon. The court was still crowded, because spectators for the first trial did not want to leave before they heard its verdict. To some extent, the Kehoe matter was something of an unexpected sideshow for the audience. It was of interest, but it was not the main event. Not only had Jim's troubles not captured the imagination of the public, there would be no femme fatale giving evidence at his trial.

A second jury was chosen, but the same judge and lawyers were involved, as were the police officers, the coroner, and most of the witnesses. At this trial, which focused on Jim's actions alone, two men said that the accused was up to no good, while two others said his character was above reproach. As was the case in the first trial, Tom Donovan was a key witness, although this time, he switched sides and testified for the defence. It was as if, because he had saved his neck by turning Queen's Evidence against Nicholas, he would henceforth secure his friendship with Jim by offering to support him. Tom claimed that even though Jim was indeed inside Old Melady's house on the night of the murder, he had nothing to do with the deaths that occurred there. Jim might have broken into the house, but it was as if he was little more than a mildly curious spectator to what had happened there. Tom had admitted that he too was in the house but, like Jim, had essentially just watched events unfold. Naturally, neither of them had done any harm.

And the strategy worked.

In all, eleven individuals took the stand, most of them for only five minutes or so, and gave abbreviated versions of the testimony they had made at the earlier trial. This was particularly true from the coroner, Nigh, Trainer, and Stephens.

Two of the men who gave evidence for the Crown had been incarcerated with Jim in Goderich and, while there, had talked to him every day, often several times each day. These conversations took place in the day room of their cellblock and in the prison yard. Both men remembered clearly what Jim had told them concerning the case at hand, and each gave roughly the same evidence when they were asked about it under oath. They recalled that Jim was reluctant to talk much when he first came to the jail, but as they got to know him, they found him more forthcoming. In the course of time he told the two that he was "in for the Seaforth murder," but initially said very little about it. Neither man told the court how they reacted to this information when they first heard it. Both claimed to know Jim well, and each recalled conversations they had with him.

Hugh McLaren was the first to take the stand. Although he was born in Scotland, the fifty-four-year-old, grey-haired McLaren now lived in Seaforth and made his living there as a baker. He admitted to being a troublemaker around town, but justified his behaviour because, as he said, it was always his temper that got him into difficulty. Seaforth Justice of the Peace Daniel L. Sills had dealt with the man and had jailed him on the combined charges of threatening and arson. There is no record extant that elaborates much on either matter, but fragmentary news items imply that the man apparently told an unnamed individual he would kill him or burn his house down. He seems to have done the latter.

McLaren was serving time for both charges and was in jail prior to Jim's arrival there. The two had not met before that, although they likely would have known of each other, as Seaforth was a small place. They became friends in jail.

During their time together in the same cellblock, McLaren had wakened a sleeping Jim when Edward Campaigne came to see him. A bit later, following his talk with the jailer, an upset Jim came back to their cellblock and told McLaren that Tom Donovan was about to turn Queen's Evidence. At the time, McLaren was sure Jim feared that Tom was going to testify that while he personally had nothing to do with the murders, Jim and Nicholas were the real killers. McLaren recalled Jim pacing the floor of the block and giving the impression that he feared for his life.

Because Jim was so upset, he told McLaren some of what had happened at Old Melady's on the night of the murder, even though he does not seem to have mentioned specifics of the matter prior to this. On the witness stand, McLaren repeated what had been said. "'Nicholas and I crawled in the cellar window, and he went up first,'" McLaren testified, quoting Kehoe. "'Nicholas made some noise, which wakened the Old Man, and he got up.'" Both men were drunk, so it is highly unlikely they would have been quiet for long. "'Nicholas shot him, and by the time I got upstairs, the Old Man was already dead.'" However, whether or not Jim was telling the truth about where he actually was is open to question. He contradicted himself in what he told another block mate who testified soon afterwards. "'I never saw the Old Woman at all,'" McLaren continued. This statement was also contradicted by Jim in his admission to the second block mate.

When McLaren asked Jim why they went to the Melady house that night, the reply was, "Our object was not murder; we just wanted his money."

Robinson listened intently to McLaren as these remarks were made. Then he asked if Jim Kehoe had said anything further about the money.

"'There was supposed to be $1000 there, but we only got $350,'" replied McLaren, again quoting. This was the first direct evidence, in either trial, of the amount of money the trio hoped to find — or at least thought they would find.

"And what did Nicholas shoot the Old Man with?" the Crown asked.

"Kehoe told me it was a double-barrelled pistol," responded McLaren. The witness was excused.

A few minutes later, Detective Trainer told the court about the pistol that had been found at the Kehoe home. Under questioning from the defence attorney, however, he had to admit that it did not look as though it had been fired recently. Surprisingly, perhaps, the Crown did not ask more about the gun that was found on the floor at the crime scene. There seems to have been a general assumption that it was the Old Man's and that it was used until it either jammed or broke.

The second inmate who had conversations with Jim in Goderich was a man named Thomas Little. He too told the court that he had not known Jim before they did time together.

Little was a blacksmith by trade, and the forty-four-year-old had been in jail for assaulting his wife. Again, it was Justice of the Peace Dan Sills who had put him there. Although English-born, Little gave his permanent address at the time of the trial as Memphis, Michigan. He went on to explain, however, that he had lived in Seaforth for seventeen years and that that was where he was when he was arrested. He never did explain why he regarded seventeen years as something less than permanent.

As soon as he established the identity of the witness and his reason for being on the stand, Robinson asked Little to tell the court certain information he had about James Kehoe.

"He told me he and Melady went in a cellar window," Little testified. This statement was almost a word for word repetition of what McLaren had said, but soon afterwards Little would differ from it.

"Is that all he said?" asked Robinson.

"He said he was in the house at the time of the murder, and said he was up out of the cellar when the Old Man was killed," replied Little. In other words, both witnesses placed Jim at the crime scene, but Little remembered that Jim had also said he was present when Old Melady's wife was killed. "He said the Old Lady was butchered with an axe. He said he was there at the time." Again, Jim seems to have portrayed himself as an innocent spectator to the killings. At no time did he ever admit that he had participated, yet he had done nothing to prevent the carnage.

The last two witnesses that testified were area residents John W. McIntyre and Peter Nevins. The former said he had known Jim "for years" and that his character was "very good and fair." Nevins told the court that he had been acquainted with the defendant for eight years, and that his character was "very good."

As soon as these men left the stand, defence attorney Harrison began his concluding remarks. In his summation of what happened during the trial, Harrison concentrated on one theme: character — the character of the accused, and the character of the two inmates who took the stand. His arguments, coupled with Tom's, claiming that Jim had nothing to do with the killings profoundly affected the twelve men who would ultimately have to come to an agreement on what had transpired at Old Melady's that night.

"Gentlemen of the Jury," Harrison began as he motioned towards Jim, "you observe that the prisoner has been testified to as being unquestionably a man of integrity."

Then the defence attorney became almost maudlin as he reminded the jury of the consequences of his client's being convicted. "He is the father of several children, who, if the prisoner is convicted, will be left unprotected. He is charged with the murder of his wife's father, a crime which he had no inducements." Harrison was certainly not about to tell the jury that Old Melady was attempting to remove Kehoe from his home or that Kehoe was upset by the move. Instead, the lawyer continued, "What evidence have you to convict him? Surely the finding of the pistol is not evidence. And remember, the constable himself said it had not been recently used."

Harrison talked about the former inmates who gave evidence. However, rather than attack what they said, he attacked them. He attacked their character, painting both as, if not the scum of the earth, then close to it. Kehoe would never have confided in such reprobates as these, he told the members of the jury. Then he told them why not.

And the twelve men bought Harrison's every word.

"The Crown's main evidence originates with two jail birds," the lawyer stated, his voice dripping with sarcasm. "The 'Little' jail bird, the second of the two on that stand, with the marks of dissipation on his face, sent to jail for assaulting his wife, then comes here to swear that man's life away." Harrison stressed the word *life* and pointed to Kehoe as if he were some- how placing his client on a pedestal. "Would my client — with intelligence beaming in his face — make a confidant of a fool?" The last word, referring to Tom Little, was said with an air of utter disdain, and Harrison uttered it without hesitation. Whether or not it was true had become irrelevant.

One or two of the jurors shook their heads in what appeared to be agreement with Harrison's show of disgust.

"I could imagine Melady, submerged in love with a pretty girl," the lawyer declared, his voice louder, "but is the story of this repro- bate probable?"

The biting insult of the attorney's shouted use of the word *reprobate* stunned the jury, but at the same time it seemed to reflect their own feelings about the wife-beater, or at least about the reason for which the man was jailed.

Harrison then walked over to the defendant, placed his hand on his shoulder, turned towards the jury, and asked, rhetorically, "Is it possible to think that *this* man should deny his guilt to all others and then confess to such a 'thing' as that man Little? Is the stream of justice to come through such a throat as *he* possesses?" Needless to say, Little was no longer in the courtroom, but even if he had been there to hear these words, he would have had no one to defend him.

Harrison paused, wiped the sweat from his forehead, carefully folded the handkerchief he had used to do so, and continued. "As for McLaren, what of him?" the lawyer asked. "He was in jail for arson. Is Kehoe likely to confess to such a braggart? No curls, no beauty to attract him. Is it probable that Kehoe was fool enough to confess to such knaves?" Harrison spat the last word, turned on his heel, and walked back to his table.

In his final plea to the jury, he played on their sympathies. "Would it not be a terrible thing to deprive this man of his life, and his children of a father, on the evidence of these two men? I hope, gentlemen, that your sense of justice will lead you to find the prisoner not guilty."

At no time during the character assassination did Judge Hagarty caution the lawyer. It was as if the inmates were so despicable, Harrison was given free rein to say anything he wished about them. By the time he finished, the jurors not only gave little credence to the testimony of the two, they seem to have come to a kind of loathing for the pair. Despite the unfairness of what the defence had to say, his words had a profound effect.

The address by Crown attorney Robinson, by contrast, was succinct. "My Learned Friend has dilated on the improbability of a confession among such characters as might be expected to be the inmates of a jail, but it is the principle of human nature to unbosom a weighty burden, even to ever so low or mean an individual," he began. It was as if the Crown were in total agreement concerning the inmate witnesses. No wonder their word was not held in high regard.

Robinson continued, "What object can a perfectly innocent man have in making a statement to the effect of being guilty? The conscience of guilt urges it to speak. There is many a man who beats his wife through a bad temper that could not commit perjury. It would not be wise to allow a man to go untried who has confessed complicity. If you believe he went with the object of robbery, the murder was committed for its furtherance. If you believe the witnesses guilty of perjury, acquit. If not, it is your solemn duty to convict."

As soon as the Crown had finished, Judge Hagarty wrapped up the proceedings. Everyone in the packed courtroom gave him their full attention.

"The entire case depends on the prisoner's admissions," he began. "You, the jury, have been told that if he went there with Nicholas to rob the deceased, and in the commission of that felony, the deceased was killed, then both men are guilty of murder. The law would call that murder." Judge Hagarty paused, as if he wanted to be sure the impact of these words was fully understood by the jury members. "But if you believe there was no original intention to murder, or to do violence, or to put down by force any resistance, then give the prisoner the benefit of the doubt and acquit him."

Finally, His Honour told the jury that their decision rested completely on which of the foregoing testimonies they believed. "If you believe Donovan, then you must acquit the prisoner. If you consider the worth of the evidence of Little and McLaren to be greater, then you must return a verdict of guilty."

The jury retired and deliberated — for twenty minutes. Then they returned and told the court that they had found the defendant not guilty. Jim Kehoe was acquitted because of two factors: first, the twelve men who were the jury believed he would not have confided in the likes of McLaren and Little; and second, they could not bring themselves to render a guilty verdict because the accused's children needed a father.

Jim Kehoe smiled broadly, but he would soon learn that his troubles were not over yet.

CHAPTER 21 | THE MOST TERRIBLE WORDS

FIVE MINUTES BEFORE the jurors returned to announce their verdict at the end of his murder trial, Nicholas Melady was led into the courtroom. He walked slowly, his eyes downcast, his shoulders hunched, never looking at the packed throng who watched his every move. Once seated, he leaned to the side and listened as Robert Harrison whispered something, but after that he stared straight ahead, a picture of dejection and defeat. His black hair was parted on the left and carefully combed. He was clean-shaven except for a neatly trimmed moustache, his thin face and long, straight nose accentuated his obvious weight loss while in prison.

As he and everyone present waited for the jury, the silence in the room was palpable. A large, ornate wall clock ticked loudly, but it seemed to be the only sound. No one coughed, whispered, or rustled so much as a single piece of paper. The passing seconds seemed interminable to everyone, but to the prisoner, they were also excruciatingly painful. He knew, as did everyone in the crowd, that when the silence ended and the verdict was delivered, his days on earth could well be numbered. And although defence counsel Robert Harrison had done his best to cheer his client, the longer the jury was out, the smaller the residue of hope. Nicholas now expected the worst and steeled himself as best he could to cope if it came. Deep down, however, he was close to despair.

Finally, a hallway door opened, and the jurors filed into the room. They too looked somehow defeated at the end of their terrible task. None of them talked to each other as they entered; none even looked at the crowd. They took their seats and sat in silence. Finally, a few seconds later, the foreman stood, faced the bench, and in a loud, firm voice said, "Your Honour, we find the defendant guilty as charged."

There was no applause, no obvious gasp of surprise, no sound of sorrow. Just silence, profound, perhaps unexpected, and lasting. Everyone watched the prisoner, who remained motionless, his face chalk white, his breathing laboured. He stared at his hands and kept his head down. The awful realization of the moment began to sink in.

He was now a convicted killer.

Judge Hagarty cleared his throat, looked at the young man who had just been found guilty, and asked, "Do you have anything to say why the sentence of death should not be passed upon you?" The focus of the crowd, which had shifted briefly to the judge as he spoke, quickly swept back to the man in the dock. Everyone waited quietly to hear what he might say.

A few seconds went by, and then, as the *Huron Expositor* reported, "The prisoner rose amidst the breathless silence of the vast audience of men, women and children, and [spoke publicly for the first time] in a clear and distinct voice." His words would not soon be forgotten by anyone in the room, and at the time, they were excruciatingly painful for all. Because Nicholas had not testified at his own trial, many in the courtroom had never heard him speak. Now, they hung on every one of the seventy-two words he said: "My Lord and Gentlemen; as I am convicted, it is useless for me to say anything, but I must return my sincere thanks to Mr. Harrison, and Messrs. Doyle and Squier, my counsellors." Nicholas paused, looked over at his lawyers, who now included a third member named Doyle, and nodded. He continued, "I have no fault to find with any of the witnesses, save for one man and one woman. Though the jury has found me guilty, God knows I am innocent, and I ask your Lordship for a merciful sentence." Deep down, the prisoner knew he was grasping at straws, but he pleaded his case and hoped for the best. He undoubtedly knew, however, that his situation was hopeless.

When he finished speaking, Nicholas stood in front of the judge, bowed slightly, and silently awaited the sentence he was about to receive. Judge Hagarty paused momentarily, collected his thoughts, and replied, "It is out of my power to show you mercy, or hold you out hope for any. Your days are numbered. You stand there convicted of the foulest deed that ever disgraced the annals of crime, patricide. I have nothing to do with preventing your application to the Queen's representatives for mercy, but there are no palliating circumstances in your case, therefore I recommend you to your Saviour, who alone can give you mercy. There is no moral doubt in my mind that the verdict of the Jury is one of the most righteous recorded." His Honour was obviously in complete agreement with the work and finding of the jury in this trial.

But then the judge deviated from his usual message; rather surprisingly, but with all the authority of his office, he stated loudly and clearly what he thought of the results of the previous trial. "Though the Jury have found Kehoe not guilty; in the eyes of God and man, he is as guilty as you." As far as we know, Jim Kehoe was not present to hear this startling assessment. Had he been tried by judge alone — or at least by Judge John Hawkins Hagarty — Jim would have met the same fate as Nicholas.

Now, though, with the observation on the record, Judge Hagarty paused, glanced down at a single sentence on a paper in front of him, and prepared to read it. He raised his head, looked directly at the man before him, and spoke the most terrible words any human being could ever hear. The judge's words were clear, forceful, and concise. They were the same words that had been used in similar circumstances on so many occasions in the past. Only the date and the recipient were different now. "You are now to be taken to the jail, from whence you came, and thence on the seventh day of December next be taken to the place of execution, and be hanged by the neck until you are dead, and may God have mercy on your soul!"

Nicholas Melady was then led out of the silent courtroom, and after he had gone, the crowds filed wordlessly into the night. The prisoner was back in his cell shortly afterwards, where, as the *Globe* would say on the following December 8, "he sat down and cried like a child." This day, for him, was truly the beginning of the end.

There was widespread, immediate, and long-term controversy, not so much about the conviction itself, but about the methods used to bring it about. The complaints went back to Coleman's statement to the *Globe* on the very first night of the inquest, when he told that paper who the killers were. This was further compounded when the same newspaper published much of the evidence four months before the trial began. The editors were criticized later by both the defence and the Crown, but by then the harm had been done. Because the story was reprinted by papers in Huron, many, perhaps most, of the jurors would have known in advance the details of the defence position and the fact that Tom Donovan would be turning Queen's Evidence; indeed, that he had already signed an affidavit saying that Nicholas "was the murderer, or one of the murderers."

Fault was also found with the police work, ranging from Bernard Trainer's planted evidence to the employment of the female detective. Her contribution was regarded as unfair by many, and as illegal by others. No matter how strongly the Crown had worked to convince the jury that Nicholas contacted Jenny first, at least part of the public never bought that explanation. Some believed she made sure the prisoner saw her during the time she worked with his sister. She was attractive to men, and had, because she was unable to get anywhere with the sister, flirted with him whenever she felt he was watching. As late as December 15, three months after the trial was over, the *Stratford Herald* was adamant that putting the woman into the jail to collect evidence was definitely entrapment.

The use of love letters at the trial was controversial, and even while the papers of the day grudgingly accepted the fact that the letters were necessary, they strongly implied that they should not have been read in the courtroom.

There was also a great deal of criticism that Janet Cooke had, in at least some of her testimony, stretched the truth when she told the court that Nicholas had confessed everything to her. The Crown had the love letters, as was stated often, but they only had Mrs. Cooke's recollection of the dozens of conversations with the accused. And even though Nicholas could have been put on the stand to dispute her testimony, the court would have had little more than his word against hers. That, coupled with the way she had impressed the all-male jury, would have meant that whatever she said would have been believed over whatever denials he might have made. After the trial was over, he did dispute what she said happened, but his words were largely ignored. And by then, it was too late to make any difference.

Then there was Tom Donovan's testimony. Despite the fact that the police and the Crown decided to put him on the witness stand, they knew they were taking a chance in doing so. As the *Globe* said on December 8, almost three months after the trial, "the counsel for the Crown at first had some scruples as to whether he should make use of him in this capacity, but at last he was placed in the witness box, and told a story which bore unmistakable marks of falsehood." In other words, as far as the newspaper was concerned, Tom lied in court about what had transpired at the murder scene. However, even though Harrison pointed this out, the jury dismissed the objection. It was as if the twelve men heard the lawyer, but believed Tom. Harrison could do nothing to the contrary.

But even the Crown attorney was skeptical about what the witness said, actually telling the jury to "receive Donovan's confession with caution." This led members of the public to claim that "even the Crown thought he was lying." For years afterwards, many clung to this point of view. They were absolutely convinced that the man had gotten away with murder.

The *Stratford Herald*, on December 15, commented at length on Tom's actions. In an article that day, the paper went so far as to describe what the man's future would likely be because of what he had done. The story, as written, was not only highly speculative, it was also obviously reflective of the time:

> It was only when wearied by the long incarceration in jail, and tormented by the probable consequences of the approaching trial that Donovan decided to turn Queen's Evidence. The agony of mind which he must have suffered for the eighteen months when he was in jail, and the thoughts that will forever torment him of having been the means, in great measure, not through any desire of seeing the majesty of the law vindicated, but to save himself from the noose which he saw hanging over his head, of consigning a fellow human being — his brother's wife's brother — a partner in a fearful tragedy — to the gallows, will be a punishment greater than many could bear. No matter where he goes, the curse of Cain will be on him, and to a great extent, he will be an outcast among men.

The newspaper did not mince words.

In Huron County, the *Expositor* commented on the murder investigation and bestowed praise where the paper thought was warranted. A lead editorial in the September 24 edition said, in part:

> The action taken by detectives in the Melady murder case has been the base of many comments, and mostly, we may add, of a disparaging nature. Why this is, we know not. Readers of the report on the trial will observe that the judge in his charge to the jury took occasion to remark, that were it not for the testimony of Donovan on the matter, the evidence must break down. Then it follows whatever led to his turning Queen's Evidence was the cause of leading to the prisoner's conviction. [In other words, Nicholas would die because of the words of a man he felt was his friend.]
>
> What then probably led Donovan to turn Queen's Evidence in this matter? Was he not told, after Nicholas Melady made the confession to the female detective, Mrs. Cooke, of what had been done? We believe he was. And is it not more than probable, that this is what led to the conviction of Melady? Such being a fact, the credit is due solely to Detective Smith and Mrs. Cooke, for the part they took in the proceedings.

Four days before Christmas that year, the *Globe* carried a story about a New Brunswick murder in which the death penalty conviction was about to be commuted to life in prison. In that case, the paper thought the killer should have been hanged, but, because he would not be, argued that other murderers deserved to have their sentences commuted as well. One of those mentioned was Nicholas Melady. By now, the paper felt "there were redeeming features" in his situation, and "most certainly" his death sentence deserved to be commuted.

And some members of the public in Huron agreed. Existing records are of little assistance in determining how much of a groundswell of support Nicholas received, but a petition for clemency made its rounds in the weeks immediately after the trial. As the *Globe* reported on December 8, "an endeavour was made by some of the people in the district to obtain a reprieve, and an application was made to the Government in this direction."

The *Expositor*, two days later, also referred to the appeal, but in addition, the paper mentioned the prisoner's demeanour during and following the trial. "After his condemnation, as before, he conducted himself in a most commendable manner, through which he won — so far as it is possible for a person in his position to do — the estimation, or rather pity, of all with whom he came in contact," the paper affirmed. "That tireless energy prompted by a sister's love was exerted in every possible manner to obtain a reprieve for an unfortunate brother. The prospects for such were at one time of a character that led the prisoner to express hope."

But the appeal did not succeed. Nor, perhaps, should it have.

Late on Friday afternoon, November 19, Huron County Sheriff John Macdonald received word that the request for clemency was denied, and that the law was to take its course. Macdonald informed jailer Edward Campaigne, who did not have the heart to break the news to the prisoner until the following Monday morning.

That morning, Campaigne went to Melady's cell, sat on the edge of the wooden sleeping bench, and talked quietly to the prisoner for several minutes. The two had long arrived at an understanding with each other, and a kind of trust had developed between them. In fact, they had become friends. So even before Campaigne opened his mouth, Nicholas knew what his visitor was going to say. The condemned man sat, listened, and kept his composure until the jailer left.

The last two weeks of his life passed all too quickly for Nicholas Melady. At first, he wept bitterly, alone in his cell, but then gradually worked through his self-pity and fear, arriving eventually at a kind of quiet resignation. "From this time," according to the Huron *Expositor*, "he devoted the greater part of his attention to his future welfare."

Nicholas asked Edward Campaigne if he would get in touch with the local parish priest and ask the man if he would come to the prison. The jailer made the request, and the following morning Father Bartholomew Boubat from St. Peter's in Goderich arrived and introduced himself to the condemned man. In the time that remained, the two grew close.

"He was constantly ministered to by his spiritual advisor," the *Expositor* noted, and "the visits of his relatives were also continual."

These last farewells were hard to take for all parties; as a reporter from the same paper noted, "at every parting, the scene was a sad one." Oftentimes, tearful conversations in the tiny visiting area of the jail were interrupted by the shriek of crosscut saws and hammering as the boards for the scaffold and stairs to it were put in place. Mercifully for the man in the death cell, the construction tumult ceased at dusk.

The *Toronto Globe*, for the time, was a big-city newspaper that had on its staff many tough-minded reporters whose outlook on life bordered on the cynical. They covered the country and reported as objectively as they could on the events of the day. Even a casual reading of the stories they filed leaves the reader with the facts, some of which were embellished for their shock value but which were rarely presented with much sympathy for either the downtrodden or the victimized. For that reason, it is almost surprising to find that the paper said some of the things that it did about the man awaiting the Goderich gallows.

"Father Boubat was assiduous in his endeavours to bring the culprit to a proper state of mind, and to realize the enormity of the crime he had committed and the necessity for repentance. The labours of the priest were not in vain," the *Globe* told its readers on December 8. "Nicholas betook himself to prayer and meditation, and though to some it may seem mawkish to speak of the perpetrator of a murder as a Christian, there is little doubt that Nicholas Melady, before he died, not only saw the error of his way, but thoroughly repented of the course he had taken."

But the prisoner's time ran out, while thousands of people from Huron and beyond prepared to make a trip to Goderich. They wanted to be there to watch him die.

CHAPTER 22 | TOGETHER IN DEATH

As soon as his corpse was cut down, family friends lowered Nicholas Melady's remains into the pine coffin that was there to receive it. They placed the lid on the container and carried it across the snow-covered ground to a nearby sleigh. Less than half an hour after the coroner had pronounced him dead, the men who claimed the body arrived at the train station in Goderich. During the trip there, it had seemed as if they were the only ones heading away from the jail. The streets were crowded with travellers coming from the opposite direction, most of whom were hurrying to watch the hanging that was already over. No one paid any attention to a sleigh they met on the way.

The horses used to transport the deceased that morning had been hired by men who knew Nicholas. They were neighbours who, despite their abhorrence of what was about to happen to him, felt they had to be present at the execution in order to show support for the family and to be of assistance during this time of turmoil. Nicholas's brother, Tom, was with them.

Once at the station, there was almost an hour wait until the train would leave, but that was long enough to get the horses back to the livery and pay for their use. The coffin would be taken to Seaforth in the baggage car, and the men who accompanied the body would ride in that carriage with it.

By the time the train had steamed some miles east towards Seaforth, news that the execution was over spread among the disappointed voyeurs outside the jail. There was a great deal of grumbling from the huge throng who had missed the show, with most of their anger directed at Sheriff Macdonald, who had personally made the decision to hold the execution at an early hour. The case had received so much publicity, for so long, and was so controversial that he felt moving the time forward would be prudent in order to prevent the possibility of protest. In retrospect, the idea was sound. Those who were disappointed because they had missed seeing Nicholas die could go back to their homes and read about his last few minutes in the various newspaper accounts that would soon be available.

The earliest out was the *New York Times*. The big American paper reported the matter the following morning, December 8, 1869, as it had the murders the Old Melady and his wife a year and a half earlier. The account of the hanging was brief, and not altogether factual as to the times that were involved. It also gave the deceased the middle initial "M," even though there is no record anywhere else that indicates that Nicholas had a middle name.

The *Globe* ran a notice of the public hanging the same day as the *Times*. In its story, the Toronto paper called the execution "one of the happily rare events" that occurred in Canada from time to time. And because these and other newspapers alluded to, but did not carry, a confession that Nicholas was said to have made shortly before he died, readers of the day began to anticipate future issues that might include the deceased's last communication.

They were not disappointed. The *Expositor* filled in the details. On December 10, the paper published the message Nicholas had written in response to a reporter's question shortly before the hanging. The last words for the public were succinct, low-key, and not accusatory in any way. Both Tom Donovan and Jim Kehoe were undoubtedly much relieved that their friend took all the blame himself and avoided mention of their participation in the murders. Almost every paper that covered the story stated that in his letter, Nicholas had been careful not to implicate anyone else. "It was for others to answer for themselves," was the way one described his sentiments.

Nicholas's statement was addressed to the *Expositor* editor, and the first part of what was said was an expression of thanks to those who had helped him during his incarceration. The Goderich jailer, Edward Campaigne, and his wife, Catherine, were specifically mentioned, as was Wilmot Squier, the family attorney.

Sir, as various rumours have gone about as to unkind treatment I received in gaol, I beg to certify that I have been treated with the utmost kindness and civility by all, but particularly so by Mr. Campaigne and lady. While Mr. Campaigne has been diligent in the discharge of his duty, he has used every effort to render my imprisonment as cheerful as possible; and for the few moments I have yet to live, I will remember with gratitude his kindness to me. And to my counsel, Mr. Squire, who made such exertions in my defence, I can but express my most profound acknowledgement. My gratitude also to those kind persons who have endeavoured to obtain my reprieve. God will give them a merited reward.

Then he made a public apology for his actions, a comment on the trial, and a declaration of his acceptance of blame. He followed that with a prayer for forgiveness.

Now Mr. Editor, as I wish to make no public speech, permit me through the medium of your columns to make one last atonement to an outraged society. I confess to be guilty of the horrible crime laid to my charge, and I wish therefore to express my exceeding sorrow thereat. I entreat all true Christians, in their charity, to pray the terrible Judge of the living and of the dead, that he may forgive me the horrible deed, as also the perjuries of which I became guilty in my endeavours to free myself from the accusation.

The evidence on which I was found guilty was weak and insufficient, it is true, but notwithstanding in that conviction I perceived the judgement of a just and holy God who has commanded us to honour father and mother, and whose name is never to be taken in vain. In connection with this however, I believe it is my duty to society, and to the rights of innocent parties to state that the principal portion of Mrs. Cooke's evidence was simply a fabrication. I neither admitted my guilt to her, nor did I state that the murder was committed between the hours of eleven and twelve at night, or any other hour. However, I forgive her and all others, as I hope myself to be forgiven.

Furthermore, I hereby retract all public or private conversations whereby I may have intimated directly or indirectly that any other person but myself had actually killed both my father and his wife or either of them.

When they read these words, Tom Donovan and Jim Kehoe must have been more relieved than they ever imagined they could be. Their friend was dead, but life for both would now go on. Neither would know a hangman's touch. Nicholas concluded his remarks:

I also wish to express my sincere attachment to and belief in the Roman Catholic and Apostolic Church in whose saving faith it is my firm purpose to live and die. May God comfort my poor sisters and my brother. Such affliction was not merited by them. And may the Lord Jesus Christ mercifully forgive my sins and receive my poor soul into heaven.

Nicholas Melady, Goderich, December 7, 1869.

The newspaper editor added, "To comment on the above would be superfluous."

It is impossible to determine how many of Nicholas's relatives knew the contents of the letter before it was published. No doubt some did, and they may even have passed the message along to the paper, but we have no way of knowing today how they reacted to it. We are certain, however, that there was a feeling that both Tom Donovan and Jim Kehoe had gotten off lightly — had gotten away with murder — and Nicholas's words probably ensured continued good fortune for the pair.

No doubt there were those in Seaforth and the area, aside from the immediate family, who shared the same point of view. But whether they wanted two more hangings is questionable. Already, even the idea of capital punishment was anathema to some, and the editor of the *Expositor* was among them.

In the same edition of the paper that carried Nicholas's acceptance of blame, the lead editorial railed against hanging, and public hanging in particular, as a solution to the problems of society. The piece was both long-winded and rambling, but its core message was blunt.

> Nicholas Melady has entered the shadowy regions of the dead. He has passed into "that undiscovered country from whose bourne no traveller returns." It is indeed a dreadful thing to die under the most soothing and calming circumstances, but to be hurled from a scaffold into eternity is too awful for the mind to contemplate. The last public execution that will take place in Canada has been witnessed. The curtain has dropped; from henceforth the dread show will be hidden from the gaze of a curious populace. This certainly is a step in advance. Let us hope that another step will be taken — that capital punishment may be abolished once and forever.
> ... [The editor then launched into a wordy treatise that touched on literature and scripture, but he finally did return to his subject.]
> ... We believe that the object of capital punishment, namely, the protection of life and property, as well as the deterring others from crime, can be attained, and all the expense attending these public executions saved, by substituting solitary confinement, with hard labour.

At this point, the editor mentioned that he intended to editorialize on this subject at another time, but quickly explained why he could not do so right away.

> We have written hurriedly on the present occasion with our feelings shocked by the brutal spectacle of Nicholas Melady writhing between Heaven and Earth — a spectacle which chilled the warm life-current of our frame — sent an electric shock of horror through our every nerve — causing the brain to reel and the senses to swim, and which made us say, most emphatically, after the dull heavy sound had died away, and we stood in the presence of a warm but dead man, we hope in the name of humanity that capital punishment may soon

> be abolished in Canada, and placed where it ought to be, with
> the grim relics of barbarous times.

The editorial may have swayed some in their beliefs, but certainly not one reader whose letter to the editor was published the following week. The unsigned missive trotted out most of the familiar arguments in favour of capital punishment for murder, but cut to the crux of the matter with one judicious phrase. "The best cure for a repentant murderer," the writer observed, "is a piece of rope judiciously applied to his neck."

When the train from Goderich pulled into Seaforth with the body of the deceased on board, it was met by another sleigh and a couple of cutters, all of which belonged to farmers who resided near Old Melady. They, along with the men who had come with the body, carefully lifted the coffin out of the baggage car and carried it to the waiting sleigh. The casket was then tied down; those who would transport it from Seaforth knew the condition of the snow-packed roads that lay ahead. Finally, when all was ready, the trip from town got underway. The train had already departed.

The sleigh with the coffin went first; the cutters followed. The three conveyances moved slowly between the train station itself and the tracks that passed in front of it and then turned right onto Seaforth's Main Street. This was the same street that Nicholas knew so well, where he had walked so often, and where he had been transported in custody shortly after the commission of the murder. Now he was again in the hands of others, but in a pine box instead of a policeman's wagon.

Up to the left, as the procession began, was the Carmichael, where Old Melady had spent the afternoon of the day he died. Across the main corner from it was Downey's Hall, the last building Nicholas had ever been in in Seaforth. To the left as well was Armstrong's store, a local retail outlet where a trio of elderly men stood talking. The three had gone to the store for tobacco, and C. Armstrong sold lots of it, along with a good selection of cigars, pipes, and pipe stems. In another week or so, he would be selling an additional item that would prove to be very popular. Souvenir photographs of Nicholas Melady would be available for all who wished one.

The sombre cortège moved on, away from the tracks of the Grand Trunk Railway, away from the station where Jenny had hidden before she fooled Wilmot Squier in order to prove to him that she was no threat to Nicholas. The trip, at first, was an easy one, as the snow was thickly packed on top of the first gravel that had been spread on Main Street the previous summer. The town seemed relatively deserted, but the few souls who were about stopped respectfully as the sleigh and cutters passed.

The cortège continued through Egmondville to the Van Egmond house corner, where it turned left, or east, and headed down the rural road, through snow that was deep in places and ground drifting that was prevalent for most of the way. Once or twice, the cutter riders had to lean far to the side to avoid tipping over. They were more fortunate than others that day. Area newspapers mentioned that there had been several upsets, with one or two resulting in passenger injuries. That was why the cargo on the sleigh had been well secured.

This road looked so bleak in the winter, much more so than it had on that summer night when Tom Donovan and Jim Kehoe met up with the deceased shortly before the three went to commit a robbery that would ultimately lead to three deaths. But now, the last of the three was being taken back to Old Melady's for a little while. As the *Globe* explained on December 17, Nicholas Melady "was waked for two nights in the house where the murder was committed."

Many expressed surprise that it was held there, but by this time it was Alice's home, and she would not agree to have her brother taken anywhere else. The coffin was carried, in silence, into the parlour at the front of the house, gently placed on two sawhorses, and then attended constantly until the morning of the funeral. The men who had transported the body of their friend paid their respects and departed. They would soon be replaced by a steady stream of others who came to the house, expressed their condolences to the family, and left. A handful of relatives and close friends remained in the room with the deceased at all times, spelling one another off for periods ranging from a couple of hours to an entire night. These mourners sat respectfully, talked softly, said the rosary occasionally, and even ducked out now and then for a swallow of whiskey. From time to time, one or more of them would stand by the coffin, say a silent prayer, and think back to what an enormous tragedy this had been for all concerned.

During the first evening, Father James Murphy arrived and led those present in prayers for the soul of the deceased. He talked quietly, particularly to Alice, Tom, and their sisters, and promised his help in whatever way it might be needed. By this time, two farmers from close by had been asked to dig a grave next to Old Melady in St. Columban cemetery.

The morning of the funeral, Thursday, December 9, a raw east wind chilled those who watched six of Nicholas's friends carry the casket to the same sleigh that had brought his body from Seaforth. Shortly afterwards, everyone piled into one of the many cutters on hand and travelled together behind the funeral sleigh to the St. Columban church, at the time the only Roman Catholic one in the entire area. The funeral for Nicholas was not held in Seaforth because the new $20,000 yellow brick place of worship was still under construction, but even had the building been complete, Nicholas and his entire family had attended St. Columban for years, so it was natural that he would be buried from there.

The St. Columban church that existed at the time of the funeral was also a yellow brick structure, stately in appearance, located on the north side of the Huron Road. The building was large, 150 feet long and 70 feet wide inside, but it was packed for the funeral mass sung by Father Murphy. All but the front pews were full by the time the chief mourners arrived.

As soon as the casket was brought to the church doors, the priest and several altar boys met it, and the customary prayers were said over the body. That done, the parish priest walked to the main altar, made the sign of the cross, and began the Mass for the dead. The vestments he wore were black, as were the soutanes of the servers. During this time, the coffin rested at the front of the church, where the immediate family took up the pews to the right. The six pall-bearers were to the left of the casket.

The service was long and, by today's standards, exceedingly sombre. The singing of what was called the Sequence, or *Dies Irae*, was particularly mournful. In translation, the words are "Day of wrath! O day of mourning, see fulfilled the prophets' warning; heaven and earth in ashes burning"; they hung in the air like a clarion call of doom. The entire mass was in Latin, as were all of the hymns and responses from the choir.

When the church services were over, the six pallbearers walked quietly to the sleigh and placed the casket on it. Then they and those closest to the deceased began the last procession.

There were many in attendance at the graveside. They stood in silence in the deep snow, huddled against the wind. Alice was extremely distraught, but most of the others who were there remained relatively composed.

This time, Father Murphy prayed, not just for the man who was about to be buried, but for all those interred in what was regarded by his church as holy ground. His words now were more uplifting than those heard that morning and must surely have comforted those who listened: "O God, by whose mercy the souls of the faithful find rest, bless this grave, and appoint thy holy angels to guard it; and release the souls of all those whose bodies are buried here from every bond of sin, that in thee, they may rejoice with thy saints forever."

Then he said a final blessing for the deceased, expressed his condolences to the family, and left the cemetery. Alice Melady lingered there for a long time, but finally she was persuaded to go as well. Tears streamed down her face as she looked back, but she knew that at long last, there was no more pain for her father and his wife, or for her brother. They were all together now, and they were at peace.

AFTERWORD

THERE ARE ALWAYS loose ends in any book about the past. Nagging questions persist. Individuals change, disappear, or die; events supersede one another; and contradictory references lead to more questions. This account of an event that happened so long ago has its share of imponderables, some of which may never be clarified. While some answers may be found eventually, with each passing decade their numbers will be fewer. For that reason, these few pages have been added to this narrative so that more light may be shone on some of the unknowns.

Initially, of course, we have to ask the question, What exactly happened in Old Melady's house on the evening of June 6, 1868? Much of this volume has been an attempt to provide the answer. And to some extent, I hope I have succeeded. That said, however, I am left with still more questions, and no records that I was able to unearth have provided complete explanations.

First, the facts: two people died that night, and three men were later charged with murder. All the investigations of the crime, flawed as they were, pointed to collective involvement. Yet only one of the trio paid with his life for what was done.

The first two charged, Nicholas Melady and Tom Donovan, were tabbed almost immediately by the police and the coroner as being the killers. Had he not turned Queen's Evidence, Tom likely would have gone to the gallows with Nicholas. The third individual, Jim Kehoe, convinced a jury of his innocence but not the judge who presided at his trial. Had Jim been tried by that judge alone, he too would probably have ended his days at the end of a rope. Judge Hagarty told the court, and the acquitting jury, that Jim was guilty "in the eyes of God and man."

So what did happen that night?

Much emphasis was placed on Tom Donovan's story, even though it was obviously rehearsed and largely concocted for recitation in the courtroom. He said he was at the woodpile during the time he and his friends all agreed to do the robbery. Then he said he stayed where he was and watched as Nicholas went towards the house and Jim towards home. Going towards either destination would have meant going the same way, so how Tom could discern the difference is questionable. Moreover, he never really told the court how he was able to see either of them going very far in the dark. Later, Jim told his jail block mates that he had not gone home at all, but that he and Nicholas had gone to the house and snuck in the cellar window. Both were drunk, so they probably stumbled into something, knocked it over, and made a racket that woke Old Melady. When he got up to investigate, he was shot, presumably with his own gun. This murder was almost certainly committed by Nicholas. He had the most to gain — or lose — if his father were to die. If his father had the gun in his hand already Nicholas could have taken it, or he could have known where to find it.

No record anywhere mentions that any of the three desperadoes had a firearm on the road or at the woodpile where the robbery plans were fine-tuned. And because three separate objects were used in the second killing, Nicholas likely used the gun until it would not fire anymore, Jim the chair, and Tom the axe he brought from the woodpile. It is highly doubtful that the first two would have had the axe with them as they squeezed through the cellar window. Tom, though, was scared, and he said he ran to the house after hearing gunshots, so he probably carried the axe in case he had to defend himself. If he really did enter the house after he heard a shot, not before, he could not have known who was shooting. After the murders, at least two of the three searched the trunk in the bedroom and left separate hand prints near the clasp. The police never did learn which two were involved. Nor did they locate any of the money Jim said they stole that night. None of it was found on the persons of the three, in the river, or at either Dave Donovan's or Jim Kehoe's homes. All of these matters led me to more questions than answers.

In due course, Nicholas was convicted of murder, and rightfully so, but what happened to the other two after his execution? Once Nicholas was out of the picture, the police decided to charge Tom and Jim in the killing of Ellen Melady. Both men were jailed, but only briefly, until the Spring Assizes in 1870. At that point, because the so-called mysterious witness to the killings had not turned up and no conviction could be obtained without such a person, Mr. Justice Joseph Morrison decided to release the pair at the Goderich courthouse. There was no trial; they were simply let go. The ruling satisfied some people, apparently. According to the *Huron Signal* of May 12, Tom and Jim "left the court amid the congratulations of their friends."

From that time on, Jim seems to have rehabilitated himself, and as far as is known, he stayed out of trouble. On October 18, 1870, one year and one month after Nicholas was sentenced to die, Jim and his wife paid Old Melady's estate $2,400 for the property they had been leasing. They farmed the land until Jim's retirement in 1892, at which time the couple moved to a house on Gouinlock Street in Seaforth. When Jim passed away on Thursday, February 1, 1906, the *Expositor* lauded him as "a quiet, industrious, well-doing man, a good citizen and an obliging gentleman." Not surprisingly, there was no mention of the murders or of his involvement in anything of a negative nature. His wife died just before Christmas in 1917. Both are buried in St. James Cemetery at Seaforth, where a large granite gravestone marks their place. By contrast, the location of Nicholas's grave in St. Columban is not only unmarked, it is also unknown.

I was not able to determine what happened to Tom Donovan.

Six weeks after Nicholas was executed, another death occurred in the family. His sister Mary, Tom McGoey's wife, died from what the *Expositor* termed "the fearful shock she received" on entering her father's house the day after the murders. From that day on, her health had deteriorated, according to the paper, "until at last she sunk under the sad affliction." The paper extended sympathy to Tom McGoey, who, as it turned out, certainly needed it. After what he had been through with the murders, Nicholas's execution, and now the loss of his wife, he felt that he had to get away from the area and start anew. In the fall of 1870, he moved to Toledo, Ohio, and did not return.

The whereabouts of most of Old Melady's descendants are unknown, although some moved to and died in the United States in the years after the unfortunate events of 1868. At least one of these, a grand-daughter of James Kehoe, used to spend the summer holidays at his home when she was young. She also visited his gravesite in 1979, but whether she knew of his past is probably immaterial. My own ancestors rarely mentioned the murders, and even when they did, they talked of them in a rather cursory manner. In reality, most never really knew much about what happened. I found in checking facts for this book that I could have been looking for information about a family of total strangers — which in fact was what these men and women were to me. But for better or worse, researching the account was certainly of interest. And while what happened was not something I treasure, it did take place and, as such, is part of the history of this land.

Most of the buildings mentioned in the volume are long gone, other than the jail in Goderich and the Van Egmond house in Egmondville. The Carmichael hotel where Old Melady drank was replaced with another of the same name a couple of years after his death, but the replacement is gone as well now, as is Downey's, the competition across the main corner in Seaforth. Another hotel is on that site today. Bummer's Roost is a vacant lot, and even the St. Columban church is a different one today — and at this writing, even it is about to be closed. The actual building where the three funerals took place was destroyed by fire following a lightning strike in the afternoon of July 15, 1909. Of the businesses mentioned, only the newspapers survive.

The lot lines for some of the properties mentioned in the book have been altered as well, and this is particularly true for the acreage where the murders took place. The barn Old Melady was having built at the time of his death has disappeared, but the location of the house is dis-cernable. As a youngster, I saw parts of the walls still standing, but that is not the case anymore. The outline of the foundation can be traced along the ground, and a section of the cellar exists, but that is about all.

After Old Melady's death, his property was divided up, and Nicholas inherited a share of it for the brief time he had to live. Because he knew the exact date his life would end, he was astute enough to put his few business affairs in order before then. Accordingly, on November 30, 1869, he drew up his will, had Edward Campaigne witness it, and left all he had to his sister Alice and his niece Catherine.

A week after the execution, the photos of the deceased were available at Armstrong's, while a pamphlet called "The Melady Tragedy" sold briskly in other stores.